Scaling the Ivy Wall in the '90s

Scaling the Ivy Wall in the '90s

12 Essential Steps to Winning Admission to America's Most Selective Colleges and Universities

HOWARD GREENE and
ROBERT MINTON

LITTLE, BROWN AND COMPANY
BOSTON   NEW YORK   TORONTO   LONDON

Library of Congress Cataloging-in-Publication Data

Greene, Howard.
    Scaling the ivy wall in the '90s : 12 essential steps to winning admission to America's
most selective colleges and universities / Howard Greene and Robert Minton.
        p.   cm.
    Includes bibliographical references (p.   ) and index.
    ISBN 0-316-32736-0 (pbk.)
    1. Universities and colleges — United States — Admission.   2. Universities and
colleges — United States — Entrance requirements.   I. Minton, Robert, 1918–
II. Title.
LB2351.2.G75   1994
378.1'05'0973 — dc20   94-5159

10 9 8 7 6 5 4 3 2 1

MV-NY

*Published simultaneously in Canada
by Little, Brown & Company (Canada) Limited*

PRINTED IN THE UNITED STATES OF AMERICA

To our college admissions deans
and
our secondary school counselors

Contents

Preface

*T*his is a revised edition for the nineties of *Scaling the Ivy Wall*. Thousands of students around the world have used our 1987 version to gain admission to selective colleges of their choice. The general principles of our Twelve-Step Plan are unchanged, but we have provided an expanded introduction that describes significant trends in the college world that have an impact on admission; up-to-date statistics; the most recent experiences of successful applicants; the latest advice of counselors; and new comments from admissions deans, directors, and their staffs. We have devoted special attention to the increasing difficulties of financing a college education — as many as 50 percent of applicants now seek financial aid. Also, the expanding enrollments of students from abroad justifies more attention than we previously devoted to this subject.

Our underlying philosophy, based on twenty-five years of experience, is that a determined student in the upper quarter of his or her secondary school can be offered admission to at least one of the selective colleges we list in Table 1 (page 7). We say *can be,* not necessarily *will be.* An understanding of admissions requirements and procedures is essential. For example, an A student may be turned down by colleges if the record shows an avoidance of honors courses. Selective colleges seek applicants who have shown a capacity for meeting demanding academic standards.

The actual experience of students from a broad range of backgrounds who came to the Educational Consulting Center in New York City and in Westport, Connecticut, continues to be a firsthand resource for much of this book. Organized by Howard Greene in 1969, the center offers professional admissions counseling and evaluation to students and their families concerning entry into secondary schools, colleges, and graduate schools. By providing important information and advice to students, the center has won the confidence of admissions deans and other college administrators and faculty, many of whom are cited as authorities.

Our concluding essay on the liberal arts tradition includes a comment on the curriculum controversy that has occurred in recent years. We believe that the better four-year colleges in the United States are providing excellent preparation for careers and for lives of public service. We also address the advantages that some selective institutions with technical, business, and other specialized fields of study offer together with a liberal arts education. Competition for admission to these institutions remains keen. Readers, we hope, will respond to the encouragements of Deans and Directors of Admissions, who are always looking for qualified, exciting students.

summarize the institutionalized sensitivity to the concerns of the diverse groups that comprise today's student body.

On some campuses this has led to administrative rules of conduct and of speech some students find highly objectionable. A number of selective colleges have had to deal with verbal and physical demands from many segments of their communities — demands for recognition, for more financial aid, and for expanded academic programs. Most high school students are unaware of the intensity of the emotional debate among college students and are puzzled by the social fragmentation they see after they enroll. The controversy engages such sensitive subjects as racism, feminism, sexual preference, and cultural bias in the curriculum or in faculty assignment of books and documents. Applicants should become aware of the impact of "PC" at particular colleges and the possibility of turbulence on campuses where it is evident. Not every eighteen-year-old is comfortable on a campus roiled by controversy.

In a graduation speech at George Mason University, the chief justice of the United States Supreme Court, William H. Rehnquist, said that traditionally "the university educates but it does not indoctrinate." But at some institutions, he said, "one senses there is an orthodoxy or sort of party line from which one departs at one's peril." According to the chief justice, ideas one disagrees with should be met by argument not suppression. However, ideas do not constitute conduct that interferes with the rights of others.

The implication is that when discussion leads to violence, this cannot be tolerated on campus any more than it is elsewhere.

CAMPUS CRIME

For a generation colleges have had to increase security to assure the safety and property of students. Still, parents are rightly concerned about the possibility of rape, assault, murder, and thefts even at the quietest of the selective colleges. The street crimes reported daily in the media are also occurring on campuses all over the country. Awareness of this problem has led to new federal laws that require colleges to report annually the number and types of crimes committed on campus or on students near the campus. This information is available on request to applicants and their families, but it is unlikely to be part of the glossy brochure describing a college's traditions, beauty, and strengths.

Another concern, not quite criminal but extremely destabilizing, is heavy undergraduate drinking, which is on the rise and in a few cases has led to death from overindulgence. Parents must be reassured by powerful evidence that professional campus security and administrative responsibility for student behavior is in place to minimize threats to the safety of their children.

THE NEW CAREER THRUST AT LIBERAL ARTS COLLEGES

Colleges cost more every year, while job prospects for their graduates diminish in a world where "downsizing" of business and government is a trend. Parents and students are understandably anxious about the benefit of a costly liberal arts education that may not lead to a career. They ask: what should a student be studying in these competitive and confused times? The claim that any major will be the basis for a well-rounded, cultivated, and thoughtful young person is belied by hundreds of personnel offices who turn away bright applicants daily.

College applicants should take note of available majors with career promises, such as engineering, accounting, business administration (which includes nonprofit and government organizations), computer science, and health-related disciplines. Double majors or interdisciplinary study are offered at some colleges. You can study bioengineering, geology, and environmental science, or business management and prelaw, among many possible combinations.

The old-fashioned insistence on avoiding any kind of trade school study has given way to a growing belief that an undergraduate education must point the student toward a feasible career. Liberal arts studies have long been the staple of future doctors and lawyers, but graduate students now tend to want hands-on exposure to their disciplines through internships or research assignments with appropriate faculty, in addition to a first-rate academic foundation. Today's college applicants must include in their college selection criteria a school's academic reputation and track record in terms of producing graduates who are accepted by top graduate schools.

THE NEW SAT!

One of the major changes has occurred at the College Entrance Examination Board. In reaction to decades of criticism from students, parents, and educators, who have objected to the SAT's potential unfairness and its limited usefulness in predicting college success, the Scholastic Aptitude Test has been revised and renamed. In March of 1994 a new SAT, the Scholastic Assessment Test, with a partially different format was introduced. Details will be found in our chapter on testing. We warn you that the new SAT, if fairer and a sounder measure of a student's readiness to do college work, is even more challenging than the old. Lower scores than expected are being predicted for many taking the test. There are strategies for meeting the new expectations created by the College Board, and these are addressed further on.

Acknowledgments

One of the great rewards in researching and writing a book is the relationships that develop between the authors and those who provide the information, personal experiences, and insights. We wish to express our deep appreciation to the college administrators, school counselors, parents, and students who made this extensive revision possible. It is their willingness to share so much of what they know and their encouragement of the steps and strategies we have developed that we believe will make this revision useful to the next generation of high school students and their parents, who need to create an understandable structure out of the complex and emotionally fraught process of college admissions.

We wish to thank those students who have allowed us to share their personal histories and essays that were a part of their successful admission process. To the many college admissions officers who provided both important application and enrollment data as well as their views of the many trends unfolding in admissions and financial aid, we express our sincerest gratitude. This is a professional group of educators truly dedicated to serving the public's best interests and needs. As the reader proceeds through this book, he or she will understand the value of the information and suggestions they have provided.

Thanks are due also to the following colleges and universities for providing valuable information: Amherst College; Bates College; Bowdoin College; Brandeis University; Brown University; Bucknell University; Carleton College; Colby College; Colgate University; College of William and Mary; Columbia University; Connecticut College; Cornell University; Dartmouth College; Davidson College; Duke University; Emory University; Franklin and Marshall College; Georgia Institute of Technology; Harvard University; Kenyon College; Lafayette College; Lehigh University; Lawrence University; Massachusetts Institute of Technology; Northwestern University; Pomona College; Princeton University; Reed College; Rice University; Stanford University; Swarthmore College; University of California, Berkeley; University of California, Los Angeles; University of Chicago; University of Michigan;

University of North Carolina; University of Pennsylvania; University of Virginia; Vanderbilt University; Wesleyan University; Williams College; and Yale University. Dr. Frank C. Leana, the Education director of Howard Greene and Associates, has made a significant contribution to this book by virtue of sharing his wisdom and expertise.

We are also grateful to our editors at Little, Brown and to Laurie Greene, Doris Forest, and Charles Bunting, whose critical eye for detail and organizational skills were of immense importance in making this revision truly "for the nineties."

Howard Greene and Robert Minton
Westport, Connecticut

Introduction

SOCIETAL CHANGES BRING SELECTIVE ADMISSIONS CHALLENGES

*I*t is less than a decade since the last edition of *Scaling the Ivy Wall* was written, but in these few short years American higher education has undergone a number of significant changes that are having an important impact on the college selection and admissions process. These changes, touching every American institution of higher education, reflect the many new conditions in American society, from the end of the cold war to rising demands to be recognized on the part of diverse ethnic, racial, religious, and economic groups. Economic recession and population shifts are making some selective colleges, public as well as private, even harder to get into and more costly to students and their families. Only the very wealthiest private and public colleges can continue to offer generous financial aid packages.

Bright students qualified for selective colleges must recognize the new obstacles to admission and to financing their education, and work to surmount them. It is our experience that there are proven strategies for admission and for financing an education at the top colleges and universities. Out of many years of professional experience Howard Greene and his associates at the Educational Consulting Center have evolved a system of guidance that has helped thousands enter the best higher educational institutions in the past, and this system, modified to meet the new conditions, will continue to be effective in the nineties. The center's files have in effect been put at the disposal of readers of this book to allow them to cope with these changes.

POPULATION DIVERSITY

A rapidly expanding, racially diverse population in the United States has brought new and greater expectations of access to higher education among

African-Americans, Native Americans, Hispanics, and various Asian groups. This has brought increasing pressure on selective colleges to provide them more spaces in entering classes. The response of the selective colleges has been aggressive recruitment of disadvantaged applicants. But total enrollments in these colleges have not risen. Therefore, fewer freshman spaces are available for so-called advantaged students, who now face stiffer competition than ever among themselves.

THE COST OF EDUCATION AND THE RECESSION

Between 1980 and 1992 college tuitions increased on average by 135 percent. During this same period family income rose only half as much, 67 percent. Many middle and upper income families have been hit hard by unemployment. And federal and state governments have cut the budgets of public universities, whose tuitions are rising at a rate of 13 percent a year. Financial aid to these institutions is dwindling. Money to pay for education will continue to remain a problem for many American families.

COMPARATIVE COSTS AT NINE SELECTIVE COLLEGES, 1993–94

	Overall cost*	Increase over 1992–93
Yale	$25,110	5.9%
Princeton	24,925	5.9
Harvard	24,880	5.8
MIT	24,800	5.2
Brown	24,618	5.4
Stanford	24,310	6.4
Dartmouth	24,249	5.5
Cornell	24,189	5.4
Penn	23,726	2.4

*Tuition, room, board, and fees.

The private colleges and universities, criticized by parents for ever higher tuitions, have limited their increases to 6 or 7 percent. But their scholarship population continues to rise, while government funding for scholarships and loans to needy students until 1994 decreased, obliging virtually all public and private institutions to dip into their endowments or raise more money from other sources. There is a limit, however, to how much additional money can be raised among alumni and corporations. Most private selective colleges are pinched for financial aid funds and so cut costs elsewhere. Even the wealthiest universities have had to abandon various sports or academic programs.

This money crunch has several consequences for college applicants.

- More students applying for financial aid forces the colleges to offer larger loan and work study packages and smaller grants.
- The era of "need-blind" admissions is over at all but a few of the richly endowed colleges, and their number is shrinking. While not publicly saying so, most admissions offices must now consider an applicant's financial status.
- Students placed on a waiting list are being told by most colleges they will not be admitted if they have serious financial need.

Because of these developments, applicants need to be forthright in asking admissions offices in advance what their financial aid policies are. There is simply no point in applying to a college that will turn you down for lack of money.

AN AMENDMENT THAT HELPS

Not to be overlooked, however, is the new way the federal government determines loan eligibility. The Higher Education Amendment of 1993 allows those applying for loans to exclude as assets family ownership of a house, apartment, or farm. This means that more applicants will be eligible for grants and loans than in the past. Yet, if the federal and state governments do not provide greater amounts of money there will be little or no increase in awards.

THE MERIT SCHOLARSHIP OPTION

Merit scholarships are offered to outstanding students in an attempt, often successful, by colleges to lure them away from prestigious colleges where they would receive a smaller financial aid package or no aid at all. Naturally this practice is questioned by some colleges whose reputation alone lures applicants, but from the applicant's point of view, it may be not only prudent but wise to consider the offer of such a scholarship. We consider this a worthy option and discuss it further in our chapter on financial aid. Obviously, in hard times, merit scholarships are going to be harder for good students to turn down.

PUBLIC LOSS OF CONFIDENCE IN UNIVERSITIES

The positive image of some great colleges and universities has been tarnished by unseemly financial practices or political upheavals. Congress has objected to excessive billing for university research and overhead, and to frivolous use of public subsidies. This has led to reduced funds for research projects and consequently to less money available for students paid to assist faculty in laboratories and in scholarly research.

Another blot on the university escutcheon has been the questionable quality of teaching, especially when done by graduate assistants. Full-time faculty have been observed on occasion to be consulting far from their own campuses. Candidates for admission have a right to ask questions about what kind of teachers they will have and how much individual attention they can expect. Applicants should not be timid about demanding to know if the colleges they apply to are really living up to the widespread acknowledgment that there has been too much emphasis on research and publishing and that not enough faculty attention has been paid to the undergraduate's classroom experience. The financial woes of many institutions are leading them to cut back on academic programs and services. Let the buyer beware when choosing a college.

A GROWING NUMBER OF SELECTIVE COLLEGE APPLICANTS

High school students and their families are targets of an enormous marketing effort by colleges all over the country. This practice is not new, but the change is in the accelerating volume of beautiful brochures, fliers, and videos distributed, and in the rising number of face-to-face sales efforts by admissions teams. Even selective colleges are involved in this applicant drive — out of a determination to maintain a large number of applicants, and to increase the diversity of their applicant pools. All this in the midst of declining secondary school enrollments! Why is this?

It is because the benefits of a degree from a selective college are perceived as giving the graduate a head start both in a career and in the enjoyment that grows out of the quality of intellectual training such institutions provide.

Unfortunately, a selective college cannot ensure all its graduates immediate career employment when the economy is slow. But its graduates are perceived to have a better chance of gaining admission to a quality graduate school that provides training in law, medicine, business, or other professions. That's why we foresee a continuing rise in applications to the colleges we discuss in subsequent chapters, especially as the number of high school graduates grows during the nineties. International students enrolled in selective American universities now represent over 400,000 places. Many are highly talented students who are attractive to selective colleges, and their numbers on campuses will continue to multiply.

PC — THE POLITICAL CORRECTNESS ISSUE

The concept of "political correctness," barely perceptible when we first published this book, has become one of the most divisive issues on many campuses, and has attracted widespread news media attention. These two words

ALERT! ALERT!

We open with this survey of changes not to alarm students or their families, but to alert them to what is happening out there in the groves of academe. Among the buzzwords of the nineties is "the real world." In the real world of admissions the selective colleges are more in demand than ever and therefore the chances of admission are not strong for students who are "on the margin." But who is a marginal student to the admissions committee of a highly selective college? The answer will surprise you: it can be a school's top graduate, it can be a high-ranking private school student, it can be a "scholar-athlete." It behooves applicants, therefore, to plan well their choices of colleges and their strategies for being standout candidates.

To the uninitiated this is a challenging situation. What we hope to do is educate our readers, to reassure them, and to instill in students who follow our twelve winning steps the confidence that they will enroll in one of America's leading colleges or universities. Students of talent with outstanding performance, there is every possibility you can win a place in a top college if you take the right steps throughout high school, but *do not* take anything for granted.

*Scaling
the
Ivy Wall
in the '90s*

Before You Begin

A WORD ABOUT OUR TWELVE-STEP PLAN

A word about what we call our Twelve-Step Plan: this logical sequence of responsibilities has been followed for twenty-five years at the Educational Consulting Center. Its practicality is demonstrated by the fact that most students who have followed it have been admitted to good selective colleges (as well as to less selective institutions when appropriate to the candidate).

While many students enter these colleges in their own way, we feel that our plan has the advantage of reducing the anguish and anxieties that are inevitable in the admissions process. More important, we know it works!

The one proviso we insist on at the Educational Consulting Center is that an applicant become acquainted with the plan. How much of it will be useful varies with the individual. Our answer to the candidate is: use what you need. You will not be marked down for not filling out every one of the worksheets.

We are blowing our own horn a bit because it pleases us so much when a client or a reader of this book expresses gratitude for our help. We must return the compliment by saying no college ever admitted a book, a counselor, or a tutor. It is only the student who passes muster on the basis of school performance, community activity, character, and other evidence of personal striving that impresses an admissions committee.

That said, we invite you to study the Twelve-Step Plan over the period of time you need to complete the admissions process. Any questions you have will be answered by calling an ECC counselor at (203) 226-4257 or (212) 737-8866.

TWO APPLICANTS WHO MADE IT

Before you begin to acquaint yourself with the Twelve-Step Plan, we would like to tell you about two students recently admitted to selective colleges who came to the Educational Consulting Center feeling very uncertain about their prospects for admission. Vincent visited the center late in the spring of his junior year in a fine high school in northern New Jersey, following a visit to Cornell, his father's college. He and his parents were troubled by an admissions officer's assessment of Vincent's chances of getting into Cornell. On the basis of his record to date, he appeared to be a weak candidate. "You should look at a number of colleges that are likely to accept you," he said to Vincent.

The family had assumed that despite a B average and combined SAT scores of 1100, Vincent would be admitted because he was the son of a Cornell man. Vincent was a varsity soccer player and vice president of his class. Why would his chances at Cornell be doubtful? Because in the competition among alumni children, Vincent's academic efforts were inadequate. If he could show more drive and less reliance on his Cornell connection, he would have a stronger chance of admission. What the Center recommended was a revised senior curriculum that made strong demands on him.

To prepare for this, Vincent attended tutoring school during the summer and worked with the Center on essay writing. His senior year program included honors courses in European history and English. Better study habits developed at tutoring school brought him improved grades — a B+ average, impressive in view of the heavier course load. When he retook the SATs in November, he brought his scores up to 1190, still 60 points below the average of Cornell freshmen, but competitive with alumni children. On three SAT Subject II Tests in his senior year he averaged 590 (out of a possible 800).

The Twelve-Step Plan he was following calls for an understanding of admission procedures and knowledge of different selective college characteristics. Instead of wanting to go to Cornell because his father went there, he learned to evaluate a number of colleges and compare them with Cornell. Knowing that a successful candidate must persuade each college of his particular distinction among many applicants, he decided to play up his photography, a hobby rewarded by prizes in local contests. At the center's suggestion, he visited the University of Rochester, whose close relationship with Eastman Kodak makes it possible for students to take courses in optics and other subjects related to photography.

By March Vincent had learned from Cornell that he was now a much stronger candidate. But his interest centered on Rochester, which accepted him in April. He was wait-listed by Cornell, accepted by the University of Michigan, and rejected by Hamilton. Conferring at the center with his parents, Vincent expressed a strong desire not to wait to see if Cornell would take him off their waiting list, and to accept Rochester. His father realized that his son had come to this decision reasonably and that he was indeed fortunate to be going to a fine university about which he felt so warmly.

Martheil's case is somewhat different. Her mother is French and until eighth grade she lived in France, where her American father was in charge of an international marketing company. At her private day school in Pittsburgh,

Martheil had no trouble getting As in French (800 on her Subject II French Test), but English proved difficult and pulled her average down. She scored 500 and 525 the two times she took the verbal SAT (610 and 620 were her SAT math scores). Martheil is very pretty, and the school noted that her interest in boys was causing her to neglect her studies in favor of frequent dating. The college counselor suggested that she apply to a college where the academic pressure is minimal. Her mother was not pleased.

An interview at the Center in the summer following her junior year brought out the fact that in France Martheil had been a much stronger student. The combination of a new culture and a sudden popularity with boys was working to undermine her natural academic ability. Secretly she yearned to live up to her academic potential and to resist the peer pressure of popularity. After grasping the essence of the Twelve-Step Plan, she agreed at once to accept the challenge of reading a book a week for the rest of the summer; the center provided a book list. Then with the Center's help, Martheil set some goals for herself: she would try to bring up her academic performance senior year to make her competitive for a selective women's college, where popularity with boys is less important than at a coed institution; she would practice SAT tests to improve her verbal score on a third try (it worked, and she scored 580 on the verbal and 610 on the math — it is not unusual for a score to drop slightly on a second or third test); she would become more active on the student council; and she would try out for the varsity tennis team, which she easily made.

By Christmas Martheil had brought up her grades to put her in the upper 20 percent of her class. Having visited several colleges in the fall, she submitted applications to Sarah Lawrence, Mount Holyoke, Smith, and Scripps College in California, a place she was unaware of — the Center recommended she apply there because of that excellent small college's interest in enrolling good students from the East. In her applications she stressed her unique experience of being brought up in France, including difficulties she had overcome. "I feel that I have been 'stretched across the Atlantic,' " she wrote in her essay.

Among the colleges, she favored Mount Holyoke, where she eventually enrolled. What helped her admission there was her specific interest in the college's connection with Mystic Seaport in Connecticut, an interest that stemmed from summers of sailing at Arcachon, near Bordeaux. She was also admitted by Scripps and Sarah Lawrence (and rejected by Smith). Martheil is majoring in French and hopes to work in an international corporation as a marketing specialist.

Neither Vincent nor Martheil is a *typical* applicant, for the simple reason that every applicant to a selective college is unique. By following the Twelve-Step Plan both students were able to rise above mediocrity through their own efforts. An important factor in their admissions was their understanding of the need to communicate to the colleges their own individuality: that is, assurance they would make the most of their higher education and be assets on their campuses.

By following the Twelve-Step Plan as these students did, you can gain admission to one or more selective colleges that are right for you. Doing this will require time and effort, but you will be a stronger person for it wherever you enroll. We have yet to know a student who regretted this exhilarating experience.

A COURSE IN ADMISSIONS

The Twelve-Step Plan to College Admissions is essentially a course in what it takes to get over the ivy wall and into a selective college. It has been carefully worked out to cover admissions requirements, procedures, tests, essays, campus visits, interviews, applications, financial aid, and enrollment in a logical sequence that demystifies the admissions process and reduces anxiety about getting into college. Conceiving of this book as a course you give yourself will fix your mind on essential things to do progressively as you move steadily toward an achievable goal: acceptance by at least one selective college you really like — not a backup or a safety, but an institution to which you have chosen to apply because it suits your abilities and your tastes.

It is our experience that when good students approach admissions the same way they approach a course in history or algebra, they stop wondering whether or not they will get into one or two colleges in particular. Instead, they begin to see that surely they are going to get into a very good college, because they have earned their place there by hard work and commitment. What they have to do is show the right colleges who they are. The Twelve-Step Plan is designed to help them do just this. If you are among those whom teachers and counselors have urged to apply to a selective college, the Twelve-Step Plan can make college admissions an experience you will enjoy.

THE SELECTIVE COLLEGES

A selective college is defined as (1) one receiving many more applications than the limited size of its freshman class; (2) one whose applicants have combined SAT test scores of approximately 1100 or higher; (3) one whose applicants' grade point averages place them in the top half of their classes in high school. (Note: the SAT is optional at a few very selective colleges.) A selective college offers a higher quality of education than most because of an outstanding faculty, excellent facilities, capable students, and a tradition of the highest ideals and expectations for its graduates. Being selective does not mean being exclusive. On the contrary, selective colleges seek to admit the broadest variety of applicants to achieve a balanced class that reflects the diversity of the nation. Selective means that each college is able to select from a large number of qualified applicants with high test scores and class standing, students it seeks for its own campus, and this is possible because so many

Table 1

THE SELECTIVE COLLEGES

Amherst College	Lawrence University
Barnard College	Lehigh University
Bates College	Lewis and Clark College
Boston College	Massachusetts Institute of
Boston University	Technology
Bowdoin College	Middlebury College
Brandeis University	Mount Holyoke College
Brown University	New York University
Bryn Mawr College	Northwestern University
Bucknell University	University of Notre Dame
California Institute of Technology	Oberlin College
Carleton College	University of Pennsylvania
Carnegie-Mellon	Pomona College
University of Chicago	Princeton University
Claremont McKenna College	Reed College
Clarkson University	Rensselaer Polytechnic Institute
Colby College	Rice University
Colgate University	University of Richmond
Colorado College	University of Rochester
Columbia University	Saint Lawrence University
Connecticut College	Sarah Lawrence College
Cornell University	Scripps College
Dartmouth College	Smith College
Davidson College	Stanford University
Denison University	Swarthmore College
Dickinson College	Trinity College (CT)
Duke University	Tufts University
Emory University	Union College (NY)
Franklin and Marshall College	Vanderbilt University
Georgetown University	Vassar College
Hamilton College	Villanova University
Harvard University/Radcliffe	Wake Forest University
College	Washington University (MO)
Harvey Mudd College	Washington and Lee University
Haverford College	Wellesley College
College of the Holy Cross	Wesleyan University (CT)
Johns Hopkins University	Williams College
Kenyon College	Worcester Polytechnic Institute
Lafayette College	Yale University

students believe that only a small number of the many four-year colleges offer the training and educational experience that promise a more rewarding life after graduation. We have compiled a list of selective colleges and universities, which appears in Table 1.

THE SELECTIVE STATE UNIVERSITIES

University of California (all campuses)	State University of New York (all campuses)
University of Colorado (Boulder)	University of North Carolina, Chapel Hill
University of Connecticut	
Georgia Institute of Technology	Miami of Ohio University (Oxford)
University of Illinois (Urbana, Champaign)	Pennsylvania State University
	University of Texas (Austin)
University of Indiana (Bloomington)	University of Vermont
	University of Virginia (Charlottesville)
University of Michigan	
University of Minnesota (St. Paul)	College of William and Mary
	University of Wisconsin (Madison)

Because of its reputation for educational quality, a selective college attracts more applicants than it can accept in a freshman class limited to a certain number. Moreover, applications to the more selective colleges are increasing, despite the decline in the number of high school graduates from a high of 3.2 million in 1975–1976 to 2.5 million in 1990–1991.* With only one applicant in every six or seven being admitted to Stanford, Harvard/Radcliffe, and a number of other selective colleges, even the best-qualified applicants face stiff competition.

Selective college applications are on the increase for the foreseeable future because (1) these colleges are held in high regard by employers and graduate school admissions committees; (2) more parents believe that degrees from selective colleges will insure their children's success, and therefore such parents strive to assure their children of good college preparation as one of the major things they can provide; (3) newly prosperous families can afford the high cost of private colleges and at the same time add to their own social prestige by sending their children to them. Incidentally, many admissions deans and directors have told us that the growing popularity of their colleges surprised their administrations, which had anticipated a drop in applications corresponding to the drop in the number of high school graduates.

Still, the competitive situation is not nearly so overwhelming as the figures suggest. A fact often overlooked by high school students is the rise in the number of selective colleges in the past twenty years. Even among the finest private schools in the country, the long-held fixation on a few traditional, prestigious colleges has given way to emphasis on the top state universities and dozens of colleges that have attained selective status in recent years. These colleges are the beneficiaries of improved quality in high school college preparation programs. Better students attracted stronger faculties, and alumni responded with large benefactions. All of which means that any student in

*SOURCE: U.S. Department of Education.

THE MEANING OF IVY

Ivy was introduced into the American colonies by the British, who for centuries used it to cover the brick walls of English churches, homes, public buildings, and universities. Older colleges like Harvard, Yale, Princeton, Dartmouth, Brown, and Pennsylvania planted much ivy around their buildings and campus walls, and the practice was imitated by newer institutions. Ivy has become a symbol of quality education, although merely decorating a building with this leafy, climbing plant hardly suffices to make an institution selective.

The phrase "The Ivies" refers to a few of the oldest highly selective eastern colleges. We have chosen "the ivy wall" as a symbol of the selectivity that characterizes a narrow range of excellent private and public institutions.

The Ivy League is an athletic league consisting of Brown, Columbia, Cornell, Dartmouth, Harvard, Penn, Princeton, and Yale. They have a common agreement on admission of athletes, athletic practice schedules, and financial aid — no athletic scholarships are allowed.

While ivy is associated in some minds with exclusivity and elitism, our intention is to associate it with excellence, pure and simple.

FACULTY SALARIES AT SELECTIVE COLLEGES

One assurance of a quality education is the caliber of the faculty, and this can be measured in part by professors' salaries. At MIT, instructors earn over $35,000 a year, which is as much as full professors are paid at some colleges. MIT pays its full professors $88,000 a year, well above the national average for institutions with doctoral programs. While such information is not likely to be carried in college catalogues, applicants should feel free to ask what the faculty is paid at colleges they are visiting.

THE RANGE OF FACULTY SALARIES
Here are some top salaries of full professors at selective colleges.

Harvard	$96,500	Chicago	$86,900
Yale	$90,200	Northwestern	$82,600
Princeton	$92,700	Rice	$77,900
Stanford	$91,200	Amherst	$71,700
MIT	$88,000	Pomona	$71,000

the selective applicant pool, the upper 20 percent of each year's high school graduates, will be proud to attend any one of the colleges on our list.

There really are an adequate number of freshman places in the best colleges for the best students in the country. For the student with a strong admissions strategy, this broader selection offers new and exciting opportunities.

THE SELECTIVE COLLEGE APPLICANT

Selective colleges all seek students with strong academic records, who also have demonstrated an excellence in sports, extracurricular activities, or community service.

What is a strong academic record? At least a B average and combined SAT scores above 1100. But we know, and probably you do too, that students with a C average and combined SATs of 900 are sometimes admitted to very good selective colleges. The reason for this broad range of definition lies in the strengths such students have nonacademically. They have a talent in the arts, or they are outstanding athletes, or they have been honored for an exceptional social service commitment. The numbers of such students are small, a handful in a freshman class. Yet knowing that such a group exists should encourage any student with an interest in selective colleges to ask about applying to some of them.

The best way to determine your prospects is not to trust your own judgment of your chances for admission, but to talk to a guidance counselor or to the

---

ADMISSION RATIOS

Harvard/Radcliffe and Princeton admit one out of five applicants or fewer.

Amherst, Brown, Dartmouth, Rice, Stanford, and Yale admit one out of four.

The following colleges admit one out of three: Bates, Bowdoin, Cal Tech, Columbia, Cornell, Duke, Georgetown, MIT, Pomona, Swarthmore, Wake Forest, Washington and Lee, and Williams.

These colleges admit between 40 percent and 50 percent of applicants: Boston College, Carleton, Colby, Colgate, Connecticut, Davidson, Hamilton, Haverford, Lafayette, Middlebury, Northwestern, Tufts, University of Chicago, University of Pennsylvania, Vassar, Wellesley, and Wesleyan.

Ratios for out-of-state applicants to state universities: University of California at Berkeley and University of North Carolina (Chapel Hill) admit one out of five; UCLA, University of Virginia, and College of William and Mary admit one out of three; University of Michigan and University of Wisconsin (Madison) admit two out of three.

NUMBER OF APPLICANTS FOR THE CLASS OF 1997

Amherst	4,302
Brown	12,371
Colby	2,848
Connecticut College	3,035
Cornell	19,227
Dartmouth	8,600
Davidson	2,375
Emory	8,506
Harvard	13,865
Kenyon	2,275
University of Michigan	19,086
MIT	6,411
University of North Carolina (Chapel Hill)	15,050
Northwestern	12,300
University of Pennsylvania	12,394
Pomona	3,000
Princeton	13,218
Smith	2,925
Stanford	13,600
Swarthmore	3,239
University of Texas (Austin)	14,325
Trinity College	3,057
UCLA	23,342
Vanderbilt University	7,800
University of Virginia	15,848
Wellesley College	2,894
Wesleyan University	4,771
Williams	4,188
Yale	10,705

admissions offices of colleges that interest you. There are levels of selectivity, and you may be surprised by the encouragement you will get to contact or visit colleges looking for just your kind of student.

Selective colleges look for evidence that you can do their academic work and that you have some absorbing nonacademic interest. They do not have any automatic cutoff level of grade point averages, class rank, or SAT scores. If you have any interest at all in any of the colleges we have listed, we suggest you follow it up. Don't take yourself out of the running on the basis of hearsay, a hunch, or statistics suggesting that you have to have a specified combined SAT score to be admitted to a selective college.

If encouragement from your advisor is not forthcoming, seek confirmation from the colleges themselves. The worst that can happen is that the admissions office will advise you that your chances are very poor. The admissions offices

SOME COLLEGE ENDOWMENTS

Endowments do not tell the whole story about selective colleges, and some colleges with open admissions have substantial endowments. But in general the selective colleges have endowments that give them advantages. Here are some of the larger ones as of 1992.

Harvard/Radcliffe	$5,778,257,000
Princeton University	3,286,327,000
Yale University	3,219,400,000
Stanford University	2,853,366,000
Columbia University	1,846,600,000
Emory University	1,763,518,000
Massachusetts Institute of Technology	1,752,943,000
Washington University	1,687,413,000
Northwestern University	1,308,363,000
Rice University	1,302,576,000
University of Chicago	1,224,036,000
Cornell University	1,214,600,000
University of Pennsylvania	1,095,796,000
University of Texas System	1,094,659,000
University of Notre Dame	828,554,000
Vanderbilt University	800,632,000
University of Michigan	797,149,000
Dartmouth College	743,670,000
Johns Hopkins University	725,035,000
Duke University	669,443,000
University of Rochester	656,178,000
University of Virginia	634,600,000
California Institute of Technology	626,575,000
Brown University	572,644,000
Wellesley College	485,115,000
Swarthmore College	442,298,000
Smith College	435,565,000
Carnegie-Mellon University	404,531,000

SOURCE: The National Association of College and University Business Offices as cited in *The Chronicle of Higher Education*, February 9, 1994.

When reading literature about a college, look for the endowment figure. And ask for it when visiting colleges. Keep in mind that the size of the endowment should be viewed in relation to the number of undergraduates in the institution. Higher per capita endowments than those of larger universities may enable some smaller colleges to provide an excellent faculty/student ratio (10 to 1 or lower), and a more substantial scholarship program.

of selective colleges will sometimes suggest alternative colleges you should investigate if your academic record is not at the level of students the selective colleges accept.

Sometimes, a top student fails to be admitted to one of the most selective colleges when these same colleges have admitted students with less impressive academic statistics. No explanations are available for individual cases, but we know that admissions offices, in seeking diversity, never fill their classes with all of the brightest students who apply. When a bright student is not accepted at Princeton, for example, it is because of the nonacademic profile; in the judgment of admissions, the student does not fit into this particular freshman class.

There is no doubt that you can compare academic statistics of freshman classes and observe that some, such as MIT, Yale, and Wellesley, enroll more of the stronger academic performers than others. But there is no way to quantify the nonacademic qualities of those admitted to any of the selective colleges.

Keep in mind that very bright students always are accepted by some excellent selective colleges. A Harvard/Radcliffe admissions officer told a faculty member of Concord Academy, one of the leading private schools in Massachusetts, that if all of the applicants were to enroll elsewhere, an equal number of applicants just as qualified could be chosen from those rejected. Such students will be found at Amherst, University of Chicago, Berkeley, and many other excellent institutions.

WHY SELECTIVE COLLEGES WANT YOU

No one would be so foolish as to claim that the chances of being rejected by Stanford, which had over 13,600 applicants for the class of 1997, are not high when only 2,841 were admitted that year. But even the most selective colleges have urged us to communicate the fact that there are many good selective colleges seeking students who follow the plan we propose.

Selective colleges are quality colleges, which want quality undergraduates. You can demonstrate that you will be a quality undergraduate, and you can be a winner in the admittedly complicated and often baffling college admissions competition.

You are unique. Admissions offices will come to recognize your uniqueness and see how you would fit into their particular upcoming freshman class. So many applicants seem alike. We will show you how to create an impression of uniqueness that makes a college say, "We want this applicant."

The diversity of a balanced class creates "a catalytic effect," acccording to a former Director of Admissions at Dartmouth. Richard Stabell, Dean of Admissions and Records at Rice University, says, "I'm really looking for a student who enjoys learning, not just getting high grades. . . . We're not looking for a class with well-rounded students. We're looking for a well-rounded class" (*College Bound,* vol. 7, no. 10). The concept of a balanced class works very much in your favor when you analyze the colleges and apply for admission to those that seem most suited to what you have to offer them. We think of Elizabeth in rural New Hampshire, who wanted to attend an urban college outside New England. Her personal statement appealed very much to the admissions office of Northwestern University in metropolitan Chicago, and though her academic record was little different from those of the majority of applicants, her mastery of French made a strong impression, and her goal of a foreign service career was unusual. She was accepted because her uniqueness fitted into that particular college's class balance. It would not have fitted into Georgetown's because so many Georgetown applicants aspire to the foreign service and she would not have contributed significantly to the class balance there.

To get a balanced class, the selective colleges go into the field and persuade students to apply who would otherwise not consider themselves candidates. Roland, whose widowed mother had limited means, was planning to commute from the suburbs to a large metropolitan university that had an environmental studies program. A newspaper report of his prizewinning air pollution research project caught the eye of a Princeton alumnus, who notified the Princeton admissions office. A member of the staff persuaded him to apply to a college he considered impossibly expensive. He was awarded a Naval ROTC scholarship after acceptance at Princeton. Princeton valued his particular uniqueness.

Harvard/Radcliffe, which turns down almost six out of every seven applicants, nonetheless is out looking for candidates. An applicant for the class of 1990 was discovered in upstate New York. He was an extremely bright student, yet no one in his school had urged him to apply to any selective college, and he was astounded by a visit from a staff officer of Harvard/Radcliffe's admissions office. He was the first in his school ever to apply to Harvard. And there are many such firsts every year. A valedictorian, who went to MIT from a Dallas high school, says that no one in the school had ever heard of MIT. MIT was delighted to balance its class with this student from Texas, who now is a computer programmer for a software company.

Selective colleges like to balance their classes with students who have discovered their own uniqueness and displayed it. Some examples in our experience include a boy who learned Arabic in order to work eventually for a construction company with contacts in the Middle East, another boy who became an accomplished quilt maker, a girl who gives magic shows for parties, a collector of rare books, a juggler who juggles hatchets instead of balls, and a breeder of prize cattle. Through this Twelve-Step Plan, you will learn to make this "principle of diversity" work for you. With this book's guidance, you will plan to apply to *several* selective colleges, with the objective of being admitted to one or more of them precisely for the diversity you will contribute to a particular freshman class.

AN UPBEAT APPROACH

Applicants who approach college admissions with a "can do" attitude largely avoid the jitters that afflict many candidates in today's anxiety-ridden atmosphere. *A Guide to the College Admissions Process,* published by the National Association of Admissions Counselors, says: "Self-assessment, evaluation, patience, persistence and above all good humor and perspective are the elements of a happy transition from high school to college."

Dean Whitla, Director of Educational Evaluation and Research at Harvard, who has conducted a summer institute for admissions officers for twenty-five years, says, "There are so many good selective colleges, sound applicants should canvass widely. There is really no basis for so much worrying if you approach admissions with an open mind."

A certain level of anxiety about college admissions is inevitable, even useful in pumping up the adrenaline that will help make the Twelve-Step Plan work for you. You will find as you proceed that your self-assurance will grow, and instead of asking, "Will I get in?" you will be thinking, "Which college will I choose when I am admitted to two or even three?" The belief that there is a place for you in at least two selective colleges will grow stronger as you go through the Twelve-Step Plan.

In twenty-five years of professional counseling of students, Howard Greene and his associates have never had a high school senior who followed this Twelve-Step program fail to gain admission to an appropriate college of his or her choice.

WHEN TO BEGIN

The Twelve Steps do not require a single time frame for completion. Most students begin the admissions process in the fall of junior year; a few even take the Preliminary Scholastic Assessment Test (PSAT) in the fall of sophomore year. For the majority the process runs until the spring of senior year, but those who apply for Early Decision may be admitted in December. You are free to create your own schedule, bearing in mind application deadlines and test dates.

HOW TO USE THIS BOOK

We have tried to make this book readable, but that does not mean it can be read once and put aside. It is a handbook that should be used as part of your college preparatory program. In other words it is the kind of book Francis Bacon said should be "chewed." This means it should be read carefully and each section should be read more than once.

We suggest you acquaint yourself with it by first reading over the table of contents. Then read to the end of Step Three, underlining as you go, making notes of things you should do: classify yourself; list colleges you might apply to; list admissions requirements at all these places; consider the advantages of applying for Early Decision or Early Notification; answer the Student Questionnaire; plan your demanding curriculum; focus on those activities and talents that matter the most.

Read the succeeding chapters in a sequence that fits your schedule. Mark your twenty-month calendar to include reading and reviewing relevant chapters. Do your worksheets as you go along. Yes, they really do help you to keep your ideas and information organized.

YOUR SYLLABUS: THE TWELVE-STEP PLAN SUMMARIZED

The Twelve-Step Plan is a course you are going to give yourself in getting into college. Our book is your text, and the Twelve Steps we now summarize are your syllabus.

STEP ONE: KNOW ADMISSIONS REQUIREMENTS AND PROCEDURES

In this step you will learn why it is important to be thoroughly knowledgeable about admissions requirements and procedures. Such knowledge will help you to (1) clarify reasons to apply or not to apply to a college, (2) make your applications for admission and financial aid more complete, and (3) discern the kinds of information that will be most useful to the admissions office in making a decision in your favor. It can help you determine courses to take in high school if you have not already committed yourself for a particular term (you might conclude that a fourth year of a foreign language would be more appropriate than an elective in anthropology). Knowing how an admissions office selects its freshman class is the beginning of your own self-education as you prepare for your college.

Jean Jordan, Associate Dean of Admissions at Emory University, advises, "Read all the information. Don't assume you know everything. The applicant pool is always changing. Keep in touch with the school to make sure nothing has slipped through the cracks or been lost."

STEP TWO: DETERMINE YOUR STRENGTHS

To know who you are, to know what you really want in life, to know what you do best are fundamental factors in decisions you will be making to insure acceptance by a selective college. We have prepared two questionnaires to help you and your parents in this quest for a clear vision of your strengths.

Admissions offices are mightily impressed by applicants who show genuine self-insight, because from experience they have learned that when college students know their strengths they are most likely to develop them.

STEP THREE: FOLLOW A DEMANDING CURRICULUM

All selective colleges push their students academically, and so the most important requirement they ask of applicants is that they take challenging courses in a four-year liberal arts curriculum. You should know what the selective colleges consider to be the basic minimum of strong high school courses. Such questions as how many honors courses need to be taken, how valuable foreign language fluency is, what you can do to make up for required courses not taken will be answered in Step Three, which goes to the root of college admissions. You must go beyond the minimum requirements for a high school diploma to enter these selective colleges.

STEP FOUR: MAKE COLLEGE BOARD TESTS WORK FOR YOU

In this step you approach the revised SAT I and SAT II Subject Tests (formerly called Achievement Tests) in a somewhat less tense mood than is usual, and you recognize that Subject Tests offer an opportunity to improve your academic record. You first learn to appreciate why, despite criticism, the SAT endures as a fundamental part of college admissions. Accepting the SAT as a given, you see how its importance varies from college to college. You will discover how it is possible to improve your scores, and by how much. In Step Four, you learn to accept the level at which you test as only one indicator for admission to college. You use the Subject Tests to bolster the record. A special strategy on taking Subject Tests over a longer period will give you an edge over some students who take them all at once.

STEP FIVE: EXCEL OUTSIDE CLASS

Selective colleges are seeking well-rounded classes, not the well-rounded student. To be a member of a number of boards or play several sports or take part in theater productions will not make you a strong enough candidate compared to the editor-in-chief, the varsity lacrosse player, and the student who gets the lead in plays or conducts the school band. Even in senior year you can commit yourself to an endeavor that tells a college you stand out. You don't have to be an All-American to satisfy a selective college. You do have to go all out in some activity at school or in your community.

STEP SIX: KNOW THE COLLEGES

Amazingly, applicants will write in a personal statement that they plan to major, for example, in business when in fact the college has no undergraduate business program. In Step Six you are not asked to know all the colleges; you must know only those you are considering as possibilities for your strengths and tastes. It is recommended that you acquaint yourself with a dozen or even fifteen colleges, visit as many as you can, and narrow your focus to seven or eight, which you will get to know very well from catalogues, brochures, films, visits, and from talking with others who know them. The more you know about colleges, the sounder will be your choice of those to which you will apply.

STEP SEVEN: MAKE THE MOST OF CAMPUS VISITS

Campus visits turn abstraction into a reality. Visiting a variety of campuses, you will compare facilities, academic programs, and the social atmosphere and keep a useful record of your impressions. In this step you will learn why it is important to stay overnight in a dorm. You will rate the colleges you visit on a scale of 1 down to 5, and use this rating to help you later decide to which colleges you will actually apply.

The subject of the interview is discussed, and you will learn why the interview is not necessarily an important factor in admissions decisions, but is important to help you learn if a particular college is right for you.

STEP EIGHT: FIND YOUR PLACE IN THE CLASS PIE CHARTS

Every selective college is made up of groups of students in such a way that you can construct pie charts dividing it into categories. By locating your position within such pie charts, you will learn where competition is great, and where it is slight. Finding your particular place in the class pie chart of each college will allow you to adopt sensible application strategies. You will learn in Step Eight to apply to colleges where your chances for admission are good.

STEP NINE: WRITE AN EXCITING ESSAY

Selective college applications ask students to write statements and essays that reveal aspects of their nature and of the lives they lead. Here is a further opportunity to display your uniqueness. In Step Nine you will see how other students have shown admissions officers their feelings and their experiences in a way that reflects their characters favorably. You will learn to choose a topic and write an account that awakens the reader's interest. You will learn to respond to questions on applications in brief, concise, meaningful terms. You can win over many an admissions committee with the right essay and personal statements.

STEP TEN: PLAN YOUR SELECTIVE COLLEGE FINANCES

Knowing college costs and financial aid procedures, you can plan how to pay for the higher tuitions charged by selective colleges. Procedures are somewhat complex and will require a certain amount of time. You will learn how the College Scholarship Service analyzes need, of the importance of completing thoroughly and on time the long Financial Aid Form, how aid packages vary, where to find unusual sources of scholarship funds. Your financial plans will influence your decision about applying to one college or another. You may be surprised to know that some families with a $90,000 income qualify for aid, and others who do not qualify benefit from a variety of college financing programs.

STEP ELEVEN: MARKET YOUR STRENGTHS

In Step Eleven you will see from examples just how students have successfully made extra efforts to insure recognition by admissions committees, faculty, and coaches. Marketing means selling yourself, something you will be doing later when you apply for a job, seek public office or a place in graduate school. Learning to do this as you apply to college will have a lasting value.

STEP TWELVE: ENROLL IN THE RIGHT COLLEGE FOR YOU

The final step in the plan for getting into college is enrolling in the right college for you — where you will be happy. Faced with two or more letters of acceptance, you have to choose the college that you feel will help you to do your best. Being happy in college is important because it allows your strengths to flourish. In Step Twelve you will see how some students have made their choices of college work for them. Special situations like being wait-listed are covered under this important final step.

PROFITING FROM THE ADMISSIONS PROCESS

The college admissions process has much to teach you. You will be learning how to make important decisions that bear on your future. You will learn a good deal about American higher education and the opportunities it offers. You are going to be meeting educators who are interested in you and want to learn something about you. You will discover new things about yourself, positive qualities that will please you — improved self-expression, more confidence in talking with strangers. It is our experience that students applying to selective colleges enrich their lives as they prepare for those exciting four years of higher education. The search for colleges, the interviews, the essays, and the follow-up self-marketing you will be doing should add up to a sense of real accomplishment on that day when the colleges respond to you with their offers of admission. Heed the advice of an admissions officer at the venerable College of William and Mary: "Relax and have some fun in the process of applying to colleges. Be serious about the effort, but don't take yourself too seriously."

STEP ONE

Know Admissions Requirements and Procedures

A STRATEGIC START

*O*ver the years, the selective admissions process has evolved to distribute thousands of outstanding high school graduates among fewer than one hundred of the country's top colleges. You can immediately establish a strategic position in this process by learning how a number of selective colleges expect you to prepare yourself academically for their demanding work, and by knowing how particular colleges select their freshman classes from among many qualified applicants.

To begin with, you will familiarize yourself with the admissions requirements of a number of selective colleges. Why so many when your chief interest may be in only two? A key feature of the Twelve-Step Plan is that you will increase your chances of admission to a selective college of your choice by applying to a variety of schools where you believe your particular strengths give you a unique advantage. To do this, you will need to learn about a variety of selective colleges.

BEGIN WITH COLLEGE CATALOGUES

You can acquaint yourself initially with a variety of colleges by looking over catalogues, viewbooks, and other published material available at your school or public library. Send away for information you cannot get otherwise. (Harvard/Radcliffe receives over 40,000 applicant queries a year!) Colleges are anxious to help you learn about their institutions.

THE CLASS PROFILE

Every college publishes a profile of the freshman class and distributes it to alumni and guidance counselors. Useful data such as the number of applicants admitted by class rank, test scores, and regions of the country can help you position yourself as a candidate for the colleges you are considering. Your guidance counselor should have such profiles, but if not, write to the college for one, or contact the local alumni representative.

THE COLLEGES' REQUIREMENTS

As you read through the material, take particular note of the admissions requirements of colleges that interest you, and record the information in the notebook you should be keeping on your admissions procedures. Or use the worksheet on page 24, a copy of which appears in the Appendix.

RELATIVE SELECTIVITY

Selective colleges' requirements can be rated in three broad categories: Exceedingly Demanding, Very Demanding, and Demanding. Table 2 lists the selective colleges and their classifications. Be sure your research includes colleges in *at least two* categories.

A student applying to competitive colleges should be aware of the nature of the selection process at each of the colleges or universities to which he or she applies.

> Richard Skelton, *former Director of Admissions,*
> BUCKNELL UNIVERSITY

If students have questions, they should contact the admissions and financial aid officers and look to them as aides, not adversaries, in the admissions process.

> Jennifer Rickard, *Associate Dean of Admissions,*
> SWARTHMORE COLLEGE

Do your homework! Know what your own strengths and weaknesses are and what you want out of a college or university. Gather sound information during your search, ask lots of questions, seek advice from several sources, and visit different campuses before you make your final choices.

> *Admissions Officer,*
> UNIVERSITY OF PENNSYLVANIA

INFORMATION SOURCES

If you cannot find a specific college catalogue, write to the college for one. Should the college happen to be out of catalogues, or want you to pay for one, ask the admissions office to send you their requirements for admission. No college can expect an applicant to apply without knowing its requirements. Your counselor is another source for this kind of information, but remember how busy counselors are, and do not be surprised if the counselor suggests you get this information on your own.

One of the effects of the increased interest in selective colleges is the occasional inability to keep up with the demand for costly catalogues. Viewbooks and brochures are cheaper to produce, but their information is often a summary, an overview, and they do not provide the kind of specifics you must have. Software programs in your school's resource room may or may not provide a thorough statement of requirements. When they do, print them out and paste them into your notebook. Videos often reveal institutional priorities.

Even though you may believe yourself highly qualified and a good candidate for Bryn Mawr, Stanford, Williams, or others that are Exceedingly Demanding, for instance, you can never be certain of admission to such colleges and should consider some Very Demanding ones you would be happy to attend.

Or, if you think that only a Demanding college will take you, you may be selling yourself short by not considering Very Demanding institutions as a possibility. You could be surprised to discover that a college you thought was beyond your reach would like to admit you for reasons you haven't considered.

PRELIMINARY SELF-CLASSIFICATION

By going through various colleges' requirements in your notebook and comparing them with your curriculum and your performance to date, you can arrive at a preliminary classification of where you are in the selective college pool. You may already have such a classification in mind, but now you are in a position to evaluate it realistically. This self-classification will help you establish admissions goals and work toward them systematically.

For instance, if you believe you can be admitted to a Very Demanding selective college, on the basis of your academic workload, then you can concentrate on what such colleges expect of you. Whatever your preliminary self-classification, the Twelve-Step Plan will help you focus your energies and fulfill the necessary requirements. You may find, as we have found many times, that you have a good chance of getting into a college you may have

COLLEGE REQUIREMENTS WORKSHEET

Name of College	1. ___	2. ___	3. ___	4. ___	5. ___	6. ___
Level of selectivity (Demanding, Very Demanding, Exceedingly Demanding)	___	___	___	___	___	___
Units of high school courses required (1 unit = 1 year)	___	___	___	___	___	___
English	___	___	___	___	___	___
Mathematics	___	___	___	___	___	___
Science	___	___	___	___	___	___
Languages	___	___	___	___	___	___
History or Social Studies	___	___	___	___	___	___
Electives advised	___	___	___	___	___	___
Total units required	___	___	___	___	___	___
Is SAT I or ACT required?	___	___	___	___	___	___
How many Subject Tests required?	___	___	___	___	___	___
Tests recommended	___	___	___	___	___	___
Advanced Placement policy, if any	___	___	___	___	___	___
Is credit given for college courses taken while still in high school?	___	___	___	___	___	___

identified as "too demanding." That's why the first self-classification is *only* preliminary.

Let us look at the way three different students went about their preliminary self-classification.

ANTHONY

Anthony came to the Educational Consulting Center shortly after receiving his PSAT scores of 66 verbal and 68 math. This tall, thin boy was the leading

Table 2

RELATIVE SELECTIVITY OF THE SELECTIVE COLLEGES

Key

E = *Exceedingly Demanding*
V = *Very Demanding*
D = *Demanding*

E Amherst College
V Barnard College
V Bates College
V Boston College
D Boston University
E Bowdoin College
V Brandeis University
E Brown University
E Bryn Mawr College
V Bucknell University
E California Institute of Technology
E Carleton College
V Carnegie-Mellon
E University of Chicago
V Claremont McKenna College
D Clarkson University
V Colby College
V Colgate University
V Colorado College
E Columbia University
V Connecticut College
E Cornell University
E Dartmouth College
V Davidson College
D Denison University
D Dickinson College
V Duke University
V Emory University
D Franklin and Marshall College
E Georgetown University
V Hamilton College
E Harvard University/Radcliffe
   College
V Harvey Mudd College
E Haverford College
V College of the Holy Cross
E Johns Hopkins University
D Kenyon College
V Lafayette College

D Lawrence University
V Lehigh University
D Lewis and Clark College
E Massachusetts Institute of
   Technology
E Middlebury College
V Mount Holyoke College
D New York University
V Northwestern University
V University of Notre Dame
V Oberlin College
E University of Pennsylvania
E Pomona College
E Princeton University
D Reed College
V Rensselaer Polytechnic Institute
V Rice University
D University of Richmond
D University of Rochester
D Saint Lawrence University
D Sarah Lawrence College
D Scripps College
V Smith College
E Stanford University
E Swarthmore College
V Trinity College (CT)
V Tufts University
V Union College (NY)
V Vanderbilt University
V Vassar College
D Villanova University
D Wake Forest University
V Washington University (MO)
V Washington and Lee College
V Wellesley College
E Wesleyan University (CT)
E Williams College
D Worcester Polytechnic Institute
E Yale University

RELATIVE SELECTIVITY OF THE
SELECTIVE STATE UNIVERSITIES

E University of California (all campuses)	D State University of New York (all campuses)
D University of Colorado (Boulder)	E University of North Carolina (Chapel Hill)
D University of Connecticut	D Miami of Ohio University (Oxford)
E Georgia Institute of Technology	
D University of Illinois (Urbana, Champaign)	D Pennsylvania State University
	D University of Texas (Austin)
D University of Indiana (Bloomington)	D University of Vermont
	E University of Virginia (Charlottesville)
V University of Michigan	
D University of Minnesota (St. Paul)	V College of William and Mary
	D University of Wisconsin (Madison)

WRONG ASSUMPTIONS ABOUT THE
ADMISSIONS PROCESS

A 1992 survey on admissions trends suggests that "students' desires are closer to reality than their perceptions of how the process actually works," according to the National Association of College Admissions Counselors (NACAC). Of 3,485 students at public and private schools nationwide, 34 percent ranked SAT or ACT scores as the most important factor in college admissions.

But 84 percent of NACAC member colleges listed admission test scores *after* grades and college prep courses. Students who test well but whose class performance is mediocre are at risk of rejection by selective colleges, which insist on the high quality of their undergraduates' secondary school training.

basketball player for his large regional Vermont high school, and his coach was talking to him about colleges that might offer him an athletic scholarship. But his college counselor was urging him to consider selective colleges, where there is no financial enticement for athletes — scholar-athletes as they are called — but where good athletes have a competitive edge in admissions.

At the Educational Consulting Center he identified himself as one of the top students, ranked in the upper 10 percent of his class, interested in scientific research at a college such as Duke or the University of Chicago. He recognized, though, that he had so far taken only one honors course, chemistry, and no Subject Tests, so that he really did not qualify for such colleges yet.

He had begun to consider others like Colgate, Lehigh, and Johns Hopkins. But even they would expect Anthony to show his capacity for college-level work. So he agreed to take three more honors courses during the remaining three terms of school, in spite of the demands of basketball (he dropped out of the a capella choir to get more time for the extra studying).

Thus his preliminary self-classification was that of an applicant with a good chance for admission to an Exceedingly Demanding college if he could handle the challenge of a heavier academic schedule. And if the competition proved too strong, the probability of his getting into a Very Demanding college was excellent.

PAULINE

Pauline attended a private day school near Boston that looks to the Educational Consulting Center for college counseling. Her first self-evaluation came at the end of her sophomore year while she was drawing up her junior curriculum. Seeing herself as unexceptional, she talked vaguely of junior college and of taking a year after high school to "find herself." She did rank in the middle of her class, but she had gotten As in Spanish. Was she underestimating her potential? The question intrigued her. By the time she took her SAT in the spring of her junior year, getting a combined score of 1175, she had raised her sights to the point where she was considering several Demanding colleges.

An A− in history and an 800 on the Spanish Subject Test led her to wonder if she had a chance for an Ivy college. The Center let her answer her own question in the negative. That would be overreaching. She concluded that she would have little trouble getting into a Demanding college, but that the competition for places in Very Demanding colleges might be too stiff. Her self-evaluation came down to a borderline candidate between the least competitive colleges and the next level. With the Ivy fantasy out of her mind, she was accepting herself as a good but not brilliant student. This preliminary classification allowed her to take on without anxiety a course load of one college-level course per semester.

PETER

Peter was the familiar golden boy, an achiever near the top of his class in a high school on Philadelphia's Main Line. He was captain of the baseball team, and a wonderful camp counselor. He listed his college choices in his junior year as Princeton, University of Pennsylvania, and Duke. Aware that a dozen classmates were applying to Princeton, which in the past had taken no more than half that many from his school, he got the uneasy feeling (characteristic of many top candidates) that he might not get into his favorite colleges. His list was therefore expanded to include Georgetown, Vanderbilt, and Penn State.

OUT-OF-STATE APPLICATIONS TO PUBLIC INSTITUTIONS

Recent figures suggest the strong competition between out-of-state students applying to public universities.

In 1993 the College of William and Mary, part of the Virginia state university system, admitted 1,711 out of 3,351, or 51 percent, of its Virginia applicants, as opposed to only 1,396 out of 4,564, or 31 percent, of out-of-state applicants.

The University of Virginia (Charlottesville) had almost twice as many out-of-state applications (10,426) as in-state ones (5,422) in 1993, and accepted only 25 percent of them, as opposed to 51 percent of Virginians. Of the total enrolled class, 39 percent are from out of state.

The University of California at Los Angeles accepted 807, or 34 percent of its 2,368 out-of-state applicants for the class entering in fall 1992. However, these 807 students represented only 3.6 percent of the total 22,165 applicants; this includes 19,797 California residents. UCLA, as do many state universities, uses SAT score cutoff levels to eliminate a portion of their candidates automatically without considering grades or extracurricular accomplishments. In 1992 the UCLA cutoffs for out-of-staters was 601 verbal and 689 math.

In addition to requiring other measures of high academic achievement, the University of California at Berkeley states that in general it considers only out-of-state students who rank in the top 4 percent of their high school class. In 1993 only 12 percent of the enrolled students at Berkeley were out-of-staters.

Which is one of the toughest public universities to get into if you apply from out of state? The University of North Carolina at Chapel Hill. While 64 percent (4,122 out of 6,418) of the North Carolina applicants were admitted in 1992, only 1,377 out of 9,696, or 14 percent, of the out-of-state applicants were admitted, making it just as selective as the most selective Ivies. However, if you were lucky enough to be the child of a UNC–Chapel Hill alumnus, you stood a much greater chance, 51 percent, of being admitted as an out-of-stater in 1992. The middle 50 percent of out-of-state candidates who enrolled in fall 1992 at UNC–Chapel Hill presented combined verbal and math SAT scores well over 1200.

In the summer after his junior year he decided not to return to camp but to take an enrichment course at the University of Pennsylvania. His senior-year curriculum included two honors courses and two advanced placement courses. Taking the SAT a second time, he had combined scores of 1250. His self-evaluation led him to conclude that he might get into Pennsylvania and Duke, probably not Princeton, and that he would easily get into any Very Demanding college. His foresight was accurate: Princeton wait-listed him and never took him off the list. He was accepted by the other five colleges. (Colleges put a number of candidates on a waiting list in order to assure themselves of enough freshmen to fill the class in case too few of those accepted agree to enroll.)

YOU AND YOUR GUIDANCE COUNSELOR

Some counselors in large high schools have as many as 300 to 500 students to counsel, including those applying to selective colleges. Even in private schools counselors may be pressed for time. If you find that your counselor is not being as helpful as you expect, give your counselor a hand by putting in writing a brief résumé of your achievements, interests, colleges you are thinking about, and problems on your mind. Include your preliminary self-classification and get the counselor to react at your next session. Is your self-evaluation on target, or not? A constructive dialogue should ensue that may cause you to reconsider your first judgments about yourself as a selective-college candidate. Thereafter, keep your counselor informed with brief notes about your progress. Pass on your impressions of colleges you visit or your reactions to test scores.

If a counselor is to be helpful, he or she must know you. Fleeting visits with someone who counsels several hundred students are insufficient to establish a genuine understanding of who you are and what you aspire to be. By communicating in writing you get the counselor's attention and you make your file more personal. Knowing how motivated you are, the counselor will respond with more attention, because eventually he or she will bask in your reflected glory. Counselors take great pride in students who are admitted to selective colleges.

In the back of your notebook, keep a short diary of your meetings with your counselor and of notes you send. This will serve to show how constructive your relationship is, and it will let you see how frequently you are in contact. There is nothing to be gained by taking up more counseling time than you really need. Your demands will increase as you near application-filing time in your senior year. Then it will be important for you to make sure that your teachers send copies of their recommendations to the counselor as soon as possible.

REQUIREMENTS VS. PROCEDURES

Requirements describe what a college expects you to accomplish as you prepare to go on to higher education. Procedures are the specific things you must do from junior year on, such as taking tests, visiting colleges, being interviewed, and making out applications for admission and financial aid.

You can begin learning different selective colleges' high school course

MODEL PUBLIC SCHOOLS

It is a painful fact that wealth and tradition can offer great educational advantages. You don't necessarily have to come from a wealthy family to attend excellent schools in New York suburbs. And what examples they set! For instance:

- Bronxville, on the outskirts of New York City, pays teachers on the average over $65,000 a year.
- Byram Hills in Armonk, NY, sends 90 percent of its graduates to four-year colleges.
- At Chappaqua's Horace Greeley High School, 15 percent of the senior class win National Merit Scholarships. The staff/pupil ratio is 11 to 1.
- In Scarsdale more than 90 percent of the teachers hold masters degrees. Twenty-five percent of the town population is international, including 20 percent Japanese. About 14 percent of the seniors score 5 on Advanced Placement exams.

We cite these examples to confirm our view that excellence in public education is attainable and that more communities should be pushing their students the way these schools do.

requirements at any point in your high school career. The earlier you do, the more sure you will be that your academic work conforms to what several colleges expect. While the better high schools direct college-bound students toward a liberal-arts- or science-oriented curriculum, it remains the obligation of the student to satisfy the requirements of colleges to which he or she applies.

MEETING REQUIREMENTS IS THE KEY

Of course, there is more to getting into college than meeting academic requirements, but how well you meet them will determine in part how desirable you are as an applicant. As we will see later, admissions officers use the first round of applications readings solely to determine whether, and how well, the applicants have met the college's admissions requirements. *Now* is the time to study the requirements of those twelve to fifteen schools, and to tailor your curriculum and test schedule accordingly. At the very most selective institutions, the absence of a required essay or course or Subject Test can be used to weed out candidates from so well qualified a pool.

So make it your very first priority to be sure you can meet the minimum requirements of several selective colleges. They are your initial foothold on the ivy wall!

Harrison, for example, was interested in the University of Virginia even

SOME SELECTIVE COLLEGE REQUIREMENTS

While selective colleges all urge applicants to take English, math, science, foreign languages, social studies, and arts courses, you should read admissions requirements information in catalogues or brochures carefully to make sure that your curriculum conforms to expectations of the colleges you like. Here are selected passages and summaries from a few catalogues.

University of Rochester. "A strong secondary school program usually includes four years of English *with continuous practice in writing* [our emphasis], four years of social studies, at least two years of foreign languages, three to four years of mathematics, two or more years of laboratory science." *Note:* the applicant who takes four years of math and three of science is competitively stronger than the one who settles for three years of math and two of science. You must read your catalogue with the competition in mind.

University of Pennsylvania. "Penn is one of the most selective and competitive colleges and universities in the nation. Students who apply for admission typically have outstanding records of academic and extracurricular achievements. Because Penn seeks a talented, diverse, energetic, and creative student body, many factors are evaluated for admission. Academic ability and the secondary school record are the most important factors. Other criteria considered include special talents, outstanding personal qualities, evidence of motivation, leadership, and commitment, and recommendations from counselors, teachers, principals, and headmasters. Although there is no required high school program, Penn recommends a thorough grounding in English and foreign languages, social sciences, mathematics, and natural science. Scores from SAT and three Achievement [now Subject] Tests are required of all candidates."

Emory University. Applicants need a minimum of three years of math and two years of foreign language, but the university would prefer them to take three or *four* years of foreign languages. It is recommended that those expecting to concentrate in science or math take three years of science and four of math. Rarely does a college demand; it recommends and suggests a strong curriculum, leaving the door open for the admission of an unusual and worthy student who for one reason or another has not covered traditional secondary school ground. The good selective college applicant should not be misled by any lack of insistence that recommended courses be followed. The sound rule is to take the high road and push yourself to the utmost of your capabilities.

Reed College. "While the College expects that its applicants will receive a secondary school diploma prior to enrollment, exceptions are occasionally made." This is a more liberal expression of the idea that a selective college is prepared to admit any student who can do college work and make a contribution to campus life. A potential opera star with inadequate school credits might be a good candidate for Reed. The requirement here is that the applicant be in some way exceptional.

Colgate University. ". . . Sets no limit on the number of students admitted from a given school." (The italics appear in the Colgate catalogue.) While this may not seem to have anything to do with requirements, it is related in the sense that you should not be discouraged from applying just because you are not as strong a candidate as some others in your school. Colgate looks for evidence of academic and intellectual maturity in the selection of courses, such as the number and difficulty of courses chosen each year. Four full-year courses are a minimum course load. The senior year is most important, as the courses selected for the last year should reflect previous preparation.

Similarities in requirements do not obviate the need to read the requirements sections in all descriptions of admissions. The better students are those with an eye for subtle distinctions. Questions any requirements raise in your mind should be put to interviewers at the college (or wherever you are interviewed). If you are not satisfied, your counselor will get an answer for you from the admissions office.

---

before high school, because his mother had gone there. In his freshman year he wandered into the resource room at his high school in the Washington suburbs and leafed through the Virginia catalogue. In chapter 2 he was startled to read this sentence on admissions: "Because full-time students at the University take five academic courses each term, the committee recommends that students take no fewer than four and preferably five academic courses (English, math, history, science, and foreign language) in grades nine through twelve." He was taking only four courses. His counselor had said nothing about "stretching," which is what UVA asks applicants to do. During his sophomore, junior, and senior years Harrison took five courses, including four honors courses and one advanced placement course. Eventually he did go to *the* University, as they call it in Virginia.

Marjorie began looking through college catalogues only in the fall of her junior year. In her private Seattle school one of her teachers had talked about Scripps College, outside Los Angeles. Having already looked at ten college catalogues, she got hold of the latest Scripps *Bulletin,* which says that among admissions factors considered are "independent study and college level work." It continues: "Individuals who wish more specific information or advice regarding acceptability of specific programs are invited to contact the Office of Admissions."

How would Scripps react to her independent language and art studies? She had studied art history in Italy during a summer vacation and had gained some fluency in Italian. Now she was planning to spend the vacation before her senior year in Paris to deepen her understanding of painting and to become more fluent in French. Her counselor suggested that Marjorie write to Scripps admissions describing her projects. Her letter stated that if admitted she would major in either art or French. The admissions office response was encouraging,

---

Admissions officers complain about the following faults in applicants who disregard requirements:

- improper investigation of the college
- not reading material put out by the college
- never questioning college officials during a visit
- not meeting minimum academic requirements

---

and it included information on Scripps's strong international relations and studies abroad program. An alumna called at her home to interview Marjorie, listened to her describe her summer projects, and reminded her of the importance of consistently outstanding academic work in her senior year. Marjorie ranked in the upper 15 percent of her class. In her senior year, she got an A in French for the first time. She was admitted to Scripps and three other selective colleges.

ADMISSIONS PROCEDURES

To meet admissions *requirements* you do academic work over a four-year span. Admissions *procedures* are intermittent and are followed from the fall of junior year until you are admitted. These are the components:

1. Tests (College Board or American Testing Program)
2. Campus visits
3. Interviews (not obligatory for most colleges)
4. Applications, which include:
   the student's school transcript
   personal statements and essays
5. Recommendations by teachers, counselors, heads of schools, alumni, and others
6. Financial aid applications if needed
7. Letters of acceptance, of wait-listing, of rejection

Admissions procedures vary in some respects from college to college, as you will find out as you read catalogues and other material from a number of them, but they vary within the seven categories listed. You may know these general procedures already, but what you have to know cold is what each college's procedures are, and particularly what their deadlines are for submitting applications. Each procedure is covered thoroughly in a later chapter. For our purposes here, let's draw up an admissions schedule, showing how all these procedures fit into our Twelve-Step timetable:

ADMISSIONS SCHEDULE

Junior Year

October   Take Preliminary Scholastic Assessment Test/National Merit Scholarship Qualifying Test (PSAT/NMSQT)

Winter   Review PSAT results with college counselor
Begin planning campus exploratory visits for spring
Discuss senior curriculum with counselor
Draw up schedule of College Board tests for March, May, June

Spring   Narrow list of colleges to visit to a manageable number — eight to ten
Start visiting colleges
Take tests per schedule
(If I become an early candidate, I must take SAT and Subject Tests by June)

Summer   Make summer wonderful and productive
(more on this in Step Six: Excel Outside Class)
Have formal interviews at those colleges that emphasize or encourage them

Senior Year

Fall   Take as many honors-level courses as I can
Complete campus visits
Register for November (or October in certain states) SAT four weeks in advance of test date
If I am an Early Decision or Early Action candidate, verify the application deadline, which is usually November 1, but can vary through December and even January. Submit application by the appropriate deadline, and give those who send in recommendations three weeks' advance notice
Begin working on applications
Take lots of time on essays and personal statements
Register for December SAT if I decide to take another SAT
Keep in close touch with college counselor about transcripts to be sent out
Begin planning college finances, get Financial Aid Form at school

Winter   Complete applications in December
If I apply for Early Decision and am deferred, prepare for follow-up self-marketing at other colleges
If I apply for Early Decision and am admitted, withdraw all applications previously filed
File Financial Aid Form if I need aid
Market myself with additional information to be sent to the colleges

Spring   Decide which selective college I will attend
         If wait-listed, decide whether or not to wait
         Take advanced placement tests for college I will attend
         Complete financial aid plans according to nature of aid package

You need not at this point know all the details about what is listed on this schedule. As you go from step to step these procedures will become clear to you. There is obviously a great responsibility imposed on you, the candidate, to follow the procedures. You must meet the schedules the colleges require of applicants, and the way to do this is by making a schedule for yourself and checking it regularly. This schedule will make your conferences with your counselor productive.

If you have already completed some of the schedule, such as taking the PSAT, revise the schedule accordingly.

SEATTLE CONFIRMS ADMISSIONS TRENDS

Seattle, Washington, has in recent years become one of the most desirable places to live in the USA. It is not surprising that there is considerable interest in selective colleges located in the Northwest.

Dr. Wendy Ellison Mullen, Director of College Counseling at Lakeside School in Seattle, reports that in the past ten years the number of college applications completed by its students has risen by 50 percent. This highly regarded private school sends many of its students to the University of Washington, but after that local institution come Stanford, Harvard, Pomona, Brown, Princeton, Berkeley, Whitman College, Yale, and Penn — in that order.

The 1993 graduating class of 106 students applied to 136 colleges and enrolled in 55. One of the more startling developments is that the University of Washington decreased its offers of admission to state residents from 91 percent in 1990 to 75 percent in 1992 because of the increase in resident applications. "More families are choosing to send their children to state institutions due to the rising cost of colleges," Dr. Mullen says.

A new trend at Lakeside is taking a year off before college. Seven members of the Class of 1993 did not go to college or school until the fall of 1994. About a third of the Class of 1993 applied for Early Action/ Early Admission, of whom almost half were accepted. Only 30 percent of Lakeside applicants applied to four schools or fewer. More than half applied to between five and ten schools. Eleven percent of all applicants resulted in placement on a wait list, but of 71 wait-listed, only 8 were eventually accepted and only 3 enrolled in one of the schools.

More than a third of Lakeside graduates usually enroll in selective colleges in the Northeast. About 20 percent enroll in colleges in Washington State, 20 percent in California, and the rest in other parts of the country.

In addition to the standard procedures, there are a couple of specific procedures that we'll consider here.

SPECIAL PROCEDURES — EARLY DECISION

THE PROS AND CONS

Admission to selective colleges by Early Decision has developed as an advantage to the colleges and as a convenience to the right student. Early Decision means that you, the candidate, request a decision on your application in the fall, before the end of the first academic term of senior year. The conditions imposed are two: you request Early Decision from only one institution; you agree if admitted by Early Decision to apply to no other institution thereafter. In short, you have been admitted and are de facto enrolled almost a year before you actually matriculate. If you are not admitted early, your application is deferred for final decision in early April.

Before you jump to the conclusion that Early Decision can put an end to all your worries, you should realize that there are as many potential disadvantages as advantages in taking this admissions route. To begin with, only very strong candidates should even consider Early Decision. You need high grades in a good curriculum, a breadth and depth of nonacademic interests and activities, College Board scores that would place you in the top 20 percent of those applying to that college (not the top 20 percent of your school class, the top 20 percent of *all* applicants). If you are just below these criteria but have much to offer the college, you can possibly gain some attention and leverage by applying for Early Decision. You may be deferred, but you may also be favored among candidates admitted in April. Students are also urged to investigate enough colleges to be absolutely sure that the college from which they are asking an Early Decision is their true first choice and not a college they happen to know will accept them. We have seen too many students jump at the chance for Early Decision from a college they are not happy to attend. Haste is the besetting evil of the Early Decision decision.

THE EARLY DECISION PROCESS

You should understand how colleges use Early Decision in an effort to enroll top students in their freshman classes before some other institution gets them. The great majority of colleges will not review and evaluate the large number of regular applicants' credentials until February, March, and April. By that time the admissions office has closed off applications, and so the committee knows how many applications are in and just how many admission letters can be sent out. Each applicant can be evaluated against the caliber of the total batch of applications.

When applicants are judged for Early Decision, the admissions office has no idea what the total application pool for the year looks like. So the committee looks at the early applicant as only representative of the best of the lot. Such applicants must be deemed to rank between the top 10 percent and 20 percent of the class: the freshman class, we again emphasize, not the secondary school class. The exception can be the outstanding athlete, class leader, or performing artist who is sought after by many colleges.

You can see that if Bowdoin, Middlebury, Colgate, and Penn can get top students in Early Decision, these are students Yale, Amherst, Dartmouth, Stanford, Harvard, Princeton, or other highly selective colleges will not take from them. Applicants, particularly those who rank very high in their classes, should recognize that not only are they competing among themselves for places in freshman classes of the best selective colleges, but the best selective colleges are competing among themselves to enroll as many top students as possible. While the competition for admission is stiff, there is a limited number of highly qualified candidates to go around.

It pains Princeton very much to lose about half those it admits to Harvard, Yale, Stanford, and a few other colleges. It pains Amherst to know that students admitted to both Amherst and Princeton are more likely to enroll at Princeton. Early Decision is a kind of admissions aspirin to relieve selective college administration pain. In this sense the applicant who is very strong is in the driver's seat. Like the World War I poster of Uncle Sam pointing a finger, saying, "Uncle Sam wants you," Early Decision is saying, "College USA wants you." The question then boils down to: do you want College USA?

As the total number of selective college applications grows, so does the number of Early Decision applicants. Let no strong applicant rush to judgment without reflecting on all the implications.

For Greg the question was not whether he would be admitted to an Ivy college, but which Ivy college would be most likely to take him. In a major Long Island high school he stood in the upper 5 percent of his class, had a combined SAT score of 1460, Subject Tests in the low 700s, an AP 4 out of 5 score in American history. He was president of his school's Model UN, and had interned for a congressman. In his interviews at the Educational Consulting Center he listed Yale, Princeton, and Brown as his first choices.

But these colleges are overwhelmed with applicants from the New York area. Dartmouth is not. Moreover, Dartmouth's Nelson Rockefeller Institute for Political Studies is ideal for a student like Greg, interested in political science. A visit to the college convinced him that he would love it, and he followed Dartmouth admissions' advice to apply for Early Decision, which, if successful, would mean forgetting about any other college. In so advising him, Dartmouth was shrewdly taking an applicant who might have beaten out competition at one of their rivals like Brown, Yale, or Princeton. Thus Early Decision was a perfect fit for applicant and college. Greg was admitted to Dartmouth in December of his senior year.

REQUIREMENTS FOR EARLY DECISION

An interview. A personal interview is either encouraged or required by the majority of colleges. You should ask whether the interview was a success and make sure that the college understands just why it is your number one choice.
Tests. SATs and three Subjects must be taken by June of junior year. If you feel that you will do better in your senior year, you can still apply early, but be certain to arrange to retake SATs and Subjects in your senior year; you may very well be admitted by spring of senior year, having been deferred on the early plan.
Teachers' recommendations. Usually two recommendations are required. Will teachers you already know give you very strong reports, or will you get better reports senior year, based on what you know about your teachers? Be careful that teachers do not send in boilerplate recommendations — that is, one recommendation per student sent in Xerox copy to every college to which the student is applying.

CAVEATS

Don't try to beat the Early Decision system by secretly applying to another college if admitted by one through Early Decision. You can get burned when the college that first admitted you finds out and withdraws its offer of admission.

Don't sell yourself short by being drawn into an Early Decision at a college that seems less exciting or less selective than one or two you hope to attend. You should give yourself every opportunity to apply to colleges that you truly want to attend.

THE ADVANTAGES OF EARLY DECISION

If you have a genuine, heartfelt first choice and are a very strong candidate, you put yourself in a very good position by declaring this in the form of an Early Decision application. Either you will be admitted then and there, or your name will be flagged as one to take a very good second look at later. The fact that you applied for Early Decision and did not make it is in your favor because of your commitment to the college. *Be warned that this holds true only for the very best student, or close to the best.* Ultimately every applicant is judged on the record.

And, speaking of the record, the colleges love the students they admit by Early Decision because of their great performances in college and thereafter. And so colleges would like to take in more of them, and wish that the best students would apply early. Example: Dartmouth turned down four out of seven candidates for the class of 1997, most of them exceptional applicants. Some of those they rejected would have been admitted had they applied early. By spring there were no places for them. For the class of 1993, Dartmouth had 1,003 Early Decision applicants. Approximately 30 percent of them were admitted because of the high quality of the group. Some were deferred and admitted in the spring.

So, to sum up: apply for Early Decision only if you are among your school's best students, and apply only to your very first choice of college.

FINANCIAL AID

You will have to fill out a "short version" of the Financial Aid Form. When admitted by Early Decision you will, in most cases, learn right away what your aid package is. No waiting all winter to find out how you will fare. Another plus for Early Decision.

SPECIAL PROCEDURES —
EARLY ACTION AND EARLY NOTIFICATION

Not to be confused with Early Decision is the Early Action or Early Notification process available at some colleges, such as Yale, Princeton, Harvard, Brown, Georgetown, and Northwestern. Usually students apply for Early Action or Early Notification to colleges where they are reasonably sure of admission. Accepted early, they need file no other applications. However, unlike Early Decision, which rarely results in a rejection and almost always defers the decision on a candidate's application if he or she is not accepted, in Early Action you can be rejected or deferred.

Another big difference between Early Decision and Early Action or Early Notification is that the candidate is not under obligation to discontinue all other applications. By the same token, the applicant does not become the same premier candidate for spring admission he or she becomes if deferred in Early Decision.

Applicants for Early Action and Early Notification run more of a risk than those for Early Decision because of the severe screening process, which is an effort to eliminate marginal candidates. We recommend against Early Action or Early Notification applications if there is the slightest chance of your not being admitted. Usually you can get an idea from the admissions office whether such an application is really welcome.

Heather came to the Educational Consulting Center after Georgetown had rejected her when she applied for Early Action. It was pointed out that she really did not qualify as an Early Action candidate, but need not feel so crushed by Georgetown's decision, for there are several Catholic colleges more suitable for her. Her 550 Verbal SAT and B− grades in English courses, none of them honors, could not be offset by a solid 610 math SAT and A− and B+ in science courses. She was overestimating, too, the strength of her athletics. Being on the swimming team of a small Maryland high school showed character, but she could not expect to compete at the college level. Heather applied to Villanova, Notre Dame, Boston College, and William and Mary (not a Catholic college) for regular admission and was accepted by Villanova, Notre Dame, and William and Mary; BC wait-listed her, and she enrolled at Villanova. Her Early Action mistake was unpleasant but not fatal.

INSIDE THE ADMISSIONS OFFICE

Far from being confined to back-room reading of applications, admissions officers canvass schools, talk to counselors, interview applicants, and meet

---

WISDOM FROM A DEAN OF DEANS

Fred Hargedon, Princeton's Dean of Admission, is one of the most respected members of the admissions world. In May 1993 he took the trouble to compose a three-page, single-spaced letter to all prospective applicants, presenting his observations not just about Princeton admissions but about applying to any college. Here are some excerpts.

Begin your college search by taking some time to think hard about why it is you want to go to college in the first place.

Set aside some quiet time to reflect frankly on your strengths and weaknesses.

Sketch out a tentative plan of what it is you wish to accomplish in college.

Try to imagine how well a given college will meet your needs and interests as a junior or senior, not just what it offers as a freshman.

Try to avoid falling into the trap of thinking about one or another college solely in terms of a few descriptive adjectives or traits.

I happen to believe that the saving grace of college admissions as a whole in this country is the fact that we don't all agree on precisely the same students to admit in a given year.

In applying to a college with more qualified applicants than there are places available in the freshman class, there will be some factors affecting the ultimate decision on your application . . . over which you have no control and for which you should not feel responsible.

Don't let the college application process so preoccupy you that you miss out on all that your school has to offer you during your senior year.

with alumni committees who help conduct interviews. In this way, they become acquainted with thousands of secondary schools. These contacts are the admissions staff's way of keeping in touch, finding out what is happening in schools. "Quality dropping here," one may note of a particular high school, or "This school is developing stronger candidates," or "The students who enroll from this school always seem happy or successful."

Admissions officers spend much time, too, on the phone, answering questions candidly, even bluntly, if a counselor asks about a certain candidate's chances. The staff is approachable — by applicants, parents, counselors, or media — up to the time of the big crunch that begins in January, as applications are reviewed.

HOW APPLICATIONS ARE REVIEWED

There's no secret about what happens to applications. "We read every single application at least once," says every selective college admissions dean or director. During the first reading two things happen: the most promising candidates for admission are identified, and those who must be immediately rejected are also identified. This second category of applications gets a cursory second glance from another member of the staff, and unless considered a possible candidate, is filed and not reviewed again.

The few immediately identified as acceptable require confirmation by others on the staff and by the director, but they seldom take up much time. It is the big group of possible acceptances that will be pored over, discussed, and argued about. At the most selective colleges, between 5 and 10 percent of applicants are more or less instant admissions, and 10 to 20 percent more or less are instantly identified as not to be admitted, leaving thousands of folders

---

PORTRAIT OF AN ADMISSIONS STAFF

An admissions office at any college consists of a small staff of professional educators, teachers, or administrators, who like meeting families, talking to counselors, and helping the college pick freshman classes. "An individual who does not enjoy biography probably would not enjoy being an admissions officer," says an assistant dean for admissions at Columbia School of Business, a statement that holds true for undergraduate admissions too. Most colleges staff their admissions offices with their own alumni because of their knowledge of the college and loyalty to it, although, increasingly, young professionals are attracted to certain colleges for their specialized knowledge. You should ask in an interview why they like to work at their particular institution.

for a small staff to consider. (You can see how important it is that your application distinguish you favorably from the start!)

SPECIAL ROUNDS CONSIDERATIONS

During the winter, admissions offices consider candidates by categories known as rounds. There are minority rounds, alumni and faculty children rounds, athletic rounds, foreign student rounds, and miscellaneous rounds depending on applications — handicapped students, for example. There are no geographical rounds as such, but the staff considers the advantage to the college of accepting students from parts of the country they want represented in the class balance. Regional representatives of the staff make pleas for top candidates from their territory. They win some arguments and lose others.

Special rounds, in effect, weight the chances of the applicant favorably against those who are not part of the round. Alumni children have a better chance of being admitted than non-alumni children, or an athlete may have a better chance than a nonathlete with higher academic qualifications. At the same time, there is competition within the rounds. Not all alumni children who apply are admitted, nor are all athletes, all minorities, or all of any group that is considered separately. Special rounds are covered in more detail in Step Eight.

Alumni play an active role in helping admissions committees identify candidates and in interviewing them. Alumni trustees, fund raisers, and benefactors sometimes put in a good word for an applicant, and this will have considerable weight in some folders and in others very little. In either case, candidates do well to understand that in the American college system, public and private, alumni support, financial or otherwise, is critical to the continuing excellence of the college.

RATING SYSTEMS

Each college has its own rating system, but few reveal their exact character. We know that Princeton and Amherst rate candidates on a scale of 1 to 5, and Dartmouth on a scale of 1 to 6 — 1 being the highest rating. Those who read folders for Yale admissions are asked to rate candidates 1 if they recommend acceptance, 2 if they recommend acceptance with reservation, 6 if they recommend rejection with reservation, and 7 if they recommend out-and-out rejection. Rating systems exist for the convenience of admissions committees. There is really no way a candidate can discover how he or she has been rated. Such information is confidential and is used only to classify candidates for committee discussion.

A former Yale admissions staff member reports that each folder is read by two people: one is a generalist concerned with the composition of a class as a whole, the other a regional specialist who reads only folders of candidates

RATING SYSTEMS AT PRINCETON AND AMHERST

In the system introduced at Princeton and adopted by Amherst, candidates are rated on a scale of 1 down to 5 in two categories, academic and nonacademic qualities. Any folder that turns up a combined total rating of more than 6 is considered a "non-admit." This means, for example, an academic 4 and a nonacademic 1 will probably be admitted to Princeton or Amherst.

Some folders require several readings when the committee gets down to cases and discusses decisions as a group. Then the appeals of faculty, coaches, alumni, benefactors, and others may be considered. Henry Bedford, former officer of admissions at Amherst, told a *Wall Street Journal* reporter that such pressures are "trivial" compared to the pressure of getting all applications decided on by April. But later the reporter noted that one applicant under consideration could not be turned down until the president of the college knew about it and could prepare for an alumnus's possible complaint.

from one part of the country. Alumni children's, minorities', and athlete candidates' folders are read a third time by specialists in these three categories of applicants. Most of the discussion is about candidates rated 2 by both readers, candidates on the borderline of acceptance. There is some discussion when the area reader wants to accept and the general reader has reservations about a candidate. Rarely is there any discussion if the candidate is rated 1 or 7 by both readers. Such candidates are admitted or rejected in less than one minute of committee time.

Any committee member may request discussion of any candidate. A folder rated 6/6, reject with reservations, may be discussed because of an 800 math SAT score. A minority candidate rated 2/6 may be discussed at the request of the minority reader who favors admission. At Yale one or two faculty representatives are present for every vote, which is recorded anonymously and tabulated electronically.

A rating system like Princeton's reveals how self-evaluation determines the nature of the candidate pool of a highly selective college. For the class of 1997 only two applicants were rated 5 academically and nonacademically. Very weak candidates rarely apply to Princeton. And exceptionally strong candidates are equally rare: there were only six applicants for the class of 1997 rated 1 both academically and nonacademically.

HOW FAIR IS THE ADMISSIONS PROCESS?

In a word, very! Admissions staffs have been established as autonomous committees, which constitute a kind of high court beyond which there really are no appeals. Admissions committees are, by intent, relatively impervious to the influence of prestige, high office, and wealth in considering applicants. (At Princeton, some years ago, the admissions office received a call from the White House about a candidate, but even this failed to improve the candidate's chances!)

A well-meaning party attempting to influence the committee on your behalf may end up feeling rebuffed or even insulted if his or her recommendation doesn't result in your admission to that college. We would hope to spare you *and* your admirers this sort of embarrassment. (Of course, the attempted influence we're talking about here is quite different from letters of recommendation, which *do* carry weight with admissions committees in the proper course of the admissions process.)

As a result of the scrupulous fairness of selective admission, the great colleges of our country are open to all who qualify by virtue of their own efforts. You, who follow the Twelve-Step Plan, can feel confident that your application will receive the same consideration as any other. The selective admissions process is fair to all, and neither influence nor gimmickry can subvert it.

WHAT ADMISSIONS OFFICIALS RECOMMEND

We asked eighty selective college deans and directors of admission for any message they wished to convey to future applicants. Here is a representative sample of their responses.

Bates. Preparing for admissions to Bates takes time and thought, for we truly do read all applications carefully. Essays should show that you have considered your response(s) before beginning to write, rather than dashing off some hasty all-purpose answer. Visit Bates if it is at all possible, to have an interview and see the campus. Our interviews are evaluative in nature; they are part of the admissions process. If you cannot come to Bates before February 1, by all means request an alumni interview.

Brown. Turn TV set off and read, read, read.

Bucknell. A student applying to a competitive college for admission should be aware of the nature of the selection process at each of the colleges or universities to which he or she applies. The quality and content of the academic performance attempted, the quality of performance and achievement, and sustained extracurricular contribution over a long duration are increasingly important in the decision as to who will be admitted. We would urge students to work hard, be intensively involved in a few things rather than to be spread too thinly over many things. We like to see productive follow-through with activities rather than a long list of marginal contributions and activities.

Carleton. Take the most challenging program available in your secondary school. Don't be afraid to take risks. Prepare your application and essay carefully. Schedule an interview if at all possible.

Carnegie-Mellon. Select the most demanding courses for which you are prepared (and which are available to you) in your high school. Grades are very important.

University of Chicago. With the increased interest in quality secondary education, students have available increasingly strong high school programs. Students who choose the best program in the most rigorous courses will have an advantage in admission to the most selective colleges. We have seen an increase in applications with a continued increase in quality and we think the top colleges will continue with this trend.

Colgate. If the school offers top courses and you are qualified, you really must elect to take them. Try to concentrate on being excellent — don't fall into the well-rounded trap, where you have some talents in a lot of areas, but none of them strong enough to stand alone. Remember that admissions is a human process and that we don't expect perfection; most people stumble once in a while. Don't worry about the interview or trying to second-guess what admissions is looking for. All we look for — beyond the customary qualities of intelligence, curiosity, sense of humor, motivation, sensitivity, and appreciation for others (tolerance) — is what the student is. What every student is can only be where he or she is at this time.

Columbia. Relax; for the most part it's a buyer's market except for about fifteen schools.

Connecticut College. Take advantage of all available opportunities to learn, through involvement in academic and nonacademic (extracurricular, work/ volunteer experience, etc.) programs. Develop talents, make commitments, and derive as much pleasure as possible from the things you do.

Cornell. Take challenging courses, do the best you can, attempt to excel in one area important to you, apply to few colleges — those that meet your needs.

Kenyon. Take the most demanding program you can handle, which should include four years of math. Look at all parts of the country, not just the East Coast, unless you enjoy rejection.

Lewis and Clark. Be aware of international issues and follow current events.

Trinity. The quality of the curriculum is not something that can be thought of only in the senior year. Planning *must* start in grades eight and nine.

Tufts. Be responsibly active and contributing in your school and community, and maintain a quality curriculum throughout all high school years. Also apply for financial aid when in doubt.

Washington and Lee. Worry more about program, personal productivity, and performance, and less about standardized scores.

Williams. Go for the three Ps — Program, Performance, Potential — i.e., take the best schedule, do well what you are doing, give the college a good sense that you have ability and potential and that you are willing to use it. In writing up your application, give a good sense of what has meaning to you;

GRADE POINT AVERAGES AND SAT SCORES OF UNIVERSITY OF CALIFORNIA AT BERKELEY APPLICANTS

For the Class of 1996

Grade point average (GPA) intervals are listed vertically and Scholastic Achievement Test (SAT) composite score (mathematics plus verbal) intervals are listed horizontally. Each block in the chart represents a pool of applicants with GPA and SAT scores within the specific intervals indicated.

GPA is defined as a student's GPA in the core academic courses as calculated by a UC admissions evaluator or, if the evaluated GPA was not available, the student's GPA as self-reported on the application for admission.

The campus overall total includes freshman applicants whose GPA or SAT composite score (or both) were out of range or unavailable. Data were compiled in September 1992.

GPA	ALL PROGRAMS EXCEPT ENGINEERING SAT Composite					
	490–790	800–990	1000–1190	1200–1390	1400–1600	OVERALL
2.82–2.99			131/21	39/0	3/0	173/21
			16%	0%	0%	12%
3.00–3.29	179/11	500/79	729/127	304/50	26/7	1738/274
	6%	16%	17%	16%	27%	16%
3.30–3.59	173/24	608/165	1133/247	569/136	44/21	2527/593
	14%	27%	22%	24%	48%	23%
3.60–3.89	116/15	573/160	1489/408	1081/449	125/111	3384/1143
	13%	28%	27%	42%	89%	34%
3.90–3.99	11/3	97/23	332/104	325/219	47/45	812/394
	27%	24%	31%	67%	96%	49%
4.00	39/12	345/115	1908/769	3363/2770	997/980	6652/4646
	31%	33%	40%	82%	98%	70%
OVERALL	518/65	2123/542	5722/1676	5681/3624	1242/1164	17063/7326
	13%	26%	29%	64%	94%	43%

GPA	ENGINEERING PROGRAMS SAT Composite					
	490–790	800–990	1000–1190	1200–1390	1400–1600	OVERALL
2.82–2.99			17/2	5/0	0/0	22/2
			12%	0%	0%	9%
3.00–3.29	25/0	42/0	78/2	42/7	0/0	187/9
	0%	0%	3%	17%	0%	5%
3.30–3.59	13/0	75/0	153/10	110/14	12/2	363/26
	0%	0%	7%	13%	17%	7%
3.60–3.89	19/0	94/5	231/22	232/75	41/20	617/122
	0%	5%	10%	32%	49%	20%
3.90–3.99	2/0	22/0	68/11	81/30	10/8	183/49
	0%	0%	16%	37%	80%	27%
4.00	8/0	60/4	393/87	870/523	387/353	1718/967
	0%	7%	22%	60%	91%	56%
OVERALL	67/0	293/9	940/134	1340/649	450/383	3409/1204
	0%	3%	14%	48%	85%	35%

SOURCE: An informational booklet distributed by the University of California, Berkeley

write from personal experience. And show where you have exhibited follow-through.

Yale. If a college is selective, all six factors are important: application and essay, school recommendations, extracurricular activities, grade point average, board scores, and quality of curriculum.

Certain themes run through all these remarks: the importance of a strong school curriculum, the need to push yourself by taking demanding courses in which you do well, the uselessness of being all-around anything instead of excelling at one or two things, the absence of any reference to SAT scores except by Washington and Lee, suggesting that admissions offices pay less attention to them than to grade point averages.

Despite these similarities of outlook, each college has its own agenda, its own approach to admissions that you must recognize. As you complete Step One, you will be learning the nature of the selection process at a number of the schools that interest you. Columbia's statement that except for fifteen colleges it's a buyer's market is, in our view, encouraging, but to be taken cautiously. Relax, yes, we're all for that — as long as you're following the Twelve-Step Plan!

Certainly the selective process does not consist of marking folders with numbers weighing grade point averages over board scores or essays over school recommendations. As one director observed, it is the folder with "internal consistency" that is the most highly considered as an "admit" or a "possible admit." Colleges, after all, admit a whole person, and they want to make judgments based on how much of the whole person a folder reveals.

Let us sum up what admissions directors are telling you.

1. Study hard and make sure you take demanding courses and follow a strong curriculum.
2. Excel in one or two things outside class: sports, extracurricular activities, or community service. Don't spread yourself too thin.
3. Get to know how each college you apply to evaluates your folder. Find out how important SATs are, and find out what talents the colleges may be seeking. *Believe the Bates statement that says preparing for admissions takes time and thought and a willingness to ask for information at admissions offices.*

Step One will be completed gradually and will underlie the other steps you take in the Twelve-Step Plan. The agenda you create in this initial step begins the action program that will admit you to one or more selective colleges. Let's move on to Step Two.

Step One Checklist

1. Begin to use your notebook on college admissions to record key information.

2. Consult a variety of college catalogues that may interest you; list their admission requirements in your notebook.

3. Give yourself a preliminary self-classification, estimating how well qualified you think you are to apply to colleges with requirements that are Exceedingly Demanding, Very Demanding, and Demanding.

4. Send to your counselor a brief summary of your college interests. Include your preliminary self-classification.

5. Draw up a schedule of your admission plans for tests, campus visits, applications.

6. Discuss with your college counselor and with the appropriate admissions offices the advisability of Early Decision or Early Notification.

STEP TWO

Determine Your Strengths

MAKING A CHOICE

Choosing a college is really your first major decision in life. The process involves discovering, among possibly a hundred or more places you've never seen and know little about, a handful where you think you will be happy and productive for four years. What's more, you are asked to prepare yourself at one of these colleges not for four years, but for the rest of your life. You are, in effect, laying the foundation on which you will build your career and your life's work. And the quality of that foundation rests on identifying your personal and academic strengths.

John Sloan Dickey, former president of Dartmouth, once said: "The first requirement of being genuinely well educated is to have the capacity of being useful." Admissions committees of selective colleges seek to enroll students who will be useful to themselves, their fellow students, the colleges, and society.

But how do they identify such students? Actually, admissions officials look for applicants who identify *themselves* as useful. These are students who know their strengths, and who are therefore likely to be motivated and directed by them.

Contrast these two self-assessments.

Ricky, a junior in a competitive high school near Richmond, Virginia, wrote the following statement for Howard Greene in the spring of his junior year.

> I would like a career in journalism. I have had this idea ever since my uncle visited us from California years ago. He is city editor of a daily paper in a small city, but he made me feel that the whole community depended on his work. For example, he described how his paper handled a racial zoning problem and avoided a potential race riot.
>
> My uncle suggested that I read a daily paper and study lots of American history. My 640 score on the History Subject Test is one result that

should help me get into a top college. As I have indicated, I am in the upper 12 percent of my class.

I have tried to make my writing for the Scripture, our school paper, an influence in school. My articles on drug abuse were reprinted in our town weekly paper. Perhaps somebody is avoiding drugs because of those articles. I am hopeful that I will be elected editor senior year.

My grades and SAT scores are good enough for Chapel Hill, according to my counselor. This college appeals to me because of its history department, and because it is a large urban university in a high tech area where things are changing. I believe I can acquire the background a good newspaperman needs — although I might wind up in radio or TV — at such a great university as North Carolina. I would like suggestions for other comparable colleges I ought to apply to in case I don't make it to Chapel Hill.

Jacqueline, a junior in a private day school in Milwaukee, ended her questionnaire for the Educational Consulting Center this way:

I am a typical all around person. I believe a person must make a contribution in life, so I take part in as many school activities as possible. My best sport is tennis — I am number six on the team and play doubles in matches with other schools. I also play field hockey (jayvee), and basketball (intramural). As a member of the Student Council I am responsible for advising on Robert's Rules of Order. In my church I attend Youth Group meetings monthly and have helped Asian refugees find jobs, two at our hospital where I volunteer. I am not sure yet just what college to apply to. It will depend on how much I can bring up my SAT scores next year — I know I am really not an 1100 student. I hope you can help me test better.

Ricky clearly had a handle on himself, and did indeed go to North Carolina. Jacqueline was less mature at the time. She learned to concentrate her energies during her senior year, spending much of her free time at the hospital. Doing that suggested the possibility of a nursing career. She learned to accept the fact that she was not going to score much higher on her tests, and that the important thing was to develop her warm feeling for people into a usefulness to society. She was admitted to the University of Wisconsin, which in her junior year had hardly seemed a likely possibility.

ACADEMIC STRENGTHS

Academic strengths are easily recognized and quantified by grades, class rank, and test scores. These are reinforced by teachers' comments, and here's where you can turn weaknesses into strengths. The natural tendency is to read over those comments that praise your work, and merely glance at those that criticize it. But it is critical comment that can teach you to overcome bad habits and force you to master material you find difficult or unpleasant to learn. So your procedure should be first to note your obvious strengths from grades, test scores, and comments. These will be apparent to an admissions committee, too, and so you should continue efforts to keep these strengths. But you should also reflect on your teachers' criticisms for clues to ways to improve your record. Awareness of your academic strengths will give you confidence to accept criticism and act on it.

EXTRACURRICULAR STRENGTHS

Identifying obvious fortes such as athletic achievement, election to class offices, success on the school paper or in the drama club is a simple matter. But you should be careful not to confuse mere activity with strength. Participation is not a strength in itself. Admissions committees are unimpressed by laundry lists of activities in school or in your community. Rarely is any student strong in six areas. Even in athletics today, the demands of a single sport make it difficult for a good athlete to be outstanding in several sports.

What colleges look for are standouts: 20 percent of the class of 1997 at Williams had been distinguished athletes, some 30 percent achieved distinction in music, 18 percent had been heads of a service organization. By identifying one or two of your strengths, you clarify your extracurricular goals and assure yourself of the possibility of becoming an accepted student.

YOUR STUDENT QUESTIONNAIRE

To help you discover more about your abilities, we have adapted a questionnaire that has proved of great value as students embark on the Twelve-Step Plan to college admissions. In it, you are asked to examine your academic performance and personal qualities, and to rate the features of colleges (size, geographical location, and so on) according to your preferences.

Reflect on the questions, and jot your answers in your notebook. The questionnaire is intended to take time and thought as you fill it out. Some points you've probably been thinking about already; others you may be reflecting on for the first time. For instance, let's say you live in the East and are thinking of applying to Stanford, where your mother went, and to Middlebury, where your father went, as well as to Vanderbilt, where last year's valedictorian went. The first question asks you to check priorities of locations. Already you have to think about which of these colleges you would prefer, and to deal with such thoughts as "Will Mom be offended if I don't put Stanford first?"

In saying that you should get to know yourself for the purpose of successful college admissions, we are not suggesting psychoanalysis or therapy. Knowing your strengths is a matter of looking at palpable records — your grades, SAT scores, extracurricular accomplishments — as well as your tastes. Your school

ACTIVITIES OF APPLICANTS TO TWO
SELECTIVE COLLEGES

WILLIAMS

Head of student government	89
Distinction in music	179
Distinction in studio arts, theater, dance, or creative writing	149
Research or honors in sciences	149
Distinction in athletics	209
Head of service organization	189
Debate captain, editor in chief of yearbook, newspaper, or literary magazine	169

CARLETON (SAMPLING OF INTERESTS)

Took first place in the Tour De Wolf mountain biking competition
Played Russian chess master Gary Kasparov to a draw
Published an article in *Ad Astra,* the magazine of the National Space Society
Rescued sea turtles in Costa Rica
Was named state Gatorade Soccer Player of the Year
Worked at sod farming thirty hours a week for three summers
Won one of eighteen Malcolm H. Kerr Scholarships to study in an Arab country (Tunisia)

records are a known quantity, but do you prefer a small, medium, or large college? Or a college that is within a university with graduate schools? At first you may say a university, because it's supposedly more stimulating. And then you visit Pomona or Lafayette and wonder what could be more stimulating than either of these fine small colleges.

The questionnaire can reveal what your individual strengths are and help you concentrate your efforts where they will be most rewarding and useful. As you know your powers better, they will serve you better, not just in getting into college, but in all that you do.

ANSWERING THE STUDENT QUESTIONNAIRE

The questionnaire appears in worksheet form in the Appendix. Let's take a look at the questions, to start you thinking about them before you actually fill out the worksheet.

Question 1. You may already have a clear vision of the kind of college you would like to attend. But perhaps you haven't given much thought to second

STUDENT QUESTIONNAIRE

1. What type of college do you see yourself in? Please look over the characteristics listed below and review them with your parents before checking anything.

   GEOGRAPHICAL LOCATION (number choices 1, 2, 3, etc.)

   Northeast _____ Middle Atlantic _____ Midwest _____

   South _____ Far West _____ Does not matter _____

   EXACT LOCATION (please check)

   Urban _____ Suburban _____ Rural _____

   Does not matter_____

   SIZE (please check)

   Small (under 2,500 undergraduates) _____

   Medium (2,500–6,000) _____ Large (6,000–10,000) _____

   Extremely large (10,000–25,000) _____

   Do you prefer a college (undergraduate only)? _____ A university (undergraduate, graduate, and professional students)? _____

   Does not matter? _____

   Coeducational? _____ Single Sex? _____ Does not matter? _____

   What characteristics would you prefer in a college?

   What characteristics would you like to avoid?

   How important a consideration is institutional prestige?

   How intensive an academic workload and grading system do you want?

2. Intended major (or possible majors, if you are undecided)? Specific academic interests apart from your major? Extracurricular interests you intend to pursue in college (please list in order of importance):

3. Will you need financial aid? _____ Do you want a part-time job? _____

4. Father's college and class _____

   Graduate school(s) _____

Mother's college and class _____

Graduate school(s) _____

Does either of your parents teach or work at a college or university?

Are any relatives significantly involved in any college of possible interest to you? Which ones?

5. At this time are there any colleges in which you are particularly interested? Which ones? Why?

   Have you already ruled out any colleges? Which ones? Why?

6. How would *you* assess yourself as a student?

   What do you consider to be your areas of academic strength and weakness?

   Do you think your transcript and counselor/teacher reports, if any, are a fair evaluation of your academic abilities?

7. How would you characterize yourself?

   What kind of person are you?

   What kind of people do you like to be with?

8. Please list your *most important* extracurricular pursuits (specify years of involvement).

   School activities:

   School sports:

   Outside activities:

   Work and summer activities:

   Hobbies and pastimes:

   Awards (academic and extracurricular):

   Please indicate, after reviewing the items above, the one or two that interest you most.

and third choices. We want you to reflect on them because there are so many good college opportunities in different sections of the country.

For instance, let us say you live in the East and your father went to Amherst. You believe you have only a 50–50 chance of acceptance there, so you are considering Wesleyan, Hamilton, Bates, and Colby. We might ask you to think about such alternatives as Carleton in the Midwest, Reed in Oregon,

Kenyon in Ohio, Pomona in California. There are also Pennsylvania colleges to be aware of: Bucknell, Lafayette, Lehigh.

You still may end up putting Northeast as your first preference, but you will have a second and third choice after considering other places.

Characteristics you prefer might be a strong college spirit, proximity to ski slopes, opportunities for political action, permission to live off-campus.

Characteristics you might like to avoid might be a heavy emphasis on fraternity/sorority life, a strong major sports orientation, fundamentalist religions on campus, a place with coed dorms, extreme weather conditions, many wealthy students, large numbers of alumni children, limited course selection, or large lecture courses.

We ask, "How important a consideration is institutional prestige?" to make you think a bit. Granted admission to Harvard/Radcliffe and Princeton, 75 percent will accept Harvard; 50 percent will accept Princeton. Most of those turning down Princeton's offer will go to Harvard/Radcliffe or Yale, which are older and have more prestige in applicants' eyes. To attend a prestigious college is to benefit from what the late Calvin Lee called the "halo effect." Lee, a Columbia graduate, was an academic dean at Boston University and, later, chancellor of the University of Maryland. He believed that a good student can get a good education at dozens of places not considered particularly prestigious.

Our own feeling is that the reason why any college has prestige is that it has exceptional qualities that add up to an exceptional educational experience. But merely having a prestigious undergraduate degree will not guarantee self-fulfillment, admission to a prestigious graduate school, or a good job. Undoubtedly, in certain circles, it may have social cachet. How important is this to you?

How intensive an academic workload and grading system do you want? This question is related to the prestige issue. Prestigious colleges expect from their highly competitive students hard work, and their professors are loath to give out too many As. Say you are used to getting As in high school. Are you prepared to settle for Bs in a college with heavy workloads, where the professors wield a heavy blue pencil? Or would you be more comfortable somewhere where you are likely to excel? To answer this question you have to know how you respond to challenge, for, make no mistake, college is in many ways unlike secondary school. In a literature course you will read a novel a week. Science courses call for labs that mean many a lost afternoon. Up to now you have been used to a few dozen books. In college you are going to have to read hundreds, and in graduate school perhaps thousands, of books and articles. If you have had advanced college-level courses already, you have an idea what it will be like in college. Now multiply such courses several times.

A man getting his Ph.D. at Michigan in theater arts presented his thesis on Sarah Bernhardt, the great French actress. The first question his advisor asked was "How many books have you read?" Flabbergasted, the candidate said he had no idea. "I've read three thousand related to your subject," said the faculty advisor. A pedant? No doubt, for merely quantifying your reading says nothing about what you have absorbed. Nonetheless, colleges are full of brilliant scholars who appreciate hardworking students. You should assess your ability to stretch your mind — and your body. Burning the midnight oil calls for endurance as well as character.

Question 2. Imagine yourself already in college. How will you spend your time? What will you major in? What courses will you take not related to your major? What sports will you play, what will be your extracurricular activities? Some students know that they want to study medicine and will major in biology or chemistry. Others plan to go to law school and say they think they'll major in history or government. Business-oriented students think of economics or psychology. Future journalists think of English as the right major.

And then many students are not sure what direction their education will take, are not sure whether they want to make a lot of money like Dad or go into the foreign service. This doubt is quite normal, and the questionnaire is not trying to push you into a premature commitment. It merely asks you to indicate *interests.* You are going to college to acquire knowledge you don't have. How does a person fix on subjects he knows nothing about? By listing interests and looking at college catalogues to see what the course offerings are. You can also get an idea of what it means to major in a field by looking at the description of departmental requirements in college catalogues.

Even in college your interests may change. A prominent anthropologist decided on his profession only after majoring in sociology. No college asks enrolled freshmen to indicate what their majors will be. You major in one particular field during your upperclass years. But you need prerequisites to concentrate in a subject, and these are taken in your freshman and sophomore years. Students enter college thinking they will major in French, get absorbed in an art history course, and decide to major in history and minor in French. So in putting down now what you think you might do academically in college, you are not casting a choice in concrete; you are simply making it easier to look at potential colleges from an academic point of view.

What else will you do in college besides study? Have fun, of course, make new friends, join clubs, fraternities, sororities, societies, go to parties. But how about going out for the campus paper, the radio station, joining the dramatic society, getting involved in campus-related community service, running for the student council? Colleges have various activities. At Stanford you might get involved in designing the elaborate card shows put on at football games. At Penn you might want to get into the annual musical comedy put on by the Masque and Wig Society. Dartmouth students put in hours in the theater production shop. Glee clubs provide a wonderful chance to broaden musical interests.

Your participation in sports will depend on your abilities. Varsity high school stars may not be college varsity material, but they can still engage in intramural sports. And students take up new sports in college: rowing, squash, water polo, rugby, organized Frisbee teams. Or you can simply exercise by jogging, dancing, swimming, climbing mountains, biking, or playing volleyball.

As you begin to envision your campus life, academic and nonacademic, you will see that there is a temptation to spread yourself thin because of the rich opportunities. Now is a good time to begin thinking about the best use of your college time for enjoyment and self-development. Overdoing extracurricular activities and sports can not only weaken academic performance, but lead to frustration — and exhaustion.

Questions 3–5. These questions are purely factual to help an advisor guide you in your choice of colleges to which you will apply. For instance, if you need financial aid, or a part-time job, some colleges are less likely to admit you than others that are "need blind" in judging applicants. Knowing where your parents went to college is to know that your chances of admission as a child of an alumnus are greater than the chances of other applicants at such colleges. If you have a parent on a college faculty, you know what a savings this means, since most colleges waive the tuition of such students.

Question 6. This provides a quick way to see your nonacademic self as you have developed in secondary school and allows you in your senior year to focus on the things you do best.

Question 7. This one asks you to evaluate your academic performance, to interpret your report cards to yourself, and to explain any unfairness you sense in what your school has said about you. It may be that a certain teacher has been unduly severe in grading you, that other students have been favored. Whether these impressions are true or not, your reactions are important and should be examined with your counselor. Personality clashes between teachers and students can weaken academic performance. But how do you prove you really deserve an A in French? You may have to spend a summer abroad and come back to school pretty fluent in French. You speak with a good accent. But still your teacher notes in your writing a lack of mastery of grammar.

A willingness to acknowledge weakness is in itself a strength and can be a step on the road to academic improvement. It's also a clue to how admissions officers will judge your prospects. They are not looking for the perfect student, but for the promising student. You may even have to respond to this question in an interview or on an application, so be prepared.

Question 8. Conclude the questionnaire with a warm-up for the all-important personal essay you must write with your application. Who are you? How would you describe yourself to a sympathetic stranger like an admissions officer? This is a chance to see yourself not as you would like others to see you, but simply as you see yourself. Here is an example from the files of Howard Greene.

Mary Ann, a senior in a Rhode Island high school, gave this response to question 8:

School activities: Principal's Advisory Committee, jr., sr. year; features editor of *The Beacon;* concert mistress school orchestra sr. year; student government representative 4 years

Sports: Cross-country team jr. & sr. years. Letter jr. year

Outside activities: Junior Achievement, Community Symphony

Work and summer activities: Hospital volunteer, music course at Community College (3 undergraduate credits)

Hobbies: creative writing, swimming, listening to symphony music

Awards: National Honor Society, Junior Achievement scholarship

Most interested in: The Beacon (school paper), violin

YOUR PARENTS' ROLE

Your parents play an important part in the admissions process. They are concerned that you attend a college where you will have a happy and successful four years that prepare you for the future. In most cases they will be visiting colleges with you. With rare exceptions their financial support is critical. As many as 80 percent of families now applying to selective colleges apply for financial aid. We have found that college admissions are a family affair, and when parents and students collaborate in harmony, the admissions experience is enhanced and results are more satisfactory.

The Parent's Questionnaire is a stimulus to encourage your parents to discuss your college admissions program with each other privately, so that they will have reflected on their expectations and will have thought more about you in terms considered by admissions offices. Parents, no less than students, need to understand selective admissions. We have found that their meetings with counselors are more satisfying if they have thought about matters raised in the Parent's Questionnaire. We suggest that each parent answer the questionnaire separately and that they then compare their responses before discussing them with anyone.

We suggest that your parents not disclose their answers to you, so that they may be as candid and realistic as possible without worrying about hurting your feelings if their views of your strengths happen not to conform to your own. The insights parents gain from the questionnaire, rather than their specific answers, will help guide them *and* you throughout the admissions process.

From your point of view the Parent's Questionnaire is a good way to involve parents in the admissions process. A parent may react strongly when taken by surprise. A girl will tell her mother she wants to go to a large state university because there will be so many people there that she will be bound to find a more interesting, more mature, more diverse student body. And her mother will ask, "Is that the main reason to choose a college?"

PARENT'S QUESTIONNAIRE

(Each parent should answer the questions without consulting the other; then they should compare answers. They should write them out but not show them to the children. They may want to use their answers when talking to a school counselor.)

1. What characteristics are you especially interested in finding in a college or university for your son or daughter? You might wish to comment on the college's type, style, atmosphere, academic reputation, and "institutional prestige," as well as its location.
2. Describe to yourself your son's or daughter's relative strengths as a student (organization, motivation, self-discipline, independence, creativity, growth potential, etc.).
3. Colleges often ask for several words that best describe an applicant. They also ask schools to assess individuals in areas such as leadership, confidence, warmth of personality, concern for others, energy, and maturity. How would you describe your son's or daughter's personality and values?
4. What is his or her greatest achievement? In what sense is he or she special in your eyes?
5. Is there anything else you feel (medical background, etc.) would be helpful to your son or daughter regarding the college selection process? Anything in the family history, its educational background, for example?
6. Please list the names of any colleges to which you plan to encourage your son or daughter to apply.

OVERESTIMATING AND UNDERESTIMATING YOURSELF

Many of us have a tendency either to overestimate or underestimate ourselves.

Some typical overestimations arise from our tendency to forgive ourselves for little faults that we like to think do not matter. Jeremy, for example, writes brilliant papers but fills them with spelling errors he could easily correct simply by reading through what he has written. He gets a B+ instead of an A, but dismisses this as meaningless because he has read that some great writer or other never could spell and that his errors were corrected by editors.

If your academic performance has suffered because of this tendency, you may not be qualified for admission into some of the most competitive colleges. Even more important in the long run, though, the habit of overestimating your capacities blurs your own vision of yourself and impairs your ability to change and improve.

The habit of underestimating yourself may arise from some prior criticism.

PARENT'S RESPONSE

1. We would be interested in a college with a high academic reputation and institutional prestige. Presumably there's a basis in fact for a school's reputation and we believe that graduating from a highly regarded college can only help one's career. However, we are also aware that the college must be appropriate for Kevin's record and abilities. We hope to identify schools that offer not only a reasonable chance of gaining admittance, but an atmosphere — personality, if you will — that will be pleasing to Kevin. A liberal arts versus a highly math/engineering-oriented institution would seem to be more suitable to Kevin; also, at this time, he thinks he would be more comfortable in a smaller, rural environment.

2. Kevin has demonstrated a sense of responsibility, independence, and self-discipline in handling homework. He manages his time by himself and, although he sometimes procrastinates, on the whole he structures his studying so that he does not have to cram at the last minute. His teachers have commented positively about the maturity he displays in the classroom. He writes well and does well in his presentation of creative research papers. In math, he tends to rush and make careless errors; and he has trouble linking logical math sequences. On the other hand, he has demonstrated a talent for foreign languages.

3. Kevin is mature for his age and thoughtful in his interpersonal relationships. He is, however, very hard on himself and frequently sets unrealistically high standards. He is not exceptionally energetic or ambitious. Although he often assumes a natural leadership position, he is reluctant to run for class office.

4. Kevin would probably consider his baseball accomplishments as being his greatest achievement. He was forced to overcome a number of disappointments and fears during his many years playing baseball. In our admittedly subjective eyes he is special because of his kindness and good humor. And he is special not just as a son, but as a friend.

5. Kevin has always done relatively poorly on standardized tests. His school performance has consistently exceeded his aptitude testing results.

6. I am a Cornell graduate and Kevin has expressed an interest in pursuing a career in veterinary medicine. Cornell has an excellent veterinary program. George, my husband, graduated from Dartmouth and would be pleased if Kevin were to apply there — but he would not encourage Kevin to apply simply because it's his alma mater; i.e., there's no arm twisting.

7. When reviewing our responses to the questionnaire, bear in mind that Kevin is only beginning his 10th grade year — opinions and views, his and ours, can change dramatically in the next two years.

A music teacher puts you in the back of the chorus and suggests you sing softly, and you conclude that you have no ear for music. This then becomes a prominent part of your self-description. "I play tapes a lot, but I have no ear for music," you say, ignoring the contradiction of your statement.

In assessing *both* your strengths and weaknesses, then, it's important to be clear-eyed and avoid the pitfalls of over- or underestimating your capacities. An admissions officer is always impressed by a candidate's self-knowledge and willingness to reveal genuine limitations without self-deprecation. We grow, in part, by confronting our weaknesses, and selective colleges are looking for students with outstanding capacity for growth.

The great reporter Theodore White thought he might become a scholar until a professor at Harvard suggested that his talents better fitted him for journalism. The behavioral psychologist B. F. Skinner majored in English because he wanted to be a writer of fiction. After college he turned to psychology and got a doctorate. Most of what he wrote is nonfiction, but Skinner was also the author of the utopian novel *Walden II.*

As you learn more about specific colleges, Step Two will help you focus on those schools where *your* strengths will be best developed. We urge you to look at your responses to the questionnaire often. Confer with teachers, counselors, and your parents to see whether you have got yourself "right," whether you can see yourself as others see you.

THE CONFIDENCE OF STRENGTH

When you know where your strengths lie, there lies, too, the basis for self-confidence and optimism. Selective colleges are training students in leadership. A leader must be confident in his or her ability to lead, whether it is in scholarship, a laboratory project, a business, a work of art, or government. Discovering what you are good at will make you feel proud about it, and it will strengthen your candidacy for selective college admission.

Step Two Checklist

1. Use the Student Questionnaire as a guide to your feelings about colleges you are considering. Change your answers in your notebook as you get to know more about yourself.

2. Involve your parents by having them fill out the Parent's Questionnaire. This will make their meetings with school counselors more productive.

3. Look for overestimations and underestimations of your strengths. As the admissions process unfolds you should find your academic performance improving as your study habits become more effective. Nonacademic

strengths grow through your focusing on what you do best. Listen to what people say about you to discover strong points in your character.

4. Think of being on a voyage of self-discovery that you are taking for the purpose of making the clearest presentation of your strengths to admissions offices.

STEP THREE

Follow a Demanding Curriculum

YOUR ACADEMIC RECORD COMES FIRST

*A*bove all, selective colleges want to enroll students who are able to do good college course work. Yes, they want their students to have other capabilities as athletes, actors, editors, managers of student organizations, and as young people who contribute to the dynamic life of the campus and the local community. But first and foremost, colleges exist to educate, and selective colleges conduct their educational programs at high levels of excellence. This is why admissions offices quickly turn to your academic record when you send in your application. They are under an obligation to the faculties of their colleges to put good students in their classrooms.

This is the high school curriculum that the most selective colleges recommend and that applicants to these colleges follow, with some variations:

English language and literature	4 years
Mathematics	3–4 years
Laboratory sciences	3 years
Foreign languages	3–4 years
United States history and 1 other history	2 years
Computer skills	½ year
Visual arts, theater, music, or dance	1 year

As many of these courses as possible should be honors level, beginning in tenth grade. Highly competitive students take six honors-level courses or advanced placement courses. Many applicants wait until junior year to take an honors course, and many are admitted to very good colleges, having taken only three honors courses.

"It's quite simple," says Dr. William Morse, former admissions officer at Yale. "If you study hard in high school, you will probably study hard in college. When your academic performance has been strong in school, you will not be overwhelmed by the demands of college courses. Yale's attrition rate is usually about two per cent."

THE ACADEMIC CRITERIA

Admissions offices judge your academic record on your curriculum, your honors level or advanced placement courses, your grades, and your Subject Test scores. Write down these four in your notebook and use them as a reminder as you prepare for college admission. Your academic record is distinct from your SAT scores, whose significance is discussed in Step Four — Take Advantage of College Board Test Requirements.

YOUR CURRICULUM

Use a page in your notebook to list your courses year by year. Even if you are a senior reading this book, you should review the courses you have taken, to look at them in the same way an admissions office will look at them. If you see that your curriculum has not conformed to the traditional liberal arts curriculum we list below, you should take note of this fact and discuss with your college counselor the significance of the curriculum you have followed. If there are gaps, some colleges may not consider you a qualified applicant, while others may allow you to fill in such gaps in college — typically, taking a foreign language course to make up for a year not taken in high school.

We list here the curriculum that is the surest road to admission to the most selective colleges. Some deviations from this are permissible, as we shall see. But this is the model to follow if you are aiming for an Exceedingly Demanding college like Stanford or Wellesley.

THE BEST HIGH SCHOOL CURRICULUM
FOR SELECTIVE COLLEGE ADMISSION

9th grade	English
	Biology (laboratory course)
	History (ancient or European)
	Mathematics (algebra or plane geometry)
	Language (1st or 2nd year)
	(2nd year for those who had an
	8th grade language course)
10th grade	English
	Chemistry (laboratory course)
	Mathematics (plane geometry or algebra II)
	Language (2nd or 3rd year)

>   History or
>   Computer science or
>   Fine arts or
>   Performing arts
>   11th grade   English
>   Physics (laboratory course)
>   Mathematics (algebra II or precalculus)
>   Language (3rd or 4th year)
>   United States history
>   12th grade   English
>   Mathematics (precalculus or calculus)
>   Language (4th year or a 2nd language)
>   (a 5th year honors level is another option)
>   Advanced science or
>   Advanced history or
>   Music, art, or drama as a major course

This curriculum does not include electives. Admissions offices recognize that students pursue their interests in high school, so such courses as economics, psychology, anthropology, mechanical drawing, and photography that appear on the transcript are not totally disregarded, particularly if you are praised in a teacher's recommendation for work in a subject that absorbs you. But it is fundamental to understand that you will be competing for admission against students who follow the curriculum we have listed.

For example, Arnold, admitted to Princeton from a Brooklyn high school, took six courses a term for four years, including four years of Hebrew and three of Spanish. These courses did not deviate from those listed above, but they made a heavier academic load than many selective college applicants carry, since he took art and music for three years instead of the conventional one (he was the school's leading guitarist). He took no electives like film or economics, perhaps because the school did not offer them. The quality of Arnold's courses and his ability to do well in them made him a very promising Princeton applicant.

If you can work as intensively as Arnold, you should — especially if you intend to apply to Exceedingly Demanding colleges. There are more assiduous students in the selective applicant pool than you might like to think.

A strong curriculum not only follows the courses we have listed — it includes honors-level courses and advanced placement courses.

HONORS COURSES

Some schools call them honors courses, others call them college level courses. Selective private schools and selective public schools, the students of which pass examinations at a high level, may offer the same courses without designating them honors courses. Admissions committees usually are aware that

ASSESSING YOUR ACADEMIC COMPETITION

Agreed that the number of applications to selective colleges is intensifying competition for freshman places, particularly at the most selective colleges like Amherst and Cal Tech, this general truth will only increase anxiety if you fail to look closely at the way academic accomplishment is distributed among freshman classes. Our survey of eighty selective colleges reveals that only among the Exceedingly Demanding colleges we identified in Step One is the academic competition so challenging that most freshmen now are drawn from the top students of secondary schools.

At Amherst, for instance, over 90 percent of 1993 freshmen (Class of 1997) came from the top 10 percent of their high school classes. The same statistic held true for Stanford. When only 4 or 5 percent of the applicants who rank lower than the upper 20 percent of their class in school are admitted, it is clear that first consideration is given to academically outstanding applicants. A few who are slightly less than outstanding will be admitted for extracurricular or personal strengths, or because they survive special rounds for alumni, athletes, minorities, and others.

This is what really catches media attention. The media select what they consider to be the news: in this case the rise in applications to selective colleges when the number of high school graduates is falling. At Tufts, 73 percent of acceptances were in the top 10 percent of their high school classes, while 93 percent were in at least the top 24 percent. Looking at it from the point of view of most candidates for selective colleges, this means that at Tufts only 27 percent ranked below the top fifth in their schools.

Not to belabor the point, but to reinforce it for you, the relevant figures for MIT's freshman class of 1993 were 94 percent in the top 10 percent of their high school classes and 100 percent in the top 20 percent. But at Kenyon, one of the finest small colleges in the country (the poet Robert Lowell transferred there from Harvard), only 38 percent of the freshman class of 1993 ranked in the upper 10 percent, and only 67 percent ranked in the upper 20 percent.

We could cite dozens of good selective colleges like Kenyon, which accept good students who are not near the top of their classes academically. We should also point out that such colleges reject half to two thirds of their applicants, so they remain selective and should not be considered havens for mediocre students.

The message, then, a reiteration of what admissions deans and directors have been quoted as telling you, is: work your hardest to make a good academic record. If you have done your best in school and you are not among the top students academically, you have no reason to despair. You will find that there are good colleges that want students like you. Your task is to identify those colleges that appear to offer you in particular the better opportunities for admission.

REVISED EXPECTATIONS OF TWELVE
PENNSYLVANIA COLLEGES

The 1987 edition of this book carried the expectations for applicants' preparation by deans of admission at twelve academically rigorous Pennsylvania colleges known as the Commonwealth Partnership. That statement, revised and expanded for the nineties, now emphasizes the importance of writing and of time management, of the capacity for fruitful collaboration with other students, and of the ability to use a computer or word processor, including familiarity with spreadsheet and database manipulations.

Six subject areas are recommended: the arts — two challenging courses in music, theater, dance, or studio art; foreign languages — to continue through four years of secondary school; history — two full-year courses; literature — a course a year; mathematics — four years including technology, graphing calculators, and statistical software packages; and science — three year-long lab courses, plus an additional advanced level course if possible.

The statement concludes:

Students who find success in a program such as the one [suggested] here will have little difficulty succeeding in college. . . . We believe that a strong curriculum plays a critical role in preparing students for college.

The four-page statement, substantiating our own suggested curriculum, may be had for free by writing to Commonwealth Partnership Consortium Office, Franklin and Marshall College, P.O. Box 3003, Lancaster, PA 17604-3003.

these schools push their students, and they give students at these institutions credit for the academic intensity of their studies.

One of the chief reasons why some students fail to be accepted by selective colleges is that they have not been willing to risk the challenge of courses on the "fast track" of college preparation. Many of the admissions officers we surveyed specifically wrote that they wanted applicants to be risk-takers, students willing to find out just how well they can do in honors courses.

Those who take the risk will be given credit for it even when their grades are less than outstanding. Furthermore, willingness to follow a demanding curriculum puts you in a position to make respectable Subject Test scores. We are emphasizing this point to prevent the discouragement that follows a natural tendency to compare yourself with those who do better academically than you. Accepting the level at which you perform is a sign of the maturity selective colleges admire, when they are convinced that you have made a wholehearted commitment to your schoolwork.

OPPORTUNITIES FOR WOMEN WHO KNOW THEIR MATH

Many women still consider math a "man's subject." As a result, most young women in high school drop math after completing minimal requirements. Doing this, of course, cuts off their opportunities later. Only 18 percent of women enter fields requiring college math. Careers in business, medicine, computer science, engineering, biology, physics, chemistry, architecture, and sociology are not possible without the requisite math background.

If families and schools were to strive to banish the notion that women cannot master math as well as men can, thousands of job opportunities would open up for women.

So, if you, as a young woman, have dropped math in your junior year, it is possible to catch up with courses in math outside your school. Try it. You may amaze yourself.

MORE ADVICE FROM ADMISSIONS OFFICES

Georgia Institute of Technology	Academic track record in high school is all-important.
Lafayette	Take a strong program of studies and work hard at it.
Lawrence University	Curriculum! Curriculum! Curriculum! Take the best courses, the most challenging courses.
University of Michigan	Take rigorous courses — and do well in them.
University of North Carolina	Enroll in the most demanding academic courses, to include English, math, and foreign languages all four years, and make the highest possible marks.

You, as a selective college applicant, should be capable of taking honors courses. How early in high school you start taking them and how many you can handle is something your counselor and teachers can help you discover.

Is there any honors course that counts more in admissions than another? No. Any intensive course that stretches your mind will be recognized for its educational value and as an indicator of your academic capacity. Many selective college applicants enrich their minds in courses taken outside their schools, at night or during summer vacation.

Be aware, too, that some schools do not have the budget to support a strong honors program, though they may refer to their more intensive courses as honors courses. In some schools, the same textbook serves for both honors and nonhonors levels, with honors assignments being longer and involving the writing of more papers. But, unfortunately, such courses do not compare with those offered by a secondary school with a strong honors program.

Find out how your high school's honors courses rate by calling the admissions offices at the selective colleges that interest you. Admissions officials can advise you whether your candidacy would be strengthened by some enrichment programs given evenings or during the summer at a college or another school. While allowances are made by admissions committees for your lack of opportunity for more intensive study, you should still take as many as you can handle of the honors courses available to you.

ADVANCED PLACEMENT COURSES

Advanced placement courses are at a level above honors courses, and they are not universally offered in public high schools, though the best public and private schools usually offer them. AP courses, as they are usually known, are college courses the curricula of which are prescribed by the College Entrance Examination Board after consulting a number of college professors. Each AP course in all schools has the same syllabus and uses the same texts. The courses prepare you for AP exams, although you are not obliged to take them. AP exams are given by the CEEB in May. Depending on your grade, the college where you enroll will either give you academic credit for this work or will allow you to take a course in the subject beyond the freshman level.

AP courses usually are tougher than honors courses, although in selective private and selective public schools the difference between them may be negligible, and good students can prepare for AP exams by taking an honors course plus some tutoring from the honors course teacher.

In any case, if you can do well in an AP course, you will be considered among the more qualified applicants. Some colleges, like MIT, require high AP grades in math and science for serious consideration. You will have found that out if you took note of such requirements in Step One.

Here is the official College Board list of AP courses. Examinations are given in:

English literature
U.S. history
Calculus AB
Biology
English language
European history

Spanish language
Chemistry
Government and politics — U.S.
Calculus BC
Physics B
French language
Physics CM & EM
Macroeconomics
Government and politics — comp.
Microeconomics
Computer science A
Computer science AB
Art history
Psychology
Studio art
Spanish literature
German language
Latin — Vergil
Art drawing
Music theory
French literature
Latin — Catullus, Horace

ENORMOUS INCREASE IN ADVANCED PLACEMENT COURSES AND SCHOOLS

Since the first edition of *Scaling the Ivy Wall,* the number of advanced placement examinations given by the College Board has risen more than tenfold. In 1967 54,812 exams were given, as against 580,143 in 1992! Likewise the number of schools giving the AP exams from 2,746 to 10,191. The average number of students per school taking the AP shot up to 57 from 20. A total of 388,142 took the AP in 1992. This reflects the increasing availability of AP courses in the high schools and the recognition by students of the twofold value of such courses: increased admission chances and the possibility of taking higher level college courses in subjects they score a 4 or 5 in (5 is the highest AP test score). It is likely that this trend will continue during the nineties.

CONCENTRATING IN YOUR SPECIALTY

There is a limit to the amount of work even the best students can do. In which subjects should you take honors or AP courses? The decision is easier if you know what your college plans are. Are you going to be an engineer, a scientist, a lawyer, a doctor, a journalist? Your answer should determine your senior year advanced course selection.

- Senior-year advanced placement math and science are for future engineers, scientists, doctors, airline pilots, and other technical experts.
- Advanced placement English, history, and a foreign language are for future lawyers, journalists, politicians, businessmen, and those going into government or international relations.
- Advanced placement math and history are a good senior-year combination for a future economist.

Advanced placement courses in these subjects taken in your senior year will strengthen your record, particularly if you have taken honors courses earlier in high school. Should you find it necessary, you may drop a fourth year of anything but English to make your course load reasonable, providing that the college you are applying to does not require that fourth year.

THE SIGNIFICANCE OF GRADES

Grades have been shown to be the single most important predictor of academic success in college. The College Entrance Examination Board, which sponsors the SATs and Subject Tests, has stated this fact repeatedly. The more As and Bs in your record, the more attention admissions committees will pay to your applications. An occasional C does not put you out of the running, but a C average is unacceptable at most selective colleges unless it is offset by achievement outside class. A potential All-American athlete with a C average has been known to be accepted by Ivy League colleges, on the grounds that the athlete probably has the character to learn better study habits.

Others admitted to selective colleges with mediocre grades are those with considerable talent: potential opera stars, remarkable actors, artists, dancers. As more and more students apply to these colleges, however, the allowances made for unimpressive academic work in high school will diminish.

No discussion of grades is meaningful without an evaluation of the intensity of courses you take. You will deceive yourself if your record shows good grades only in courses that are not at honors or college level. As we have pointed out, admissions committees tend to interpret such a record as evidence of a student's incapacity for harder work, or an unwillingness to risk getting lower grades in tougher courses. Selective college applicants must force themselves to discover their true academic capabilities by getting good grades in a demanding curriculum. Far from spoiling your record by getting grades in honors courses that are lower than those in other courses, you provide admissions offices clear evidence of your academic potential, and you will be admitted to those colleges where you can do the work.

BUILDING A RECORD OF COMMITMENT

Given what you have been given to work with in high school, have you done the best with what you have been offered?
Brown University admissions officer

Begin academic preparation in the pre–high school period. Take challenging college prep courses. Take honors and advanced placement and a strong senior program especially. Be sure to take mathematics every year.
University of California (Los Angeles) admissions officer

The single most important thing we look at is the academic transcript. The difficulty of courses, the breadth of courses taken, and the achievement in those courses, in that order, is what we review. We want to see students challenge themselves.
Wesleyan University admissions officer

"Strive for excellence," says one university admissions dean. The *College Digest* asks seniors: "Are you continuing your improvement? Demonstrating a 'recovery' after a slight slump? Or have your grades held steady? These are the questions the deans will be seeking an answer to."

Liberal arts colleges introduce students to a higher level of learning that can be absorbed only through academic effort. The results are rewarding to all — the talented, the athletes, the students of average intelligence and above-average drive. These colleges admit students with good grades so that faculty members can teach with an intensity that would be impossible in classrooms filled with mediocre students.

YOUR SUBJECT TEST SCORES

We will discuss the College Board Subject Tests in Step Four, but here we want to relate them to your academic record. As a general rule, you should take three Subject Tests in your strongest subjects as soon as possible after completing courses in the test subjects. You may take as many "Subjects" as you are capable of handling well, but you usually have to submit only three scores as part of your application to be considered for admission.

The chances of having three good test scores are excellent, provided you take the tests in subjects in which you have good grades, and particularly if the tests are taken soon after completing honors courses. The SAT II Tests test subjects you have studied. This does not mean that they are easy. It does mean you can prepare for them. Following a strong curriculum that includes at least three honors courses will give a reasonable assurance that your test scores will be good enough for selective college admission.

COMPARE YOUR RECORD WITH
SELECTIVE COLLEGE REQUIREMENTS

If you will take a moment to glance at what you wrote down in Step One under the academic requirements of a number of selective colleges, you can begin to compare these with your actual academic work. Using the four criteria of curriculum, honors courses, grades, and Subject Test scores, you will be able in the case of each college to answer the simple question: am I meeting the academic requirements? When the answer is no, it will be for a specific reason. Maybe you haven't taken any Subject Tests yet; maybe your grades look too low to compete at the Exceedingly Demanding level.

This procedure amounts to taking your academic bearings to enable you to steer a better course toward your objective.

In the notebook where you have listed your curriculum, put an H after every course taken, or that you plan to take, on the honors or AP level. How many Hs are there? Ideally, there should be a minimum of three. If you have more than three, consider every additional H as another step up the Ivy Wall. At this point, high grades are not a concern. Remember, your willingness to take and pass an honors course is one of the strongest indicators of your capacity for college work.

In her notebook under Step One, Louisa, a junior in a New York suburban high school, put down this way the requirements of colleges she was considering:

School Subject	Colleges and Years Required
English	Stanford and all others, 4 years
Math	Stanford 4, Amherst 4, Colorado 3
Languages	Stanford 4, Duke 3, Vermont 2
Sciences	Stanford 3, Lafayette 3, Reed 2
History	2 years at all colleges
Art, etc.	optional at all colleges
Second language	desirable at Stanford

Her notebook under Step Four showed that she had taken honors French II her sophomore year and had a 600 on her Subject Test in French II. She was taking honors French III now in her junior year and intended to take advanced placement French her senior year. When her advisor told her she probably was a marginal Stanford candidate, she got permission to take Spanish I in her senior year, and decided to take the risk of advanced placement math that year. Then she asked her family if they could afford to send her to France with the Experiment in International Living, a long-established student exchange program that includes a home stay with a family abroad. Her objectives: fluency in French and a topic for her essay — not "My Summer in France," but maybe "American Rock on French Radio" or "Learning to Love Pâté," which she hated but was assured by her French teacher she would love someday. (She did neither. Her essay was an amusing piece about learning to drive on French highways, entitled "What Drivers' Ed Never Taught Me.")

And she never applied to Stanford. Too far from home. She applied to Amherst for Early Decision and was admitted in December. Louisa finished eighth in her high school class of 320. Amherst wanted her because she "stretched," particularly in French, which she knows well enough to earn money as a tutor while in college.

Emilio, a B+ student in Arizona, was dissatisfied with his junior SAT scores, which added up to 1080. Feeling that the courses in his excellent West Coast private school truly reflected his academic caliber, he became interested in Bates College, near his family's vacation home in Maine. Bates waives SAT scores at the applicant's request. Shrewdly, Emilio reasoned that he must show Bates that his weakness in answering multiple-choice questions was offset by good marks in more courses than Bates expects applicants to pass with distinction.

Conferring with his counselor, he worked out a five-course senior schedule of honors and advanced placement courses in literature, calculus, Spanish, physics, and Japanese history. Because he had had no art course, he was advised to take a summer course at the University of Maine in art history. As a special project he worked for several days at the handsome new Portland Museum of Art, and wrote a paper on its colorful interior decoration. He got an A in this course, and his senior courses averaged B, excellent considering his workload. A 750 Subject Test score in Spanish encouraged him to consider majoring in that subject in college. Bates urged him to apply for Early Decision.

In case he should not be admitted to Bates, Emilio looked at the requirements of the University of California at San Diego, and of Reed and Kenyon colleges. His extracurricular activity was debating; he was captain of the debating team. He was admitted to Bates on Early Decision and applied nowhere else, but learned later that he would have been turned down at San Diego despite his grades, because his SAT scores were far below the automatic cutoff, 1200, for non-California-resident applicants. He had taken the trouble to satisfy admissions requirements for Bates, which waives SAT scores but admits only 16 percent of applicants who take advantage of this option.

BENEFIT FROM ENRICHMENT PROGRAMS

Admissions committees react very positively to students who have taken advanced courses at colleges or at summer schools. Subjects being pursued by selective college applicants include computer sciences, Asian languages, writing workshops, fine arts, and architecture, as well as traditional subjects. Here is a list of some summer college programs you may want to consider. If none of these is practical, you should explore colleges and schools near you and see what courses are open to high school students. Scholarships are available to those who need financial aid, so do not let lack of money keep you from exploring the wonderful possibilities these programs offer.

Some college summer programs for high school students:

Berkeley Summer Session
Boston University Summer Sessions (May and July)
Brown Summer Academy
California Polytechnic Summer Young Scholars Program
Case Western Reserve Summer Symposia
Cornell Summer Program for Advanced Placement Studies
Davidson College July Experience
Duke Summer Program
Emory Summer Schools Program
Georgetown Program for High School Students
Harvard Summer School for Secondary School Students
Johns Hopkins Center for Academically Talented Youth
Purdue Summer Programs
Skidmore College Summer Session
Tufts Summer Session
University of Pennsylvania Precollege Program
Yale Summer School

Among more specialized programs there are:

American Academy of Dramatic Arts
American Farm School, Greek Summer
Bennington College (creative arts)
Brandeis Summer Odyssey
Carnegie-Mellon University (science)
Cornell School of Architecture
Harvard Career Discovery Program in Architecture and Design
Mount Holyoke "Summermath" Program for Women
National Science Foundation Research Projects
Northwestern University (journalism, theater, music)
Rhode Island School of Design (arts)
Skidmore College (creative arts)

The National Science Foundation offers, on a competitive selection basis, programs on college campuses across the United States. These are open to talented high school students who work on research projects with college faculty members.

These are some of the major boarding schools offering enriched academic and arts programs in the summer:

Choate–Rosemary Hall School
Culver Academy
Hotchkiss School
Northfield–Mount Hermon School
Phillips Andover Academy
Phillips Exeter Academy
Saint George's School
The Taft School

There are also many programs abroad for enriched study of foreign languages, cultures, politics, and arts.

WHO SHOULD TAKE ENRICHMENT COURSES?

Ideally, every applicant to a selective college would benefit from some kind of academic enrichment outside secondary school. We recognize that this is not universally possible, yet large numbers of candidates apply with an enriched background that strengthens their chances for admission to more selective colleges. How do those who have not had this opportunity meet the competition and overcome a disadvantage? The answer lies in stretching in your own school. There is that extra honors course you can take if you are applying to Exceedingly Demanding or Very Demanding colleges.

Take Alex as an example. A student in the upper 10 percent of his private day school class in Connecticut, Alex had taken three honors courses and planned to take two more in his senior year. He spent six weeks at Harvard during the summer before his senior year in a special program for high school students interested in architecture. This not only gave him enrichment in a new field, it provided an opportunity to show Dartmouth an added range of academic diversity when he applied for Early Decision. In the fall he sent to the admissions office six drawings of an urban development project he had worked on with a Harvard professor. The professor's favorable comments went along with the drawings, a convincing way of showing capability for doing college work. Willingness to give up six weeks of summer vacation to work hard paid off, and Alex was admitted to Dartmouth in December.

Beth Ann was number one in a class of 800 in her Los Angeles high school, so it might seem that she would have been able to pick and choose any American college. Not so.

Her teachers described her as a brilliant math student, but withdrawn and socially immature. Not every college would be able to fit her into its freshman class. She would have to compete against others like her, marvelous students who compensate for shyness by pursuing solitary activities. Beth Ann, for example, taught herself the recorder, but never played in an ensemble. Her hobby was photography, which allowed her many hours alone in a darkroom she set up in her home. Her advisor's attempts to get her into another activity besides the photography club and the chess team were unavailing. "All you can do if you want to go to Yale," he said, "is outstudy the competition."

Having done all she could in high school, she began in her junior year taking extension courses at UCLA. She was, of course, recruited by UCLA, and her fame reached Cal Tech. Her record of As in all three college courses was highlighted in her Early Decision application to Yale, which deferred Beth Ann, then wait-listed her in the spring. By that time she had developed a strong liking for UCLA and accepted their offer of admission. She told Yale she would enroll if taken off the waiting list. When Yale did take her off the waiting list, she changed her mind (sacrificing a $200 deposit). She had satisfied her desire for recognition by Yale, but felt in the end she would be more comfortable in an environment she knew.

IMPROVING YOUR RECORD

What can you do if, by senior year, your curriculum hasn't been demanding enough, or your grades high enough, to assure you a place in a selective college? As we've mentioned, there are various enrichment programs that will help your academic record enormously. You might also consider a post-graduate year to improve your record.

IMPROVING YOUR GRADES

Grades reflect effort more than anything else. Consistently high grades, of course, also are a characteristic of students of exceptional intelligence. But as you have probably already discovered, you do not have to be a genius to get an A. Think of the higher grades you have received already. Were they not the result of more work, more enthusiasm in the subject matter?

Good study habits will also bring good grades. You can waste time studying if you have not learned how to organize your work and absorb what you have read. Cramming for exams is one of the most notoriously bad study habits, often concealed by success in an exam, which pulls up lower grades you have received as the result of not studying effectively.

Your effort to improve your grades will be taken into account by admissions offices. "We don't expect perfection," said one dean. "Most people stumble once in a while." So, if you should stumble, there are ways to pick yourself up and improve your grades.

There are four things in particular to think about.

Motivation. You have to feel that higher grades are important to you, in order to make the effort to change your study habits and your classroom habits too. One motive you may already have is the desire to be admitted to a college you now feel will turn you down. The reason for your doubts is probably an academic record that will not satisfy the college.

Time. We all waste time. Books have been written to teach executives how to use their time better. We can only suggest that you tighten up your schedule, reduce the amount of time spent on less important matters, and increase the time you spend studying assignments. Doing these things will not automatically lead to higher grades if your mind wanders when you read or if you fail to take notes. But combine added time to improved study habits and you are bound to bring up your grades.

Rereading. You do not have to read everything twice, not if you get it the first time. But much academic work requires a second reading. Professors do it, lawyers do it, and you will do it someday when you are engaged in your career. Figures have to be checked, novels have to be reread if you are to understand their patterns and their beauty, history cannot be learned by merely reading through a chapter.

In college you will find students who read a Shakespeare play four times in a term. Get the rereading habit now if you don't have it already.

Reviewing. Successful students constantly review their course work so that they do not have to cram for tests and exams. If you do not yet have this necessary habit, make a note in your Twelve-Step notebook now to begin reviewing for fifteen minutes a day as part of your schedule. You will find that by final exam time you need only go over material you are unsure of.

The benefits of reviewing will not only lead to grades that help you get into the selective college where you belong, they will help you to handle college work once you get there.

YOUR ACADEMIC RECORD
AND YOUR SAT SCORES

The conclusion of this step prepares you for Step Four, on how to take advantage of testing. The thought we want to leave you with is:

> YOUR ACADEMIC RECORD IS MUCH MORE
> IMPORTANT THAN YOUR SAT SCORES
> IN THE SELECTIVE ADMISSIONS PROCESS.

Not a single one of the colleges we surveyed put SAT scores ahead of a strong, challenging curriculum in the admissions process. A few said you should be less concerned about the SAT than about the quality of your academic work. "Worry more about program, personal productivity, and performance, and less about standardized scores," said William M. Hartog,

Director of Admissions at Washington and Lee University, where the average scores of those admitted are 590 verbal and 629 math.

What about the student with a mediocre academic record and exceptional SAT scores? "This situation," says Spencer Reynolds of Princeton University, "means that a bright student must develop the self-discipline to do course work in order to qualify for selective college admission."

Since the applications of minority students applying to selective colleges are considered in a special round, they compete among themselves for places. The competition is stiffest at places like Princeton, so Ruth, an African-American who ranked fifth in her rural New Jersey high school class, paid attention when she heard a visiting Princeton official advise any applicant to take as many honors courses as possible.

When her combined SAT scores added up to 1050, 100 points below those of the average Princeton freshman, she said, "I blew it." Her advisor said, "Nonsense!" And the advisor proved correct. Ruth's five honors courses, in which she earned an A, three B's and one C, were proof that she was prepared for a Princeton education.

Another case in point is that of Linda, a Chinese whose family spoke little English. As a result, Linda's verbal SAT score was only 500, while her math was 680. Linda was first in her suburban New Jersey high school class of 600 students. There is no special round for Asiatic applicants, so Linda was competing against a large number of applicants who scored well over 600 on their verbal SATs. But in addition to being her school's number one student, she also had taken six honors courses, and she had been graded A in every one of them. She was admitted to Princeton.

In a word, the challenging curriculum carried the weight.

Step Three Checklist

1. Make sure your curriculum for four years includes the best courses in English, science, mathematics, language, and history, as well as some courses in the arts and one in computer science.

2. Take as many honors courses as you can handle.

3. Take advanced placement courses if at all possible.

4. Use your notebook to compare your academic record with the academic requirements you wrote down in Step One.

5. Take enrichment courses outside school if you can — at night or during the summer.

6. Work for good grades. Weak marks are not invariably fatal, but try to bring them up by more effort and improved study habits.

STEP FOUR

Make College Board Tests Work for You

APPROACH TESTS AS OPPORTUNITIES

Your advisor and the media have probably alerted you to the new SAT. What is new is not all that different or surprising. The name has changed to Scholastic Assessment Test from Scholastic Aptitude Test, but the College Board long ago disabused the educational world of the notion that it was testing native aptitude, that is, intelligence. And the numeral I has been added to SAT to distinguish it from SAT II, the new Subject Tests formerly called Achievement Tests. SAT I tests verbal and math capabilities; SAT II Subject Tests test knowledge of specific subjects.

Subject Tests can weigh more heavily in your folder than the SAT I. They are opportunities to show your competence in specific areas. Yet psychologically the SAT remains so important as a way of demonstrating institutional success that we will devote much of this step to helping you achieve the best SAT I scores within your ability. You will be able to use your College Board test scores to display your academic strengths.

In this step you will get to know more about test taking; you will approach the SAT and the Subjects with the same confidence you have in your work in school. How will you achieve such confidence? In the same way in which you are dealing with other admissions requirements, by

1. Learning test procedures; familiarizing yourself with these tests, the nature of the questions, and the time limits for answering them.
2. Emphasizing your strengths in scheduling tests to your advantage, in the same way in which you are playing to your strengths in school.
3. Understanding the relative importance of tests in admissions decisions.

We will waste no time discussing the validity or fairness of the SATs, and we suggest that you postpone any critique of college testing until you have completed the tests. The new SAT is a response to criticism. Whether it satisfies the critics is beside the point. Our experience is that despite all the worrying, students' SAT performance tends to correspond to their level of high school performance. Colleges are fully aware why some students' SAT scores are lower than their grades, and they make allowances accordingly in admissions decisions. A student with a certified learning disability may seek permission to take untimed tests.

Those who score well on the SAT verbal and math tests concentrate on the questions, not on the issues that have arisen in public about testing. Talk to high-scoring students to verify our experience in the importance of having a positive attitude at test time.

Here's what we have been told by some students:

Aggie, now at the University of Pennsylvania: "I told my counselor that the SAT had me scared stiff because my PSAT scores were mediocre. He asked me what I had done to improve my testing ability. That's all he had to say. Instead of listening to the kids around me moaning about winding up in a community college, I got hold of practice tests and went through them. By the time I went into the test center, I was relaxed. My scores were one hundred points higher than the PSAT taken six months earlier."

Wilson, after scoring 1000 on his first SAT in his junior year at a New York private day school: "I kept grousing at home about how awful the SAT was going to be, in order to prepare my family for a shock. My father said, 'Do you know what a self-fulfilling prophecy is?' He was telling me that I was psyching myself into a poor performance. Was I really that stupid? So how do you psych yourself into a good performance? I got my father to give me a vocabulary test every week. I wasn't worried about the math SAT. Well, I got a 575 in the verbal and 625 in the math."

LANGUAGE TEST CHANGES

French, Spanish, and German tests after 1993 are given with a listening option. For the first time, Mandarin Chinese and Japanese tests are given, and in these languages a listening test is obligatory. All tests are given in November except Chinese, which is given in April. You should check with your language teachers about the dates.

These tests are administered by the schools, not at national administration centers. It is important to ask your language teacher if your school has been registered with the Admissions Testing Program of the College Board to give these tests. It is possible that your school may not be aware of this requirement. If so, your language department should contact Patricia G. Williams, Program Administrator, Admissions Testing Program, The College Board, P.O. Box 6200, Princeton, NJ 08541-6200, (609) 771-7600.

Danielle, who scored 1250 on her second SAT after tutoring school: "I couldn't believe the 1100 I got, spring of junior year." (She attended a rural Virginia high school.) She arranged to go to tutoring school on weekends in Washington, DC. "By the time I had finished the course, I had answered so many practice questions, I just knew I couldn't help but improve. I said before walking into that test center, 'Danielle, you'll get a 1200.' Somebody was listening. Me!"

Hugh: "I made a point to talk to some top seniors in my prep school about the SAT. 'Piece of cake,' they said. 'With your grade point average, you've got to do well.' I mentioned someone with good grades who got clobbered. 'LSE,' they said. 'Low Self-Esteem.' I decided to watch out for signs of LSE in others and stay clear of them. I guess I never caught the disease. That's how I interpret my 1350 scores."

ACQUAINT YOUR PARENTS WITH TESTS

Your parents can help you in this step by going over practice tests with you, checking on extra work you do to build vocabulary and to review your math. It is important that they spend some time reading through the College Board guide booklets that you will be using extensively. They will be impressed by what today's college-bound student is expected to know, and they will encourage you.

LEARNING ABOUT TESTS

There is no mystery about College Board tests. Two free guides on the SAT and Subjects are available at all schools, and you should study them as you would a textbook. They are *Taking the SAT I* and *Taking Subject Tests*. The College Entrance Examination Board urges you not to throw these guides away. (You may, in fact, wear them out, in which case you simply ask for second copies.) Even after taking a test, you should go over the guides before the next one. Your knowledge of what the tests are testing, how questions are presented, how they are scored, whether to guess or not answer questions you do not know, how much you can accomplish in a given test period — all this will build your confidence and will help you to avoid making unnecessary mistakes.

Use your notebook as a workbook as you read through these guides and later as you take practice tests.

MYTHS ABOUT THE SAT

The College Board guide dispels two myths about the SAT I. One is that the SAT measures intelligence, and the other, implied by the first, is that coaching or tutoring cannot help you improve your SAT scores. The guide states:

> The SAT I measures developed verbal and mathematical reasoning abilities that are involved in successful academic work in college. Hence SAT scores are useful to college admissions officers in comparing the preparation and ability of applicants from different high schools which may vary widely in their course and grading standards.

The assumption of admissions committees is that when a student with high grades gets mediocre SAT I scores, he or she was not as well prepared as the student with high grades and high SAT I scores. This says nothing about a student's intelligence, and indeed the colleges know this, because they are willing to admit a certain number of students with lower SAT I scores than most of their freshmen. Such students seem to overcome their weaker college preparation in one or two years, and often wind up on an academic level with those who entered with higher SAT I scores.

This fact should encourage anyone who consistently scores below 500 on the verbal or math portions of the SAT I. We cannot say too strongly that if you score low in the SAT I, there is nothing wrong with your intelligence.

COACHING OR TUTORING MAY HELP

Since the SAT I measures "developed" reasoning abilities, development can be aided by teachers, coaches, tutors, and through self-improvement: that is, practicing basic mathematical operations and reading. In *Taking the SAT I,* the College Entrance Examination Board cites results of studies of special preparation conducted by high schools, programs that have yielded improvements of as many as 30 points over average programs that occur without extra help. "Recent studies of commercial coaching have shown a similar range of results," says the CEEB *Guide.*

Tutoring schools themselves claim increases of 150, 200, 250, and more points. These claims refer to the combined verbal and math scores. If you get a combined score of 1000 the first time, you might get 1150 the second, raising you, for example, from 500 in the verbal and 500 in the math to 575 in the verbal test and 575 in the math. However, a spokesman from the Stanley H. Kaplan Educational Center, which attracts 100,000 clients a year nationwide, told us that Kaplan makes no promises and gives no guarantees, because "a student can come to the tutoring sessions and fail to absorb material, or fail to do homework." In other words, the student must work to develop the reasoning abilities tested by the SAT. No tutor can develop them for him or her.

Many of the students who come to Howard Greene's Educational Consulting Center have improved their SAT scores with the help of tutoring schools. The decision to attend one should not be casual. The course may cost more than $500. It will require self-discipline — class attendance and homework. There is no guarantee that your scores will improve after you have been tutored. If your counselor and teachers feel that this approach will be useful, and if you or your parents can afford the tuition, we would say, "Go to tutoring school." Just remember the limitations: you cannot expect a term at a tutoring school to change your scores from mediocre to brilliant.

WHAT ARE GOOD SAT I SCORES?

One subject not covered by *Taking the SAT I* is the significance of your scores. The perfect score for math or verbal is 800; the lowest is 200. All selective colleges publish freshman class profiles that provide average SAT I scores. Carleton College's 1996 class profile shows that only 3 percent of the class scored below 450 on the verbal SAT, while only 1 percent scored below 450 in the math. At the top, in the range 700 and above, more than twice as many entering freshman scored higher in the math than in the verbal — 28 percent versus 12 percent.

A glance at the accompanying pie charts shows that more than half of Carleton's freshmen scored above 600 in either the math or the verbal SAT I. But applicants with lower scores should not be discouraged from applying to this highly selective midwestern college if they have good marks and other attractive accomplishments. On the other hand, B students with low SAT scores have little chance against the competitive applicants Carleton attracts.

To take an example, Muriel, a B+ student in a suburban Chicago high school, compared her 590 verbal and 640 math SATs with the test score profiles at half a dozen colleges, including Carleton. She was assured by Carleton admissions that her test scores and her marks made her a plausible candidate. She then did everything right to assure admission — completed her application to Carleton three months before deadline, made sure recommendations and transcript were sent in on time, talked to a local alumnus as well as a neighbor who was an alumnus, and made a strong general impression on the admissions office.

So what are good SAT I scores? If both low and high qualify for admission under certain circumstances, where is the standard? It lies in what the majority of any entering freshman class achieves. You can tell from the profile that if Muriel had very low SAT results she probably would not be among those admitted. The few with low scores at Carleton or Princeton are the exceptions.

Colleges try to help students determine if they are potential candidates by listing the class standing of recently accepted candidates and their SAT scores reported either as a mean, a median, or a range of the middle 50 percent.

In the accompanying list, you can quickly tell whether your test scores

Carleton College 1996 Class Profile

Entering Freshmen with Class Rank
(Public and Private Schools)

(18% were unranked)

Top 5% 50%

2nd 5% 22%

2nd Decile 16%

3rd Decile 8%

4th Decile 2%

5th Decile 1%

Below Top Half 1%

ACT Composite Scores of Entering Freshmen

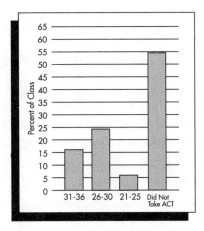

SAT Scores of Entering Freshmen

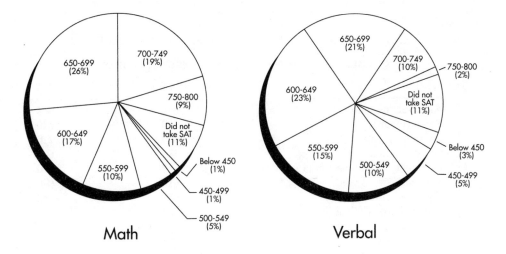

Math

650-699 (26%)
700-749 (19%)
750-800 (9%)
Did not take SAT (11%)
Below 450 (1%)
450-499 (1%)
500-549 (5%)
550-599 (10%)
600-649 (17%)

Verbal

650-699 (21%)
700-749 (10%)
750-800 (2%)
Did not take SAT (11%)
Below 450 (3%)
450-499 (5%)
500-549 (10%)
550-599 (15%)
600-649 (23%)

match up with the particular colleges and universities listed. Feel free to ask the admissions staff at any college for such information.

SAT I

The new SAT still has two parts, verbal and mathematical. The collective name for them is SAT I: Reasoning Tests. The old College Board Achievement Tests are now known as SAT II: Subject Tests. Let's look at the verbal part first.

What was called Reading Comprehension now becomes Critical Reading. The one hour allowed for completion has been extended by 20 minutes, amounting to an extra 10 seconds for each of the 95 multiple-choice questions. There are three categories of questions: sentence completion, analogies, and critical reading of four passages, from the humanities, social sciences, natural sciences, and narrative fiction and nonfiction.

CRITICAL READING

Critical Reading accounts for half the test, and instead of the traditional six passages there are four, but they are longer. Two of the passages will be related and present opposing views. An important reform, in our opinion, is the absence of antonym questions. (We said in our first edition that they "may strike you as a curious way to test your vocabulary.")

Questions test your understanding of the four passages. Since you will be

SAMPLING OF SAT SCORES FOR THE CLASS OF 1997

COLLEGES REPORTING MEAN OR MEDIAN SCORES

	Verbal	Math
Amherst (median)	642	682
Bates (mean)	590	640
Dartmouth (mean)	630	710
Smith (median)	580	600
University of Pennsylvania (median)	610	690
Wellesley (median)	610	640
Wesleyan (median)	620	660
University of California at Berkeley (median)	563	657
UCLA (mean)	555	647
University of Michigan (median)	550	630

COLLEGES REPORTING A RANGE OF SAT SCORES
(middle 50% of accepted candidates were in this range)

	Verbal	Math
Cornell (arts & sciences)	600–699	699–800
Kenyon	500–620	530–630
MIT	570–690	720–780
University of North Carolina (out-state)	510–650	580–710
Northwestern	540–640	610–710
Princeton	610–770	660–750
Smith	520–630	550–650
University of Virginia (in- and out-state)	525–640	590–710
Wesleyan	530–680	680–740

THE IMPORTANCE OF BUILDING YOUR VOCABULARY

Your vocabulary increases over the years without effort, but to give you the edge required by selective colleges you must make an effort to build it up further by keeping a pocket notebook in which you jot down new words and their definitions.

A paperback book that can help you is the Princeton Review's *Word Smart*, available in bookstores for $10. Its 823 words have been compiled from a study of their frequency of appearance in newspapers and magazines like the *New York Times,* the *Wall Street Journal, Time,* and *Scientific American.* Another source used in compiling the list was a study of College Board tests.

The claim on the cover is that this is the only vocabulary book you'll ever need. You may disagree and use other books, including, of course, a good dictionary. Comparing words you have looked up on your own and those in *Word Smart,* you'll probably find many that do not appear in *Word Smart.* A simple example is the common word *panic,* derived from the Greek god Pan, the mythical feisty goat, supposedly the cause of sudden inexplicable fears. Neither *ethnic* nor *ethnicity* is listed.

reading thousands of words in college, answers to these questions show your probable ability to understand class assignments.

ANALOGIES

Analogies are not the everyday questions you put to your friends in the cafeteria. You do not remark, "Beast is to burden as housewife is to dusting," or "Cat is to mouse as heatseeker is to jet." Analogies provide a way of discovering your ability to recognize the relationships among words you read.

There is a relationship between a beast carrying a burden, and a woman dusting her home. To understand it does not require the imagination of a poet, only the capacity of a reader of prose. In analogy questions you are asked to discern among five choices the pair of words most nearly parallel to an initial pair of words in capital letters. A cat seeks a mouse not exactly as a homing rocket is drawn to a jet engine, but there is a relationship here for you to perceive. The parallel need not be exact.

SENTENCE COMPLETION

The questions that give you a choice of words in order to complete a sentence correctly are testing your ability to see relations between parts of a sentence. Whereas analogies and antonyms test your knowledge of word meanings and word relationships, sentence completion tests you on your understanding of the logical structure of language.

By the time you were four you were speaking in complete sentences, like "I brought you this drawing I made at school, Mother, because I think you'll like it." The two parts of the sentence are automatically linked by *because*. In high school you learn that you can be misunderstood if you do not clearly establish a meaningful, logical relationship. To write in an essay, "America was settled by the Pilgrims because they came from England on the *Mayflower*," is not only unclear; it is untrue, even though the Pilgrims did come from England on the *Mayflower*. A more logical connector or conjunction than *because* would be the word *after*.

In sentence-completion questions, you may be provided with a choice of five words to complete a sentence with a blank in it, or with a choice of five pairs of words to complete a sentence with two blanks. In its 1993 edition of *Taking the SAT* the College Entrance Examination Board gave this example of a single blank question:

> Nearly all the cultivated plants utilized by the Chinese have been of
> _____ origin; even rice, though known in China since Neolithic
> times, came from India.

You are told to choose the word that best fits the meaning of the sentence as a whole from these words: (A) *foreign*, (B) *ancient*, (C) *wild*, (D) *obscure*, (E) *common*. Since *C*, *D*, and *E* would contradict the origin of rice from a specific country, India, only *A* and *B* are plausible. Test *B* and the whole sentence lacks consistency. *A* is the word that makes the best sense.

Here is a sentence with two blanks:

The excitement does not _____ but _____ his senses, giving him a keener perception of a thousand details.

Which of the following pairs would you choose to fill in the blanks? (A) *slow . . . diverts,* (B) *blur . . . sharpens,* (C) *overrule . . . constricts,* (D) *heighten . . . aggravates,* (E) *forewarn . . . quickens. B* is the only pair that works. Do you see why? Try the other four pairs and see how poorly they fit.

The Test of Standard Written English is no longer part of the SAT. Grammar is tested in the SAT II's English Composition Achievement Test.

READ TO DEVELOP VERBAL SKILLS

Invariably those who score high on the verbal part of the SAT I are skilled readers; they read a great deal and read widely. Between the time when you take the PSAT in the fall of your junior year and the SAT I the next spring, you can do much reading. But if you have not been a reader before your junior year, how do you suddenly turn into a reader? And what should you read?

We suggest that you consult your English teacher and come up with a reasonable variety of extra reading to do. Periodically you should then report to the teacher what you have read. A good teacher will observe how well you read. Unless you concentrate on and absorb reading matter, you are wasting time. To read well, do not try to read too fast. Take notes or, if you own the book, underline — magazine articles should be underlined and re-read.

Francis Bacon said, "Reading maketh the full man . . . ," and we today would add, "and woman." The more you read, the more enjoyable and useful reading becomes. Your practice tests will reveal the extent to which you must expand your reading. If you were to read a passage a day in a book like the *Norton Reader* or any other collection of prose passages, you would soon find yourself with a larger vocabulary and an ability to grasp new ideas and new information more quickly.

Such a program is an enrichment of your mind as well. Preparing for the SAT this way allows you to sample the kinds of reading you will do in a liberal arts college. You need not think of this extra reading as a means to passing a test. It is the kind of practicing that musicians do; it is how athletes perfect their running, skating, serving. It is an exercise, in this case, to develop your mind, to make you more useful to yourself and to others.

Seen in this light, the SAT reading comprehension questions become a service to you. Read passages that puzzle you, read passages you disagree with, stretch your mind and open it to the treasures of the written word. Read sophisticated magazines like *The New Yorker, Commentary,* and *Scientific American* once in a while.

And, above all, read with a dictionary at hand, take down new words, and build your own vocabulary list. A good vocabulary will help you get a good verbal SAT score. You can keep your list of words and their definitions in the back of your admissions notebook as a reminder that this will help you in your efforts to get into your favorite college. Boxes of vocabulary cards are turning up on coffee tables in the homes of college candidates. They provide amusement, even stimulation, but you do not build a vocabulary by trying to learn words in isolation. In learning a foreign language you build vocabulary as you read, as you study grammar, and as you try to understand pronunciation. Learn to deepen appreciation of your own language the same way, by reading, jotting down words you want to remember after you have looked them up in a good dictionary.

When you consciously carry on a reading program that builds vocabulary, you will find that reading assignments for your courses will become part of the program, and you will improve your course work accordingly. Some schools encourage vocabulary building by putting a certain number of new words on a chalkboard each week. Students are not marked on new words they learn, but are told that these words will help them score well on the SAT I.

You can improve your speed in the analogies if you will use your reading to put questions to yourself about the meaning of words. G. K. Chesterton made this witticism: "Art is limitation; the essence of every picture is the frame." Do you see the analogy he was making? Limitation is to art as a frame is to a picture; knowing where to stop, whether it be in a drip painting or a portrait, is all.

Discuss with friends and with your family what you are reading. When someone tells you that you're wrong, that you misread a passage, take the comment to heart. Merely to be literate is not to be a good reader. If you dislike reading or have difficulty with spelling words you have read, or words you think you know, you may have a reading disability (see the box "Advice for the Dyslexic Student"). This is no disgrace, and it is correctable. You can be tested for reading disability in school or by an outside professional organization, such as the Encyclopaedia Britannica Learning Centers. Students who have very serious reading disabilities can apply to the College Entrance Examination Board to take untimed SAT tests. The request must be accompanied by certification from a recognized educational specialist in reading disabilities.

SAT I MATHEMATICAL REASONING TEST

There are two innovations on the math portion of the new SAT: ten "grid-in" questions requiring that you produce your own answers rather than select one from a set of multiple-choice alternatives, and the recommended use of a calculator. The test remains otherwise unchanged from prior years and

ADVICE FOR THE DYSLEXIC STUDENT

In recent years many colleges have recognized that some students suffer from dyslexia, a learning disability that does not necessarily prevent the student from doing college work and even earning high honors. Famous dyslexics include Thomas Edison, Albert Einstein, and Woodrow Wilson.

Brown University has been a leader in helping dyslexic students support each other, arranging for tutoring and extending exam time. Robert A. Shaw, Associate Dean of the College, has written a brief statement for dyslexic applicants, part of which reads:

> One of the most common questions I am asked by dyslexic high school students is whether or not they should reveal their dyslexia in the college admissions process. I always advise students to inform the colleges to which they apply that they have a learning disability. This can be most effectively done by attaching a brief cover letter to the application packet, describing the nature of the student's learning disability and the specific ways in which it has affected the student's high school record. For example, many dyslexic students have particularly low grades in foreign languages. Others may have participated in relatively few extra-curricular activities because of their need to spend more time than usual on their homework.

Dean Shaw recommends that dyslexics take the SAT I both timed and untimed. He notes that fewer colleges are now rejecting applicants because they are dyslexic or learning-disabled in some other way. Of course such students would not want to enroll where there is no sympathy and thus no support for their problem.

Harvard estimates that 2 percent of its students have learning disabilities. A great many other colleges, including such Exceedingly Demanding institutions as Stanford, Columbia, Cornell, Dartmouth, and the University of Pennsylvania, have started programs to help high-achieving students who have compensated for what is now referred to as "different learning styles." Many successful applicants sit for the SAT I and SAT II on an extended or untimed basis.

consists of 35 multiple-choice questions on regular math and 15 quantitative comparisons. The quantitative questions will require study. You always have four choices instead of five. *A* signifies that the quantity in Column A is greater than that in Column B. *B* signifies that the quantity in column B is the greater. *C* signifies that both quantities are equal, and *D* that there is no way to compare the two quantities.

WORK ON MATHEMATICAL SKILLS
WITH A TEACHER

Math is not magic. You can improve your math skills with practice, but you probably need the help of a teacher or a tutor. It will not take up much of a teacher's time to show you arithmetic, algebra, and geometry books you can use to review your skills. Remember that the SAT I is based on algebra I, geometry, and on grade-school arithmetic, so you will be reviewing subjects you should already know. Some students need more directed help because of lack of skills. Think positively; you can be helped to overcome math weaknesses or anxiety.

Some students are gifted in mathematics and easily score in the 700s on the SAT math test. Most selective college applicants are well enough trained to score at least in the 500s. A lower PSAT score than 50, therefore, calls for remedial work. This will help you in your math courses, and may enable you to take an honors math course in your senior year. You may be able to get help in this work from a math whiz in your school.

A tutoring school can be particularly helpful by drilling you in the kinds of operations you will need to understand for the math SAT I. In addition, the tutoring school forces you to take practice tests, revealing weaknesses that you then learn to overcome in class sessions.

WHERE THE SAT IS OPTIONAL

In the mideighties Bates College in Lewiston, Maine, offered applicants the option of not submitting SAT scores. On the average about a fourth of the applicants did not submit SAT scores. The college found this policy successful enough in 1992 to extend the option to include all standardized tests, including the ACT and College Board Achievement (now Subject) Tests, following the example of Bowdoin College.

Sixty percent of Bates applicants requested aid, and of these, 47 percent received an aid package (a third of them grants). Bates meets all demonstrated need for upperclass financial aid. A $50-million fund-raising campaign is expected to allow this small, selective college to maintain its generous aid policy. One alumnus has contributed $2.7 million for scholarships.

Among other selective colleges that have an optional-SAT policy, Franklin and Marshall waives the SAT for those in the top 10 percent of their high school class, and Lewis and Clark candidates are allowed to submit a long paper demonstrating critical writing and analytical skills in lieu of the SAT.

TIPS ON TAKING THE SAT

The following tips have been used for a number of years by Howard Greene's students. You should start following them when you do your practice tests. They will be habitual by the time of an actual SAT.

1. Plan your time carefully. Spending too much time on a question can be as detrimental as giving a wrong answer.
2. Answer first the questions to which you know the answers. Then, if you have time left, return to the unanswered questions.
3. There is only one right answer. If you identify it, do not waste time working through the other possibilities. Go on to the next question.
4. Guess shrewdly on answers you do not know. Wrong answers carry a larger penalty than unanswered ones, but your chances for a higher score will be improved if you guess — provided you can first eliminate at least one or two choices.
5. In reading comprehension passages, underline important information as you read through the test. There is no penalty for marking the worksheets, and doing it will help you recall important information. Likewise, in mathematical sections use the white space as a worksheet.
6. Pay particular attention to words like *but, not, however,* and *therefore.* They are key words that often signal the major thoughts of a passage.
7. Wherever possible, use mathematical shortcuts, cancellation of fractions, estimation, removal of decimal points, and so forth.
8. Memorize math formulas. Formulas such as $A = L \times W$ for the area of a rectangle are often given at the beginning of the test section, but it is quicker to have them in your head.
9. Don't be sidetracked by secondary answers or answers that are true but not directly related to the central question.

Inasmuch as the SAT is given in the morning, after you have presumably had a good night's sleep, do not take practice tests at midnight or when you are tired. Take them during the day.

THE COLLEGE ENTRANCE
EXAMINATION BOARD'S ADVICE

The College Board has its own set of twelve "test-taking tips," which appear in *Taking the SAT I.* You should read and reread them until you know their gist by heart. Here is how you might fix them in your mind with key reminder sentences.

1. Questions increase in difficulty from beginning to end of each section.

1a. *Exception to above:* reading passages get harder, but the questions have no order of difficulty.
2. Omit questions you don't know at all; go to the next section.
3. Answer easy questions first before spending time on harder ones. Correct answers on easy questions count just as much as correct answers on difficult ones.
4. You don't have to answer every question. Answering 50 to 60 percent of the questions correctly can produce average or slightly above average scores.
5. Omitting some questions may not affect your score adversely.
6. Guess at the answer if you know at least one choice is wrong.
7. For a wrong answer you lose a fraction of a credit. For a correct answer you get one credit. Omitting an answer will result in neither gain nor loss of credit.
8. If you do not answer any questions in a section, you will receive the minimum score for that part.
9. You can use the test book for scratchwork, or reminders if you have time to go back to omitted questions.
10. Make no extra marks on the answer sheet! (Be sure to score the question you are answering; you can get mixed up when you omit questions.)
11. Watch out for quadruple-choice math questions. NEVER MARK THE FIFTH OVAL, E. If you do, you will get no credit for a right answer (though you lose nothing if it's wrong.) It will be treated as an omitted question.
12. Fill in the answer sheet correctly! Mark only one answer for each question by filling in the oval completely.

SAT PROCEDURES

We wish to distinguish the SAT I from Subject Tests, which will be discussed later in this step. Let's review the procedures.

1. Check with your counselor in the fall of your junior year about taking the PSAT/NMSQT. (It is sometimes taken by sophomores.) This warm-up for the SAT I does not go into your admissions folder, but you can qualify for a National Merit Scholarship if you score high enough. We recommend you take it for practice.
2. The SAT I is taken for the first time in March or May of your junior year.
3. To register you will receive a copy of the College Entrance Examination Board's *Student Bulletin,* with registration information and a registration form. You are responsible for mailing the form before

the deadline indicated in the *Student Bulletin,* together with a check for $15 made out to "The College Board."

4. The registration form allows you to mark on it answers to the Student Descriptive Questionnaire, a survey that you need complete only once.

5. The SAT is held at many test centers in each state. You are free to take the test at any center that you choose to indicate by number on your registration form.

6. Tests are held on Saturdays starting at 8:30 A.M. Arrange to be on time, and bring two No. 2 pencils, erasers, and calculator.

Your counselor will go over all this with you. These bureaucratic procedures should give you no trouble, but we are constantly amazed at how casually some students handle details. Do not be casual about the SAT I, no matter how confident you become as a result of careful preparation for the tests.

PREPARING FOR YOUR FIRST SAT I

TAKE THE PSAT/NMSQT

The Preliminary Scholastic Aptitude Test taken in October of your junior year is your warm-up. It is two hours long (the SAT I takes three hours) and is not submitted to the colleges. However, since it is also the National Merit Scholarship Qualifying Test, a high score qualifies you for valuable awards of $250 to $2000, given to 5,000 students every year. If you are among the 15,000 semifinalists, you will include this fact in your applications for admission, because colleges are mightily impressed by this group of applicants. You will also receive letters from many colleges soliciting your application, some of them selective colleges that seek as many strong students as possible.

Your PSAT scores are predictive of how you will score on the SAT I you take the following spring. They are scored between 20 and 80, so you add a zero to see what your score is likely to be in the SAT I. If you have unimpressive PSAT scores by the standards you hold, you have from December to May to develop your verbal and math reasoning ability.

TAKE SAT I PRACTICE TESTS

About a month before the SAT I, start taking practice tests. These last two and a half hours. Set aside enough time so that you will not be interrupted. The first practice test will be found in *Taking the SAT I.* Other practice tests are available in the College Entrance Examination Board's *Ten SAT Tests,* which you should definitely buy. The 300-page book costs approximately $15. There is an order form inside the back cover of *Taking the SAT I.* Taking as many practice tests as you can stand will acquaint you with the nature of the tests and give you confidence when you take the actual SAT I.

SCORE THE SAMPLE TEST AND STUDY THE RESULTS

You need not score the sample test at once. Psychologically, you would do better to put it aside and score it later, when your mind is no longer preoccupied with getting right answers. When you score it, take your time and be accurate. You gain nothing by giving yourself a mark better than the one you earned.

The board has good suggestions to follow about analyzing your performance. If you feel comfortable going over this and any other sample test with a teacher, doing that can be helpful. After taking several sample tests you will know your weaknesses and can work to overcome them. If you score in the 500s on the verbal test and in the 600s in the math one, work on those parts of the verbal test that gave the most difficulty.

TAKING THE SAT I ITSELF

After so much work preparation, the SAT I itself need not be the traumatic experience for you that it is for some students. For one thing, you already know what to expect. You know what the test will be like, and you know how you have scored in the practice tests. If you have scored 1200 in practice, you are likely to score close to this in actuality. Hoping to do better than you did in practice is not realistic, and neither is fearing that you will do worse.

TAKING THE SAT I OVER

Most students take the SAT I during the spring of their junior year and the fall of their senior year. Some take a third SAT I in an effort to improve their score. Three is enough. The likelihood of further improvement, if there has been any, is slight. There is usually some improvement between junior and senior year. Taking a postgraduate high school year will sometimes help a student make a considerably higher score. If you plan a fifth year of high school, wait until the fall of that year to take your third SAT I.

We urge you to take no more than three SAT I tests, for reasons already implied in our introduction: the SAT I is becoming less important in admissions committee decisions, so you should avoid the compulsion to try to improve SAT I scores ad infinitum. Devote your efforts to your regular schoolwork and activities. If you can show tangible results in course work or in some activity, it will count more in your admissions folder than if a fourth or fifth SAT I score is a few points higher than the last. Accept the fact that your scores tell you a certain truth about your preparation for college at this point in time. You need not think that your capacities for verbal and mathematical reasoning will remain forever at your present level. Remember that you are continually developing these powers, and that it is quite possible for you someday to surpass not only your present self but others who currently score higher than you do.

SAT II SUBJECT TESTS

Many selective colleges require candidates to submit three Subject Test scores. You may take as many as you like, as often as you like. They are given in these subjects:

English
Writing (replaces English composition)
Literature

History
American history and social studies
World history (replaces European history and world cultures)

Foreign Language
Chinese
French
German
Modern Hebrew
Italian
Japanese
Latin
Spanish

THE NEW WRITING TEST

Like the other seventeen Subject Tests, the new SAT II writing test is optional, but we highly recommend that you take it. Preparation for it is bound to have a positive impact on your writing ability. Part One consists of multiple-choice questions on usage, sentence correction, and revision-in-context — that is, revising prose passages. Part Two is an exercise in essay writing. You are allowed twenty minutes for the essay section. This test is given five weekends a year, which allows you to fit it in to your personal schedule.

Preparation for this test should include careful practice using the College Board's new sample tests in *Taking the SAT II: Subject Tests*.

Mathematics
Mathematics Level I
Mathematics Level IIC

Science
Biology
Chemistry
Physics

To an admissions committee, the Subject Tests provide more tangible evidence of your capacity to do the advanced academic work of college courses than does the SAT I. You should recognize this fact and take the fullest advantage of the fact that Subject Tests test you in subjects you know. You can prepare for them with a sense of mastery of the material on which you will be questioned.

Because Subject Tests can be taken as early as the freshman year, they offer the selective-college applicant an opportunity to make an impressive testing record. By taking a number of tests over four years, you will be in a position to choose among them the three best scores for the admissions committees' consideration. But you can also submit all your Subject Test scores, and students who begin taking them during their freshman year usually have scores that are satisfactory and often more than satisfactory from the point of view of selective colleges.

To drive this point home, put yourself in the position of an admissions committee looking at two transcripts. One shows six Subject Test scores that average 600, the other shows three Subject Test scores that average 600. The committee has to think that the student who took the extra three Subject Tests is more academically aggressive, more daring, if you like. This is what we mean by taking advantage of testing opportunities. Students who successfully exercise this testing option put themselves in a very strong competitive position for admission to the most selective colleges.

In contrast to the SAT I, which is one three-hour test, there are seventeen one-hour Subject Tests. You may choose what tests to take and when to take them. Early Decision applicants must submit their scores in the fall with their applications. Their last opportunity to take the tests is the first Saturday in November. Such applicants would be advised to take their Subjects by spring of junior year. Taking an extra Subject Test in November of your senior year will help you if your score is good. Since Early Decision candidates usually apply with the encouragement of the college, the admissions office is the best source of advice on taking Subject Tests.

THE IDEAL SUBJECT TEST PROGRAM

The ideal Subject Test program is to take as many Subject Tests as you can, starting in your freshman year, in those subjects expressly required by colleges to which you plan to apply. By your senior year you may already have compiled a record of impressive Subject Test scores. Then, as a senior, you take Subject Tests at the most advanced level.

Table 3 lists the subject testing schedule that would be the most helpful.

Table 3

CONCISE ACADEMIC AND TESTING SCHEDULE
Grades 9–12

Grade	Course Selection	Tests
9	English Biology (Laboratory) History (Ancient or European) Math (Algebra I or Plane Geometry) Language (First or Second Year)	*June:* SAT II Subject Test in Biology
10	English Chemistry (Laboratory) Math (Plane Geometry or Algebra II) Language (Second or Third Year) History or Computer Science or Fine or Performing Arts	*June:* SAT II Subject Test in Chemistry or History
11	English Physics (Laboratory) Math (Algebra II or Precalculus) Language (Third or Fourth Year) United States History Writing/Journalism	*October:* PSAT *May:* SAT I *June:* Subject Tests (in strongest subjects) Take three to qualify for Early Decision in fall.

Rules of thumb for Subject Tests:

1. Writing and Math I will most typically be required by selective colleges. They are "bread-and-butter" subjects and should be taken.
2. The third Subject Test should be in the subject that reflects college intentions: e.g., science for engineering or pre-medical students; history or foreign language for pre-law, political science, or foreign language majors.
3. If you are not certain of your future field of study, take a Subject Test in a terminal study, such as United States history or physics, a subject not continued in the senior year.
4. If you plan to take advanced-level courses in your senior year, you can leave the Subject Test until then.

Grade	Course Selection	Tests
12	Advanced-level courses in English Math (Precalculus or Calculus) Language (Third or Fourth Year) These are core courses. You may also take advanced-level courses in Science History (Russian, Chinese, Middle Eastern; or advanced European or American History) Music, Art, or Drama as a major if it fits with future college studies; or Computer Science or Economics or Political Science	SAT I November or December SAT II Subject Any twelfth-grade subject if you need to complete three or to enhance your record with extra testing results.

Rule of thumb for twelfth-grade courses:

If you have followed the suggested program the first three years, you should be able to emphasize your particular areas of talent and interest beyond English, mathematics, and language. Take advanced placement courses, if available in your school, in those subjects in which you have excelled.

Your teachers and your counselor can help you decide how many of these tests you ought to take. This schedule is often followed by students who enroll in the Exceedingly Demanding colleges.

Tests are given on five scheduled Saturdays throughout the year, as specified in the College Board registration and informational brochure *Taking the SAT II: Subject Tests*. Refer to this brochure to plan the schedule of your Subject testing.

The tests should always be taken as soon as possible after completing a course. You will see that the best time to take Subject Tests is June, after you have studied a subject for a full year. In your senior year you can take tests in December if you need to complete your requirements.

Your Subject Test scores will usually correspond to your grades in the subjects of the test. Should there be a discrepancy, a lower score than your grades would seem to warrant, you can repeat any Subject Test in an attempt to bring up your score.

By the time you submit the three Subject Test scores that selective colleges require, you should have had good or excellent scores in three out of a possible eight or nine tests. Furthermore, if you have discovered an area of concentration in which you are strong, your Subject Test scores will reflect this academic commitment, an important consideration in being admitted to the Exceedingly Demanding colleges.

If such a program is not possible for you — if you are taking Subject Tests for the first time in your senior year, for example — you still can make them count heavily in your favor by taking them in your strongest subjects.

Preparing for a Subject Test is a matter of going over material in the course you have recently completed, bearing in mind the kinds of questions you will expect from taking practice tests, just as you did for the SAT I. In fact, if you are able to take Subject Tests in your freshman and sophomore years, you will feel more comfortable about preparing for and taking the SAT I; you will be a veteran.

Use the College Board's guide *Taking the Sat II: Subject Tests* the same way you use *Taking the SAT I: Reasoning Test.* A new edition appears annually. Make a note right now in your notebook to refer to this invaluable booklet before every single Subject Test.

The guide consists of three sections: "About the Tests," "Planning to Take the Tests," and "How to Prepare for the Tests." There follow sample questions from the seventeen tests, preceded by the same directions you will find when you take the actual tests. On the back cover is an order form for the *Official Guide to the SAT II: Subject Tests,* a 380-page book that sells for $15.00. It has sample tests in each of the seventeen subjects. You should get the book and practice any test you plan to take as soon as you finish your school course in the subject, in order to allow time to work on any weakness the sample test reveals.

PRACTICE AND REVIEW

The last page of *Taking the SAT II: Subject Tests* is a schedule of the five test dates.

Plan your test schedules far enough ahead to allow you to prepare for each Subject Test. The best preparation is strong course work, of course, but you will want to take a practice test, review the course, and concentrate on any areas of uncertainty.

TIPS ON TAKING SUBJECT TESTS

Like the SAT questions, Subject Test questions get harder toward the end of a section, with the exception of questions on reading passages and diagrams. This means that as the questions increase in difficulty, you will be slowed down. So read all the questions once, answer those you know, and do not get rattled if you cannot finish a section. Many students who have respectable Subject Test scores leave questions unanswered. The unanswered questions do not count against your score.

As with the SAT I, guessing is advisable if you can identify one wrong answer.

The reading passages and diagrams are another matter. Instead of the questions' becoming increasingly difficult, the passages and diagrams increase in difficulty. The questions themselves are not presented in order of difficulty, so you may find the first question harder to answer than the last in such a section. All you can do is go through the questions and waste no time on those that completely baffle you; leave them unanswered.

TESTING: MAJOR POINTS TO REMEMBER

You will have to add SAT I and Subject Test preparation to your homework schedule. The challenge is to exercise self-discipline, for it is one thing to write an assigned paper for English class and quite another to assign yourself a book or magazine article to build vocabulary for your verbal SAT I. One solution is to write brief periodic reports to teachers on the test preparation you undertake. Doing this has the effect of obliging you to do needed preparation and allowing a teacher to help you make the best use of your time.

The success of tutoring schools lies in part in the discipline they impose on students by giving them workbooks and making them come regularly to tutoring sessions. You can prepare for tests by studying an extra half an hour a day for a month prior to a test. Be sure to allow added time to take practice tests. This kind of schedule will make it unnecessary even to think of cramming, a practice you no doubt have been told is seldom fruitful.

Step Four Checklist

1. Think of the College Board tests as opportunities in the admissions process.
2. Consider a program of self-teaching, coaching, or tutoring to improve your SAT I and II scores.
3. Read the College Board test guides and review them in preparing to take the tests.
4. Take the practice tests the College Board provides.
5. If possible, begin taking Subject Tests in your freshman year.
6. Take a Subject Test as soon as possible after finishing a course in the subject of the test.

Excel Outside Class

EXCELLENCE AS AN ADMISSIONS FACTOR

*M*ost applicants to any selective college are "average in their excellence" — that is, they excel above most of their classmates academically, but when considered in a group none necessarily excels over another. How, then, will *you* stand out from other qualified applicants within the selective college pool?

Admissions committees look to candidates' nonacademic qualifications to distinguish the students who will add high-caliber diversity to their freshman classes.

Mildred, for example, seemed to resemble thousands of selective college applicants. She played various sports, served on the student council and as a student representative to her school's board of trustees, but did not stand out in any one of these capacities. Academically, she was unexceptional, and her combined SAT score was 1150. Visiting New England colleges, she learned that her chances at many of those she liked were marginal. Disheartened, she finally sought the advice of Howard Greene.

Howard felt that as an applicant from an excellent Connecticut high school, Mildred would appeal to a college outside New England. He drew her attention to Emory University in Atlanta, which has a strong social sciences program. Among her extracurricular activities he had spotted one to which she was strongly committed, her school's chapter of Students Against Drunk Driving. "I feel," she wrote in her Student Questionnaire, "that the waste of life caused by drinking and driving can be stopped through sensitivity training." She was urged to emphasize this concern in her college applications (she applied to the University of Connecticut, Franklin and Marshall, and Villanova as well as to Emory).

Mildred's record in a national, increasingly visible social-service organization was a strong factor in her acceptance. While it was not enough to get her into selective colleges in her own region, her excellence in this area helped her to compete successfully for a place in a college that was seeking geographic diversity in its student body. Had she not emphasized her leadership role in SADD, she probably would have been unsuccessful in her bid for Emory, where she is now majoring in psychology.

An entirely different case from Mildred's was that of her classmate, Bernard, who stood in the top 10 percent of his class and was captain of his soccer team. Under Howard Greene's guidance he attached to his Dartmouth Early Decision application a long résumé of his soccer record starting with his sophomore year — 34 consecutive games as a starter, honorable mention for All-State in his junior year, membership in club soccer teams as player, coach, and referee, post-season tournament participation, his coach's comment that he was one of the committed players in his county. He even included a self-assessment: "Strengths: Intensity, vision. Weakness: Dribbling." Several newspaper accounts of his playing were attached to the résumé.

What this presentation did for Bernard was distinguish him from hundreds of applicants with similar academic profiles. Dartmouth admitted him.

In the long run, most students will finish academic work in college or graduate school and spend the rest of their lives in some kind of useful service in the professions, business, government, the arts, the media. Every selective college, with its strong body of alumni, takes enormous pride in training the men and women whose responsible leadership makes this country work. Admissions committees look for applicants whose excellence reflects an inner need to use their personal strengths, energies, and talents for a socially useful purpose.

THE SPIRITUAL QUALITIES OF EXCELLENCE

The ways in which you excel embody your personal sense of who you are, in relation to yourself and to others. You excel in ways in which no one else can. Your interests guide your choice of activities, and your personal convictions and qualities inspire and enrich your performance. No book can tell you how or in what to excel — but we *can* help you identify and emphasize your particular areas of excellence. And we urge you, above all, to listen to your own inner voice that inspires your unique capabilities, be they athletic, artistic, intellectual, political, social, or charitable.

In working with hundreds of students, we have observed (and admissions officers confirm this) that those who excel at any activity in school exhibit four qualities in common. If you recognize these traits in yourself, you can be sure that selective colleges will spot them, too.

A willingness to compete with yourself as well as with others. You ask more of yourself, striving to better your own performance. You wrestle with the devil in you that would persuade you to take it easy.

After Charles Lindbergh flew the Atlantic in 1927, he wrote a book called simply *We,* referring to himself and his plane, the *Spirit of St. Louis.* But there was another person that he recognized as part of himself. One person was the determined pilot who wanted to be the first to make a solo flight from New York to Paris. The other was the demanding physical self that urged him to sleep — and probably to crash into the ocean. Quite consciously he fought off this threatening demon, to keep flying for thirty-seven hours, to become a world hero symbolic of the pioneering spirit.

A positive outlook on life, with less tendency than others have to use drugs and alcohol. A jovial, extroverted manner doesn't necessarily reflect a positive outlook. You may be the strong, silent type like Lindbergh. Your positive outlook embodies a healthy optimism and a confidence that reassure those around you. Your competitive spirit inspires even your opponents, who trust your honest striving. You rely for stimulus on your innate optimism, rather than on alcohol.

Good organization in use of time and study habits. You have learned that there is time for everything as long as you are aware of what must be done. You do the important thing first, and the trivial takes care of itself instead of eating into the study hour. You get enough sleep, you have added energy as a result, and you get things done more efficiently.

A concern for others, which often earns you the role of leader. You have been praised for your personal qualities at home and in school, and so you respond warmly and genuinely to others. Your self-confidence and capability inspire people to have confidence in you, and to seek you out to fill leadership roles.

NONACADEMIC EXCELLENCE AS AN ADMISSIONS FACTOR

Selective colleges seek real students, of course, not paragons. What will admissions committees look for as indicators of excellence in your nonacademic record?

Naturally, it helps if you are captain of an athletic team, president of your class, valedictorian, editor of the school paper, or head of the dramatic club. The University of North Carolina had 545 varsity high school captains in the class of 1997. Washington and Lee had 55 editors-in-chief and 53 class presidents in a freshman class of four hundred.

However, while it helps to be number one in some activity, being it is not essential for admission. Selective colleges would not be able to fill their freshman classes if they restricted admission to football captains, class presidents, and valedictorians. You, too, will be an attractive candidate if, like Mildred, you have shown commitment in some activity and have been recognized for excellence. Even if you happen to be a star, you will be competing against others like yourself — athletes, editors, dancers, community leaders. *Your* excellence must stand out.

Admissions officials look for three essential characteristics in your nonacademic performance: commitment, development, and recognition.

COMMITMENT

You know the student who gets involved in so many activities that you cannot keep track of what he or she is doing — is on several athletic squads, moves scenery for one play, sings in the chorus one term, is on the school paper masthead, is jack-of-all trades and master of none. A whirl of activities does not impress selective admissions directors. They are looking for maturity, which takes the form of sticking to a few things to show positive results.

Gene, for example, swims a lot. He's always in the water. He swam on the varsity team in his small rural New York high school. He competed in the American Athletic Union's national swimming program. He was named All-State. Gene is not an Olympic-class swimmer, and he wants to be a novelist. Duke accepted him on Early Decision in part because he will fit into their swimming program, but also because they appreciate his singlemindedness that may someday bring us a new American literary voice.

Alice, in a suburban Saint Paul high school, is on the cross-country ski team, but she also has to earn money for college. Instead of taking the first minimum-wage job she could find at a supermarket or fast-food outlet, she canvassed her community for some opportunity to use her decorating talents. She found a handsome store that sells inexpensive home furnishings, many of them simple plastic containers in tasteful colors, wooden racks, occasional tables, folding chairs. She offered to join the sales staff as a decorating consultant, helping people pick items that would work well with their existing furniture, wall colors, rugs, and curtains. She makes more than the minimum wage and has been asked on occasion to visit homes and develop decorating plans. Her skill and experience have made her a semiprofessional decorator at the age of seventeen.

Walter plays football for his rural Vermont high school, but has no winter sport except recreational skiing. Knowing the basketball players, he heard them complain about lack of team support. For the last two years he has been the team mascot, wearing a bird costume to represent the eagle. A rather shy person, Walter finds that, concealed as a bird, he loses all inhibitions, and he has become such a hilarious figure on the sidelines that crowds come to watch him. His pep rallies in town have brought new fans to the school, and the basketball team for the past two seasons has won more games than it has lost. Walter is considered a factor in this success.

You have been urged to take risks academically by stretching, going for the more demanding courses, doing the extra paper that is optional, and generally going beyond the minimum asked of you. Nonacademic commitment calls for the same kind of stretching, of risk-taking, of sacrifice of time and energy.

Noel is on her school ski team in Colorado. But she also has joined a group of superskiers who are being rigorously trained in a program for national competition. Every day she finds herself skiing with far superior skiers, some of them boastful and quick to put her down. Because she is among the weak skiers, her time for the slalom run was among the slowest, and she was forced to ski with the last skiers. Her runs were made after the course was worn and icy, a Catch-22 situation — weak skier, forced to accept the worst conditions, falls a lot; good skier gets great conditions and improves technique. But Noel gets points for trying and has gradually moved up to the middle of the group. She knows she is not of Olympic caliber, but is determined to ski as well as her limitations permit. Admissions committees love this kind of commitment.

One word of caution. We do urge students not to commit themselves to any activity only for the purpose of getting into any college. If you feel you have not involved yourself sufficiently in one or two activities, make the commitment to do something you like to do, something you know will be useful to others as well as to yourself. It may be that a part in the senior play will give you a better chance of getting into Oberlin, but what will this mean to the drama coach and the rest of the cast? They want you to be part of their joint effort of putting on a good play. That's the commitment they expect. And so do the colleges.

DEVELOPMENT

Nonacademic activities should change your own capacities or outlook. Even a menial job requiring no skill can develop in you good habits such as punctuality, careful work, a cheerful manner with your associates and your supervisor. Anything that calls for skill is bound sooner or later to bring improvement in how you do it. Bernard's assessment of his weakness in dribbling means that at Dartmouth he will work to improve this.

Development usually occurs more quickly when you set goals. Agnes wanted to give up her piano lessons after six months. They bored her. But her teacher said, "It's because you don't think you're improving, and that's true. I'll make a deal with you. If you'll practice this Haydn minuet for one hour every day for a week and you don't play it any better, I'll give you up as a pupil."

Stung, Agnes grudgingly said, "Oh, all right." But inside she was saying, "I'll show her." After a week she played the little dance without a mistake, and the teacher said, "I'm sorry, Agnes, I can't give you up yet. You seem to be improving. Now do the same thing with this Mozart sonata." Agnes continued her lessons and eventually played in school recitals.

We are mentioning less conventional activities outside class, because you know already what it takes to develop yourself in sports, journalism, theater arts, or class government. Colleges do not ask that you do anything in particular with your nonacademic time, but they expect you to do something that pays off in ways that you can measure and describe, such as:

- specializing as a camp counselor in safety and lifesaving, then working as a safety volunteer in your community.
- assisting the local tennis or golf pro in summer to qualify to give lessons while in college to help pay your tuition.
- working for the local paper or radio or TV station as an intern or apprentice in order to become a campus stringer for a metropolitan paper or radio or TV news service.
- starting a part-time catering service with a plan to offer the same service for faculty receptions.
- volunteering in political campaigns to learn how to organize voters on a college campus.

All such activities show development, and this attribute will catch an admissions committee's attention. Again, your goal should be development of a skill or some personal quality, not just college admission!

RECOGNITION

When they evaluate your achievements, admissions committees rely on the recognition you've received. Keep all tangible evidence of your accomplishments, from certificates for perfect attendance to the paddle you won at camp. Save newspaper clippings mentioning your participation in community events, and consider these as possible items to be mentioned in your college applications or to be sent to the college as exhibits.

Seek recognition for your contribution if none seems forthcoming. Isabel worked in the paraplegic ward of a veterans' hospital in Indiana all summer between her junior and senior years. She was warmly thanked, the men gave her flowers, and all signed a card. When she filed her college applications, she requested a letter from the doctor in charge of the ward, describing how much her work had meant to the veterans. This letter accompanied her applications and substantiated her one-line description of this valuable public-service work.

AREAS OF NONACADEMIC EXCELLENCE

In contrast to the detailed academic requisites for admission, selective colleges' standards for nonacademic achievement are expressed vaguely. The Smith College catalogue says, "We seek students who will be productive members of the Smith community, who will be challenged by all that is offered here. . . . Because our students come from virtually every state and more than fifty foreign countries, their education and personal experiences vary tremendously. . . . The Board of Admission . . . considers each student in the light of opportunities available to her."

Chicago has only this to say: "In making admissions decisions the College consults students' academic and extra-curricular records." Clark University says that the academic record is the primary basis for admission decisions. "Secondarily," its catalogue tells you, "decisions reflect the individual experience and particular circumstances unique to each candidate."

By intention, selective colleges leave enormous latitude for accepting a tremendous variety of meaningful activities as measures of a candidate's initiative and commitment.

VARSITY SPORTS

A good athlete, as you know, will be considered for admission separately in the admissions committee's athletic round. You can discover whether you qualify for the athletic round of a selective college simply by asking your coach, the admissions office, and the coaches of the colleges. In many cases athletes know, from letters of solicitation, before they are seniors that their talents are valued by a number of colleges. The more selective colleges do not "recruit" athletes the way colleges do whose teams act as farm clubs for professional leagues.

"We don't do recruiting in the Ivy League," said Dartmouth's former basketball coach, Gary Walters, in an interview. "Student enrollment work is the euphemism we use."

Athletes give the place a tone, a Harvard dean used to say. A tone of vigor, grace, and physical control. Remember that Harvard, so often first in events, built America's first football stadium, back in 1900. No longer football powers,

---

THE EVIDENCE OF EXCELLENCE

From the Educational Consulting Center survey of admissions deans and directors here are a few figures that indicate the extent of certain accomplishments of the class of 1997.

Typically, Vanderbilt admitted 269 school editors, 82 class presidents, and 114 school presidents. Franklin and Marshall admitted 1,132 varsity captains and 49 editors. Washington and Lee admitted 69 varsity captains, 55 editors, and 53 class presidents. Bucknell admitted 645 varsity athletes, 130 varsity captains, 37 editors, and 60 class presidents. Columbia admitted 250 editors. At Davidson, 57 percent of those admitted were varsity athletes. Duke admitted 396 varsity letter holders. Georgetown admitted 1,492 varsity athletes. These figures include both men and women.

While the record is awe-inspiring, it nonetheless accounts for fewer than half those admitted to most of these colleges. Your own achievements will be recognized if you are able to identify them as such.

the Ivies have abandoned what has been called their "mucker pose," which put athletes above the scholars. Today many faculty members are former athletes. Before he became president of Harvard, Derek Bok played varsity basketball for Stanford; William Bowen, Princeton's former president, was a state tennis champion in Ohio.

If you are among the athletes destined to play varsity sports in college, you must also have a respectable academic record for admissions. In a selective college you will be a so-called scholar-athlete, even though you may never have thought of yourself as a scholar. You will be carrying a heavy academic schedule. Should you be the object of desire by two or more Exceedingly Demanding colleges, you will need the help of your coach and counselor in making decisions about the applications you will file. You should apply to several colleges and anticipate the possibility of not being admitted to a college that has urged you to apply. Coaches cannot admit anyone. They can only plead for some applicants, and they never get all they ask from admissions committees.

Many a high school star, however, is destined to try out for varsity sports in college, only to be cut from the squad: a cruel blow, but not fatal. Selective colleges have wonderful intramural sports, and you may take up a new sport in college — squash has already been mentioned, and there are also rowing, boxing, the marathon, cycling. Your excellence will find a new outlet. One undergraduate organized a horse-jumping team at Princeton. You may start your own water polo club, for all we know. The admissions office will not be surprised.

NONVARSITY SPORTS

The high school athlete who will not play on a varsity team will not be considered in the athletic round. Nonetheless, your athletic accomplishments will be a strong consideration in your favor as a nonacademic excellence.

WOMEN ATHLETES

The picture of padded women playing ice hockey is no longer an oddity.

Selective colleges have extended most athletic activities to include sports for women. Women athletes are included in the athletic round of admissions, and an outstanding woman athlete has greatly enhanced chances for admission.

Sports participation outside school, such as horsemanship, golf, or sailing, should be included in admissions applications. Comments by instructors and news reports of honors won will reinforce an impression of an active candidate.

UNDERSTANDING THE ATHLETIC ROUND

The athletic round is simply a session in which the admissions committee considers the applications of good athletes separately from other applications. This, of course, means that very good athletes with reasonably good academic records are strong candidates. But they are competing among themselves and so in the athletic round there are both admissions and rejections.

Dr. Frank C. Leana, author of *Getting Into College* (Hill and Wang, 1990) and director of the New York office of the Educational Consulting Center, warns parents and applicants to beware of the promise of admission by a coach. "A college coach does not make the final decision to admit or deny. Only an admissions committee makes that decision," he says.

No coaches are present in the athletic round, ever, though they may have talked to admissions personnel urging acceptance of certain athletic applicants. Athletes should talk to coaches at schools they are thinking of applying to to find out what might happen if they're admitted. Most coaches will tell you what they're looking for. "We need no more goalies. Sorry." Or "Yes, we could use a good place kicker. I hope you'll apply. I'll put in a good word for you." If you're rejected, don't blame the coach. He had nothing to do with it.

Most admissions officers are athletes, though not necessarily of varsity caliber, either. "When admissions officers get together, they seem to wind up talking sports," a Middlebury admissions officer told us. They love athletes, because from experience they know that athletes have the drive and optimism that will carry them to the top in many other things they do.

The Radcliffe admissions component of Harvard has a practical message for women athletes: "We have a strong athletic program and wonderful facilities, and we don't want them wasted."

EXTRACURRICULAR ACTIVITIES

There are no special rounds in admissions for editors, class presidents, band leaders, or even concert pianists. In the search for diversity, admissions committees consider each applicant on his or her merits. The more intense your commitment, the more outstanding your achievement, the more it will help you. But just as the athlete must apply to several colleges, so must the future editor of the *New York Times* (though if it were possible to identify this student, there would be competition among the top colleges to enroll him or her).

However you have excelled, you can anticipate competition from other applicants. But some college will prove to be the one that appreciates you

HOBBIES AS EXCELLENCE

Colleges are prepared to recognize excellence in just about any activity.

Dartmouth, for example, is impressed by candidates who do carpentry, cabinetmaking, and wood sculpture. Its outstanding campus shop, equipped with the best machines and tools, is filled night and day with students and faculty working with wood for the fun of it. Students who assemble radios and electronic equipment, or repair their own cars, should not fail to include such activities on their applications — especially when applying to engineering schools.

An applicant to Princeton with his eyes open included Ping-Pong as one of his competencies, observing that the university has excellent facilities he would make use of. Frisbee is not all frivolous. Intercollegiate Frisbee matches call for speed, grace, and endurance for those good enough to make the teams.

Scuba diving, wind surfing, rock scaling, or rock polishing — whatever your hobby — is of interest to colleges, as long as you can show that whatever you do, you do well and with gusto.

particularly. Your excellence will be recognized and welcomed as an addition to a freshman class diversity.

PUBLIC SERVICE AND EMPLOYMENT

Examples of what applicants submit as unrelated to school include 4-H Club membership, Bible study, nursing-home work, carpenter's apprenticeship, secondhand car salesmanship, bank teller jobs, camp counselorship, volunteer fireman duty, auxiliary policeman duty, ham radio operation, sailing instructorship, fundraising, political campaign managing, school representation at town meeting, being an extra in the opera, breeding dogs. Anything you do that you do with enthusiasm on a sustained basis is worth bringing to the attention of an admissions committee.

Routine jobs such as pumping gas, waiting on tables, or washing cars may show a willingness to work, but such activities by themselves do not demonstrate excellence. Rising in a job, even a notch, shows competence. Otherwise, it would be wise to explain why you chose to spend many hours earning a minimum wage — because you needed the money, because you were earning it for college, because your family owned a restaurant and needed your help in the kitchen.

EVALUATING YOUR AREAS OF EXCELLENCE

Recognizing your particular excellence carries Step Two — Determine Your Strengths — to another level of exactitude. You are positioning yourself to make more rational choices of colleges you would like to visit, colleges where you think you have some chances of admission.

For college admissions you will be presenting a "snapshot" of your particular areas of excellence. As we have said more than once, admissions committees want well-rounded classes more than they want well-rounded students. Your goal is to stand out in the pool of selective college applicants. Ask yourself these questions and answer them in your notebook:

1. What is my most outstanding achievement outside class?
2. How can I best call attention to this in my folder?
3. How would I rate this achievement: Excellent, Good, Fair?

In athletics your rating is often determined for you by the competition. If you are your track team's second fastest runner of the mile, you know where you stand. Other activities may have to be rated on the basis of what your teachers, counselors, or peers say of your performance. Likewise, your rating of an activity outside school may require a statement from a supervisor or someone you work with — the head of the camp if you are a camp counselor, the Red Cross director, if you are a volunteer in that organization.

4. How does my excellence match with campus activities at particular colleges (to help identify institutions that will be especially appreciative of what you do)?

Colleges want students who will participate in their programs and use their wonderful facilities.

You need not show these evaluations to anyone immediately. Think about them, revise them, then test them with your counselor or your parents. It may be that you underestimate yourself. Your counselor may ask, "Why not mention your chess?" It never occurred to you. Or your counselor may say, "I don't think sewing is going to carry much weight," if you have mentioned routine mending. But knitting sweaters with your own original patterns is worth mentioning on an application. One admissions office opened a package from an applicant to find a quilt, all the more remarkable since the applicant was male.

In Step Six — Know the Colleges — and Step Seven — Make the Most of Campus Visits — you will discover how your own areas of excellence correspond to campus opportunities and to the character of different institutions. Continue to reflect on your activities outside of class and to refine the evaluation of your performance. You are learning to know where you stand in relation to others, and if you do not stand as tall in your own esteem as you would like to, then STRETCH!

Step Five Checklist

1. Remember that being number one academically is not essential to excellence. Concentrate on excelling in your own fashion.

2. Identify the nonacademic areas in which you demonstrate the three characteristics of excellence: commitment, development, and recognition from others.

3. Stretch yourself to excel in a few nonacademic activities. Even routine jobs are opportunities to commit yourself, show development, and receive recognition.

STEP SIX

Know the Colleges

AVOID THE CLUSTER EFFECT

*T*he richness and variety of our colleges are often overlooked by applicants who have their hearts set on one or two particular schools. We want you to consider colleges of different levels of selectivity, in different parts of the country, and differing in such characteristics as size, academic programs, lifestyles, and traditions. In doing this, you will have an advantage over many applicants, who fail to diversify their applications sufficiently to avoid rejection by all of the colleges, a phenomenon known in admissions circles as the *cluster effect*. The cluster effect is fatal to the chances of many, many applicants.

Among clusters that have been identified in admissions studies are Stanford, Berkeley, Pomona, Reed, California Institute of Technology, and William Marsh Rice University in the West. Another cluster is this group of women's colleges: Wellesley, Smith, Bryn Mawr, Mount Holyoke, and Barnard. Were these colleges to accept candidates only on their academic and nonacademic merits, there would be no objection to qualified applicants' applying to such clusters. Then the western colleges would enroll mostly qualified upper-middle-class students from their region, and the women's colleges would enroll mostly upper-middle-class women from the eastern suburbs. But as we have pointed out, all colleges seek a diverse body of undergraduates — students of all economic and social levels, of varied racial origins, from different parts of the country.

Frank, for example, a good student in a Los Angeles suburban high school, found himself rejected by Cal Tech and Rice. After a year in a local junior college, he was unable to transfer to either institution, but he was accepted as a transfer by Georgia Tech. Becky, against her counselor's advice, applied only to Wellesley, Smith, and Bryn Mawr, all of which turned her down. Like many other applicants to these colleges, she was a New England boarding-school student and lived in Westchester County, New York. She ranked in the upper third of her class and had a combined SAT score of 1200. After a year taking courses at the University of London, she applied to Pomona, the University of Chicago, and Georgetown. Only Chicago turned her down, and she enrolled at Georgetown.

In all likelihood both these applicants could have made it to the colleges they are in without the anguish they went through. But they persisted, like many candidates, in applying only to colleges they knew, colleges where they thought they would feel comfortable and at home. The fact is that their images of these colleges was incomplete. Yes, of course you will find Andover girls at Smith and Beverly Hills boys at Cal Tech, but only a few of them. Apparently the changed composition of many American campuses has escaped the notice of many bright young people.

A highly respected admissions authority, Dean K. Whitla, director of the Office of Instructional Research and Evaluation at Harvard, has done research that shows a widespread tendency of applicants to cluster their applications among similar institutions, rather than shrewdly to calculate the probabilities

---

DARTMOUTH'S CLASS OF 1997

Applications	8,600
Accepted	2,090
Enrolled	1,070
Mean Verbal SAT	630
Mean Math SAT	700

Class Characteristics

50 states represented, dozens of foreign countries
175 valedictorians
90 salutatorians
600-plus in top 10 percent of graduating class
23 percent minorities
male/female ratio of 53 to 45
all admissions need-blind (rare in all but a few wealthy institutions)
45 percent of alumni children who applied were accepted (of which
   75 percent enrolled at Dartmouth, the rest went to other Ivies)

Activities and Accomplishments

Played violin for Boris Yeltsin in Russia
Captained Native American Lacrosse Team
First Place in National Peace Literature Contest
Hospital Intern in Guatemala
Worked for Thames TV, London
Organized school's Holocaust Remembrance Week
Cited in *Sports Illustrated* as scholar-athlete

PROTECTION FOR THE DISABLED

Applicants with physical or learning disabilities are legally protected from discrimination by federal law. The Rehabilitation Act of 1973 and the Americans with Disabilities Act of 1990 prohibit discrimination against disabled applicants to any college receiving federal monies.

Disabled applicants may want to query colleges about their programs and facilities. Most but not all campuses have someone responsible for coordinating special-student services. Knowing in advance what to expect, the disabled applicant can avoid disappointment and, as has often been the case, actually enhance his or her chances for admission by informing the college of his motivation and ability to overcome significant obstacles.

of acceptance and scatter their applications in what we call an *acceptance pattern.*

Jonathan, in the upper 20 percent of his class in a Chicago high school, with SAT combined scores of 1180, told his advisor in his junior year that he was interested in Carleton, Chicago, and Oberlin. This, the advisor said, was too narrow a choice, considering the competition. All three institutions accept students of Jonathan's caliber, but the students are likely to be applying from another part of the country, or they are minority students, or students with some outstanding nonacademic record, which Jonathan lacked — his forte happened to be canoeing, developed over the years at a camp in Wisconsin. Stubbornly, he insisted on applying to his three first choices, but was sensible enough to explore Colby and Bates in Maine, as well as Columbia, being attracted to an extent by a large urban university. His six applications constituted a good admissions pattern. The advisor was dead right: Carleton, Chicago, and Oberlin rejected him, Colby and Bates accepted him, and Columbia wait-listed him. He enrolled at Bates.

In a junior-year consultation with her college advisor in a Washington, DC, private school, Audrey listed as her college choices the University of Virginia, University of North Carolina, and William and Mary. He at once pointed out that these southern state universities would reject her unless she brought her SAT score above 1200 — she had scored 1150 on her second test. In the spring and summer she visited colleges in Pennsylvania and Ohio, as well as George Washington University in Washington, DC. When her third SAT added up only to 1160, she dropped her first cluster and chose to apply to Bucknell, Pennsylvania State, Miami University in Ohio, and George Washington. She was admitted to all four.

Everett was typically overconfident in wanting to apply only to Harvard, Yale, Williams, and Wesleyan. True, he was in the upper 5 percent of his

Hartford high school class, had SAT scores of 1300, high Achievement Test scores, and was a moderately good violinist, but there was no margin for error in his college choices. Howard Greene pointed out that Everett would be competing against many others whose profiles resembled his. Why would he be the one on whom fortune smiled? To the list Everett therefore added Columbia, Cornell, Swarthmore, and Johns Hopkins. Result: rejected by Harvard, Yale, and Williams; wait-listed by Wesleyan, Columbia, and Swarthmore; accepted by Cornell and Johns Hopkins. Everett enrolled at Cornell.

All three of these students were chancing a great deal by clustering their choices among colleges, one or more of which might turn them down simply because their folders were indistinguishable from many others like them. In these situations, some candidates are accepted almost arbitrarily. It is too risky a way to choose the colleges where you will apply. An acceptance pattern is one that includes at least one college you know will accept you.

Why do many, many students cluster their applications? Family pressure, peer pressure, and preconceived ideas about where they should go to college. A willingness to pioneer a bit, to go outside the circle of institutions you feel you belong in will not only create an acceptance pattern in your applications; it will broaden you. You will be a freer person for breaking the bonds of custom.

Do consider Cornell or Bryn Mawr or Stanford and others you may think might admit you, but consider, too, such wonderful places as Johns Hopkins, the University of Rochester, Colorado College, and Villanova.

In doing this you will be going against the grain of common applicant practice, and you are positioning yourself for enhanced acceptance chances. You will also be doing what many of the private-school college advisors urge their students to do. The college counselors at Choate–Rosemary Hall, for instance, make a point of getting to know a wide range of colleges around the country, so that they can counsel their students how to develop an acceptance pattern in their applications.

DISCOVERING COLLEGES

The Dartmouth director of admissions suggests that all selective college applicants should "use both chemistry and intellect to make the right choice of colleges" in considering where to apply. There is, he observes, a "match factor" to take into account when the student decides that a college may be the right place for him or her. This is a sensible approach to take in the face of the kind of competition applicants to Dartmouth and other Exceedingly Demanding colleges face: 2,090 were accepted from among 8,600 applicants for the class of 1997. "Be broad-ranging in choosing your list of colleges," he urges.

We realize that no selective college applicant begins the admissions process without some preconceptions about colleges. From your parents, teachers,

DUKE UNIVERSITY

Profile • Class of 1997

ACCEPTANCE/ENROLLMENT SUMMARY

	TOTALS			ARTS & SCIENCES			ENGINEERING		
	Early Decision	Regular Decision	Grand Total	Early Decision	Regular Decision	Total	Early Decision	Regular Decision	Total
Applications	1,051	12,738	13,789	908	10,726	11,634	143	2,012	2,155
Accepted	536	3,357	3,893	460	2,669	3,129	76	688	764
Enrolled	521	1,062	1,583	448	869	1,317	73	193	266

ACADEMIC PROFILE OF MATRICULANTS

All figures represent percentage of the first-year class.

		ARTS & SCIENCES		ENGINEERING	
High School	Top 5%	76%		83%	
Class Rank	Second 5%	14%		9%	
	Next 10%	7%		5%	
	Below 20%	3%		3%	
	Not Ranked	37%		30%	
		Verbal	Math	Verbal	Math
SAT Scores	750–800	2%	19%	2%	44%
	700–749	13%	27%	9%	39%
	650–699	25%	25%	23%	12%
	600–649	24%	16%	39%	3%
	550–599	17%	8%	16%	less than 1%
	500–549	12%	3%	6%	less than 1%
	Below 500	7%	2%	5%	0
ACT	35–36	2%		4%	
Composite	33–34	13%		21%	
Scores	31–32	23%		37%	
	29–30	30%		27%	
	27–28	15%		8%	
	25–26	9%		2%	
	Below 25	8%		1%	

INDEPENDENT SCHOOL VARIETY

It is years since private schools channeled their graduates to a handful of Ivy colleges. A recent graduating class of 322 at Choate–Rosemary Hall sent 34 on to state universities. The largest single group choosing one college was 19 — they went to Brown. Thirteen elected to go to Boston University. Nine elected to go to Yale, 7 to Northwestern, and 5 to Harvard. The vast majority of this class went to selective colleges, but it would be difficult to establish a pattern that would allow you to say that this school prepares its students for any particular place.

One reason why private-school graduates now attend such a variety of colleges is that these schools counsel their students to explore widely for admissions opportunities. Thus a Choate–Rosemary Hall student who went to Duke was admitted also to Pomona, the University of Colorado, and the University of Michigan. A student now at Harvard was also admitted to Georgetown, Lafayette, the University of Michigan, the University of Rochester, and Wellesley.

It is striking to observe that Choate–Rosemary Hall, one of the most prestigious private schools, sent this class off to no fewer than 105 different institutions. Other private schools show a similar pattern. Concord Academy sent 5 of its 1992 class to Brown, 5 to Cornell, 5 to Oberlin. It also sent 2 to the Art Institute of Chicago, 3 to the University of St. Andrews, Scotland, and 2 to Evergreen State. Exeter sent 28 to Northwestern, 19 to Princeton, 21 to Johns Hopkins, 1 to Gordon College, and 2 to Grinnell, among dozens of other colleges. Acceptances of private school students is, of course, much higher than the number actually enrolling. As many as 70 Deerfield students are accepted by one selective college, but only 26 enroll there. In 1992 more than 135 representatives of different colleges visited Deerfield to interview candidates.

peers, and from older students you have heard about colleges. Some colleges may be only names to you in the sports world; others may be part of your community. In school you have probably browsed in the career center looking at college brochures in a random way, playing with the software that helps identify colleges according to size, location, academic programs, and the like. You may already have your heart set on one or two places.

Now you are going to struggle with "the match factor," putting together a set of tangible reasons for considering any college and your gut feeling about the place — the chemistry that works to attract you to it. The procedure that may take weeks of investigation, off and on, should produce a personal list of up to fifteen colleges of varying attractiveness, a list you will reduce when the time comes to visit campuses.

HOW TO READ A COLLEGE CATALOGUE

College catalogues have a deadly quality. The prose is antiseptic and impersonal. But it is this way for a reason. A catalogue is a contract. The student can hold the college to what the catalogue says. So a catalogue should be read for what it is, a description. Most of the contents can be taken at face value. Since no one reads everything in a catalogue, it is important to read selectively.

If you list items in a column and then put the names of colleges at the top of the page, by checking the list you can quickly compare colleges to see what they have or lack according to your own needs. College A has strong government courses but is weak in science. College B has no crew. College C seems to emphasize drama and music activities. College D will not let you live off campus until your junior year.

Every catalogue puts the college's best foot forward and avoids negative comments, so the catalogues make every college sound good. The question is: Is it good for you?

Here are a few suggestions on how to proceed.

Begin with the academic qualities. You are going to college first of all for academic training, not for the social life, athletics, glee club, or mountain air. Unless you find the right academic atmosphere, the rest will be superficial and meaningless to you.

What are the degree requirements? Is there a thesis? How about interdisciplinary majors? Are there pass/fail options? The bulk of a college catalogue is taken up with course descriptions. Look for what is not offered to see if you might be short-changed. If you are interested in becoming a geologist and there are only a few courses in this field, then this college, which may be otherwise excellent, is not for you.

Special programs of study offer clues to a college's strong points. Are you interested in creative writing? The catalogue will tell you just how much academic training you can expect.

The catalogue should give an indication of the percentage of the faculty holding doctoral degrees and what the ratio of faculty to students is. Top colleges have few faculty members who lack Ph.D. degrees, and the faculty-to-student ratio is one teacher for every ten students or less. The catalogue will not tell you how many teaching assistants (graduate students) you will be taught by. Nor does it always say what percentage of the college's graduates go to graduate school, or what distinction the alumni have achieved.

Description of facilities should be scrutinized. Is there a swimming pool, hockey rink, tennis courts, a student center? How many books does the library have? Small colleges have 150,000 volumes, while universities have one to three million. Is there a science center, a theater? Whatever a college does not list, it does not have. A catalogue is an inventory of assets.

The catalogue describes living arrangements and costs. Must you take meals in common? Can you live off campus? Are dormitories large or small? High-rise or low? If there are fraternities there will be extra costs.

The makeup of the student body will tell you whether you will feel comfortable there. The number of out-of-state students may be low.

The size of the endowment may be listed. Some small colleges have higher per-student endowments than the larger ones. Obviously, they have more to offer than a college where the endowment per student is low. At Amherst the endowment per student is $184,700, and at Williams it is approximately $170,000. We should note, however, that some colleges with low endowments receive large donations for current operations.

The athletic programs listed will tell you whether you can engage in your particular sport. Not every college has rowing, sailing, fencing, hiking, and so on. In a city college, where do you work out? Is the pool open daily, and at what time?

A catalogue is no substitute for a visit to the campus, but rather an aid to the visit. Read it before and during the visit. It will stimulate questions as well as provide answers.

In addition to catalogues, colleges put out an enormous number of brochures. Some are simply promotional and must be read with caution, while others are highly informative. They are not contractual in nature like the catalogue and may be issued by a department without central-administration control. Since many private colleges are losing enrollment, reliance on sales promotion is increasing. The intelligent student will do well to "look under the hood."

If students do their research ahead of time, they will not be surprised when they get their decisions. Read the literature and ask very specific questions. Take advantage of receptions, school visits, interviews, and all contact with students and alumni.

Admissions officer,
POMONA COLLEGE

SOURCES OF INFORMATION

Without visiting a campus you can develop considerable information about a college from two general sources: people in your community and the public library or your school college and career resource center. People in your community may be your parents and relatives, family friends, counselors, teachers and coaches, college undergraduates, and alumni of the colleges.

With your list of fifteen colleges, let's say, you immediately eliminate the sense of being overwhelmed by the entire directory of 2,700 four-year colleges and universities in the country. It will be helpful to draw up a list of characteristics such as size of enrollment, cost, special facilities, academic programs, extracurricular activities, positive and negative qualities as you see them. You will soon develop a chart that is easily consulted and this will allow you to make tentative judgments — *Not for me, Possible, I will apply*.

We want your list to be far-ranging, to include places you had never thought of before, places that don't fit your original predilections. You say you want a small college. Look at some larger places. They will probably confirm your conviction, making it more convincing. Or you may decide that a bigger college offers courses not found in a smaller college; Harvard/Radcliffe offers three thousand, to take the extreme case.

Using your notebook, you can gather such information under the headings of a number of colleges, being careful to put down the source, in this way:

Columbia University

"Greatly improved undergraduate experience since the rebellions of the 1960s." *Peter Flatley, Columbia '79.*

"New York is a great place to study international relations. I used the UN like a lab." *Katherine Miller, Columbia '88.*

Smallest Ivy League college — 3,000 enrollment. *Viewbook.*

Judo-karate facilities. *Catalogue.*

"Columbia's faculty of stars actually spends much time with undergraduates. I loved it!" *Stanley Chow, Columbia '93.*

"At Columbia New York is the campus. What a cosmopolitan experience!" *Helena Ryan, Columbia '90.*

Photocopies of vital information pasted into your notebook become permanent fact sheets for quick reference when you visit colleges.

ATTEND A COLLEGE FAIR

Your counselor will probably make arrangements for seniors to attend a college fair in your area. These are usually held during the fall in a number of regions in each state. Thousands of students, counselors, and parents may show up at one fair, to mingle with admissions officers and other college officials at booths and tables.

You have no obligation to attend a college fair, and it will have no impact on your chance of getting into a selective college. Still, we think it will reveal to you the intensity of the competition among institutions for applicants, and the breadth of opportunity for specialized training.

Some fairs are held on college campuses, others at high schools, or in civic auditoriums. You will probably come home with more brochures than you will ever read.

It is useful to look at the available general literature such as *Barron's Profiles of American Colleges, Lovejoy's College Guide, Selective Guide to College* by Edward B. Fiske, *Peterson's Annual Guide to Undergraduate Study,* the *College Admissions Handbook,* the *College Board Index of Majors.* Most schools have software programs to consult. Among the best of these are *Peterson's College Selection Service* and *College Explorer,* put out by the College Entrance Examination Board.

THE ATTRIBUTES OF THE COLLEGES

Expanding the information about each college on your list, you should include in your notebook any special programs or facilities the college singles out in its literature. Columbia's viewbook discusses the Lamont-Doherty Geological Observatory, a research facility on the Hudson River that has "strong ties with the University's instructional program and with the Department of Geological Sciences." Here is a tip for an applicant with an interest in geology, oceanography, seismography, marine pollution, and related subjects. On a campus visit, an applicant who expressed a desire to know more about the observatory would be sent by the admissions officer to a campus representative. This event could lead to a faculty recommendation for admission.

What does the college say about itself? The Colby catalogue says: "Students are strongly encouraged to consider graduate study following Colby." Here is another tip: applicants who have already decided on careers in medicine, dentistry, law, business, education, engineering, the arts, or the ministry should make a note to tell the admissions committee of their plans when they visit the Colby campus. Obviously their applications will be viewed with considerable favor.

What is your special interest? English literature? You will see that Lafayette boasts of being the first American college to teach this subject. Expression of a genuine interest in Shakespeare or in any English author will elicit a warm response during a campus visit.

Needless to add, your interest in what a college has to offer must be genuine.

COMMUNITY SERVICE OPPORTUNITIES

Brown University has forty public service organizations on campus and prides itself on being a good neighbor to Providence. This should be of interest to students committed to community service projects.

At Trinity College in Hartford, one half of the students do internships and one quarter do community service or outreach programs.

Your attention must be drawn by some attribute that answers your personal need. Just to strike up a conversation on some new laboratory you have read about is not going to help you. Colleges have long experience in assessing the sincerity of applicants' statements.

It may take considerable investigation to find a college that has a facility, a discipline, a program, or an activity ideally suited to your needs. We have listed on pages 229–230 a few facilities and programs to suggest the possibilities a little digging will bring to your attention.

KNOW THE TRENDS

Do you realize that the percentage of freshmen planning to major in computer science has dropped in the past decade? One response might be "If that's the trend, count me out of computer science." For a selective college applicant interested in computer science the response *should* be "I will find out what selective colleges have lost computer science majors. I ought to have a good chance of getting into one of them as a computer science student."

There is also new interest in selective colleges in training elementary and high school teachers. Prospective teachers should keep this fact in mind as they build their lists and make plans for college visits.

MED SCHOOL WILL BE A STRETCH IN THE NINETIES

After college comes grad school, right? But not every grad school will be after you when you graduate, especially not medical schools. Applications to medical schools shot up 14.4 percent for 1993–94, according to the Association of American Medical Colleges. There were 42,808 applicants to the country's 126 medical colleges in this period, the highest number in history, surpassing the 1974–75 peak by 187.

Of these students, 17,362 were accepted. This competition means that those applicants with the strongest academic records will have the best chance of admittance. Many doctors began focusing on science in high school. Top grades in biology and chemistry are a must for med students.

Despite the tremendous cost of a medical education — $75,000 at a private medical college, four years after you get your bachelor's degree — there are many more who want to go than will go.

But if you're a competitor and like to be of service to humanity, go for it!

PUBLIC COLLEGE OPTIONS

Generally speaking, only a small number of universities or their satellite institutions can be called Exceedingly Demanding. Yet they present a problem to the mediocre student, who may be shut out of a place because it is reserved either for a higher-paying out-of-state applicant or a high-performing in-state candidate. A small state like Vermont enrolls half its students from out-of-state because these students pay $8,600 tuition, as opposed to $6,150 for Vermont residents.

We have mentioned elsewhere that at the University of Washington the enrollment pattern has changed from 91 percent state residents to only 75 percent because of the increase in resident applications. The University of Colorado (like Vermont, attractive for its quality of life, diverse curriculum, and proximity to ski slopes) is keeping resident enrollment to 50 percent for the sake of the increased revenue out-of-staters bring.

But consider the University of Connecticut, where applications from out-of-state students dropped slightly in 1993, presumably because of the recession and the 12 percent rise in out-of-state tuition. Neighboring New York, however, saw a 10 percent rise in all applications that year.

Can a trend be discerned nationally? Well, most state systems report more applications, probably because their tuitions are anywhere from half to one quarter as much as those of the private colleges. What this means to applicants is that some state systems are no longer the fallback safeties they used to be for mediocre students. High schools should take heart that this situation can spur students to better academic work.

Even rejection by a state university may be offset by attendance at a community college and a transfer into the state university system, providing the student has met the minimum standards for admission.

The presidents of several Ivy League colleges have stated that the major competition today and in the future are the first-rate state universities, particularly those listed in Table 1 (p. 8).

COMPARING COLLEGES
AND PARING THE LIST

You will not visit twelve or fifteen colleges, so you are going to make some fundamental decisions about attractive institutions that you must disregard. A small Midwest college like Oberlin looks awfully attractive to a New Yorker interested in majoring in art and performing in the college orchestra, but Hamilton is so much nearer home that Oberlin has to be stricken from the list of considerations.

Columbia could be a terribly exciting place, but New York seems too overwhelming for a girl from Portland, Maine, and she strikes it out, while leaving Boston College on her list.

You can compare colleges in a number of ways, such as:

- relative competitive admissions chances
- academic offerings
- facilities
- location
- size
- social environment
- access to faculty
- faculty/student ratio
- cost
- tradition

You may ask what the presence of graduate students adds to an undergraduate experience. Climate can be a factor in deciding to exclude a place that may be too hot or too cold for you. You may include a college just because of some unique quality — Dartmouth's Outing Club appeals to those who like to hike, climb, and camp. Or you may exclude any college with fraternities or sororities. The prospect of working in the community after graduation attracts some students to an institution like the University of Vermont, located in a high-tech area. The emphasis on spirituality and social service may put a college like Davidson high on your list.

THINKING OF GRADUATE SCHOOL

The bachelor's degree, B.A. or B.S. has become so commonplace (in 1994 more than a million graduates have them) that by itself it no longer guarantees entry to a career. Not only engineers, doctors, lawyers, and educators must do graduate work to enter their professions: virtually all future professional specialists will need advanced training. Planning their undergraduate training with this prospect in mind is critical. Now more and more undergraduates are considering postgraduate training in view of the difficulties of getting a decent job after graduating.

It is therefore not too early to be thinking of graduate school when you apply to a selective college. Because of the considerable difference between graduate and undergraduate education, we have written a volume on this subject called *Beyond the Ivy Wall* (Little, Brown, 1989).

In this work you will find the rationale for excellent college work as a qualification for acceptance by a good graduate school, and an examination of the case for attending a selective college as a help but not a guarantee for acceptance by highly selective graduate programs at institutions like Harvard Law School, Cornell Medical School, Tuck School of Business at Dartmouth, and Stanford or Berkeley's engineering divisions.

And do not forget the chemical factor that a former admissions director at Dartmouth mentioned. Include in your list those colleges that "feel right" for you and take note of those that make you uncomfortable. The emotional response is important and you need not apologize for it, whether the "preppy" look of students pictured in a brochure turned you off, or the description of the warm fellowship on campus moved you. You still may want to visit a campus that gets a low rating from you, and the visit may change your mind. Just let the chemistry work and trust your feelings.

What you are doing is learning about your own tastes, your preferences, and your possibilities, and at the same time you are making decisions on your own. You are in the driver's seat. It is not selective colleges deciding about you, but you deciding about them, for a change. And do not think that because the number of applicants to many of these colleges is increasing that they do not need yours. Even the most selective college loves to see its applications increase. So you can take momentary satisfaction in deciding not to consider MIT because by comparison to Cal Tech it's too big for your taste.

Enjoy this search for places you would like to visit and consider seriously how you would like to spend four years at each of them. The ones that appeal to you most are the ones you will visit. That is the next step in the Twelve-Step Plan.

Step Six Checklist

1. Continue your research into a variety of selective colleges by reading published material and by talking with teachers, alumni, and undergraduates you know.

2. Consider selective colleges with a wide variety of characteristics, to develop an "acceptance pattern" among the schools that interest you. Remember the "chemical factor," too, and consider colleges you feel good about.

3. Note facilities or programs of special interest to you at these colleges and follow up on these features later on during your campus visits.

4. Ask teachers and your college advisor about new trends in higher education and find out what opportunities these present at different selective colleges.

5. Draw up a list of about fifteen selective colleges you may visit, taking care not to "cluster" your list.

6. Begin comparing the colleges' attributes and gradually paring the list.

STEP SEVEN

Make the Most of Campus Visits

LOOKING UNDER THE HOOD

*V*isiting college campuses is an old tradition among applicants for admission, but it has become more than a pleasant ritual. Both colleges and secondary schools now look on a campus visit as an opportunity for enlarging a candidate's understanding of what four years of university training can be like. A few hours spent touring the campus and gathering random impressions is mere tire kicking. The potential candidate should look under the hood. For an understanding of the unique character of each college visited, a day ought to be devoted to each of the colleges that deeply interest you. If possible, you ought to spend one night in a dorm.

Philip Smith, Dean of Admissions at Williams, suggests that you subject each college to the 10:30 test. You stay overnight and observe what happens after 10:30 P.M. on a weeknight, when students drift out of the library or begin closing their textbooks in their dorms. Is there obsessive studying until 2 A.M.? Are students playing beer-can hockey or discussing politics? Is there much drinking? How does the atmosphere suit your own tastes, and could you get your work done and survive socially?

Campus visits can have a powerful influence on your motivation. When you are told that your academic performance does not stand out enough to make you a strong candidate, you may determine in your senior year to make an all-out effort to exceed your past performance in class. You may have been so stung by an interviewer's observation that you show insufficient commitment in your extracurricular activities, that thereafter you have concentrated on one or two in a convincing way.

One of the best things a student can do is visit a campus, go to class, eat a meal, and stay overnight.
Dr. Nancy Cable Wells, *Dean of Admissions and Financial Aid,*
DAVIDSON COLLEGE

You have to see places. Not just a one-hour tour; rather, take advantage of overnights and extended visits and see how campus life really is.
Carol Lunkenheimer, *Director of Admissions,*
NORTHWESTERN UNIVERSITY

COLLEGE IMPRESSIONS

One professional group now arranges six days of visits to New England campuses, including most of the region's selective colleges. Amherst, Bates, Williams, and Bowdoin have publicly complimented the College Impressions program of Campus Consultants Inc. of Randolph, Massachusetts. A structured tour for no more than eleven students includes an interview at each admissions office, a night seminar, and recreation. Under the guidance of two high school counselors, the students write a practice application essay, learn about financial aid, and are taught admissions strategies.

Arthur P. Mullaney, who founded College Impressions in 1980, is Director of Guidance in the Randolph public school system. "These visits can make all the difference to an applicant," he says. "Until a student visits a campus, college is just an abstraction. They learn to distinguish among colleges with similar academic programs by comparing the milieus, the life-styles. Some of the students become so committed that when they resume school in the fall, their marks go from Bs to As."

YOUR TURN TO CHOOSE

All through the admissions process you are concerned about being admitted to a good college, which has the power to choose you from among a number of good applicants. Now the situation is reversed. You are the one who chooses to apply to one college and not to another, and it is the college that is concerned about getting your application. Yes, even as the numbers of applicants rise, the most selective colleges want more applicants. The colleges lose to other colleges over half of the applicants they admit, so they are anxious to impress you on your campus visit. They are the sellers; you are the buyer.

Take advantage of this situation to discover as much as you can on your campus visit. Test the claims made in brochures. See for yourself how good the library will be for your particular interest. Will you be able to talk to the great professors, or are they available only to seniors and graduate students? What sports programs will be open to you? Is the social atmosphere congenial to your personality?

All selective colleges are good for most of their students, but not all selective colleges will be good for you. A campus visit will provide the essential basis for your judgment when the time comes to fill out applications — and later when you must decide where to enroll. Take notes on each visit, using the College Visit Summary Sheet. Additional copies appear in the Appendix.

PREPARING FOR CAMPUS VISITS

Experience proves that campus visits are most productive if you will take the trouble to follow a few tested routines.

- Before each visit, quickly review any notes you have made about the college in your notebook, so that you arrive on campus "briefed," as it were, and prepared to enlarge your knowledge or alter preconceptions about the place.
- From your long list of colleges you have considered, pick a reasonable number, eight to ten, that you can feasibly visit.
- Phone ahead several weeks for each admissions office appointment. Letters take too long and often result in inconvenient appointments.
- Visit your first- and second-choice colleges after visiting others. Your eye will be keener, your questions more probing because of your experience.
- Work out a timetable so as to be prompt for appointments. Study road maps, plane schedules; get directions from the college.
- Know where you will stay overnight. If you do not plan to stay in a dormitory, line up your lodging in advance to avoid anxiety en route.
- Dress appropriately. Show that you take the interview seriously. This means, for one thing, no sneakers or track shoes, no T-shirts. You should look clean and well groomed. Boys ought to wear jackets. Neckties are optional. On a hot day, if the interviewer is in shirt-sleeves, a boy can take off his jacket. Girls should avoid flamboyance — no glamorous makeup or attention-getting hairdos. In short, look natural and seek no "special effects" that will distract the interviewer. Admissions officers interview many students, and, like most people, retain first impressions in their minds long after an interview. The impression you should leave is that of a self-confident young person who cares about appearance but does not strive to make a unique statement with a garment, hairdo, makeup, or handbag.

COLLEGE VISIT SUMMARY SHEET

Upon completion of your visit, write in your responses to the issues contained here. Do this for each college visited, and then compare your summaries for each.

Name of College _____ Location _____

Date of Visit _____ Interviewer _____

STUDENT BODY

(Impression of student body in terms of appearance, style, degree of interest and enthusiasm, diversity of their social, religious, ethnic background.)

ACADEMIC FACTORS

(How serious about academics is the school and its students? How good are the facilities for academic pursuits? How varied is the curriculum? How strict or flexible are the requirements?)

CAMPUS FACILITIES AND SOCIAL LIFE

(How complete and modern are the facilities such as dormitories, dining room, student center, cultural center, athletic facilities? How active is the social life? How diverse is it? What are the parietal rules for students? Is it predominantly a commuter or dormitory campus?)

OVERALL IMPRESSIONS

(What you liked least and most; what seemed different or special about it. What type of student do you feel would be happiest here? Are you the type?)

RATING

On a scale of 1 to 5 (with 1 being the top grade) rate the college on the basis of your interest in it.

An extreme example of what not to do would be for a boy to arrive wearing a cape, or a girl decorative hosiery.
- Have a game plan for each campus, listing what you want to see and do, but leave spare time to accept invitations to an athletic event, a student play, a party, or some other activity.
- Try to talk to one or more faculty members, to a coach, to a student editor or radio station manager, to a theater arts director, or someone involved with the activities that interest you.

WHEN YOUR PARENTS
VISIT CAMPUSES WITH YOU

Parents are wonderful allies in the admissions process, but like you they need to understand how admissions decisions are made. Anxiety can spoil a campus visit and prevent you from absorbing the experience. To allay their tension — and your own — discuss your concerns frankly, and be sure to tell your parents how much you appreciate their help and caring. Pass on some of the facts and information from Step Seven, and anticipate some of the concerns your parents will have. For instance, parents should not feel offended because they are not invited to sit in on the interview — the interview is with the candidate. Warn your parents that you may prefer not to discuss the interview immediately after it is over, especially if it has revealed that you probably have a low chance of being admitted at that college.

Explain how spending a night in a dormitory will be useful, so that on some campuses you may accept an invitation to stay in a dorm instead of a motel. Make plans to meet your parents in the morning in such cases.

Incidentally, the way to arrange for a dormitory stay is first to try to contact an undergraduate you know and ask to be put up for the night. If you know no one, the admissions office will be glad to find some undergraduate willing to let you stay overnight.

Following a visit, do not elicit too many opinions from your parents. Tell them your reactions first, so that they will be cautious about dampening your enthusiasm. Let their criticism of the dormitories or the economics lecture come, if it does, after you have had your say. Then weigh their observations, even note them in your College Visit Summary Sheet as something to consider later. This approach will prevent you from taking views contrary to theirs just to assert your independence.

THE COLLEGE PEER GROUP IMPACT ON YOUR
DEVELOPMENT

In deciding where to enroll, you should consider among other characteristics the kind of students you will be thrown together with. According to Professor Alexander W. Astin's study of over two hundred institutions, the impact of the peer group is the most pervasive of 190 environmental characteristics that affect the individual student's development. Professor of Higher Education at UCLA, Astin studied more than 20,000 students and 25,000 faculty members for his 1993 book *What Matters in College,* a sequel to his acclaimed *Four Critical Years.*

The peer group's values will have the strongest influence. If you see telltale signs of a "party school" atmosphere at a college, unless your resistance is strong, you can be drawn into time-wasting, debilitating carousal.

Another surprising finding of the Astin study is that college faculties oriented to research rather than to teaching turn off students, whose cognitive development consequently suffers. This is not to say that if you personally are oriented to research that you will not benefit in a research atmosphere. But the average student will do well to recognize the possible influences the students and the faculty of an institution may exert. Appropriate questions during campus visits can flush out the negative impacts Astin has observed.

THE BEST TIME TO VISIT

The best time for visiting campuses is when they are in session, in spring of your junior year or fall of the senior year, but not on a big football game or house-party weekend, nor when exams are being held. You want to be on campus when there is neither unusual excitement nor intense seclusion, to see what normal everyday college life is like.

More and more students visit campuses during the summer, because this is the only time when they can get an admissions office appointment. We have found, for example, that by September almost all the most selective colleges have no appointment openings in the admissions office until the following spring — for applicants to the next freshman class. If you visit in the summer, you ought to return during the fall to see the campus when students are there.

WHAT TO LOOK FOR ON CAMPUS

Having worked with many students after fruitful campus visits, we find that they usually return with new impressions and different thoughts about places they knew only from written material, pictures, and what people had told them. These changed ideas are most valuable when the student organizes them into a coherent pattern that can be used in later decision making. To return and say "I had no idea Trinity College was such a neat place" is all very well, but it is not particularly helpful when you are asked to compare it with another "neat place." Why is it neat?

The College Visit Summary Sheet in the Appendix should be photocopied in enough copies for all your campus visits, and you should fill it out immediately after the end of the visit. Students who have used this sheet tell us that they take notes during the visit and then consult them when filling out the sheet. (See the box on page 137.)

To gather the kind of information you will need, you should put questions to the admissions staff, students, faculty, coaches, alumni, and employees like campus security personnel. The following questions have been used by applicants who have worked with Howard Greene on admission strategies. There are too many to ask of any one person, such as an admissions officer, and you may not be able to ask all of them at every institution. After a couple of visits, you will develop your own investigative routine.

THE SOCIAL CONCERNS

1. What are the living arrangements in dormitories or fraternity or sorority houses? What options are there for choosing roommates? Is off-campus housing available at reasonable rents?
2. If there are fraternities or sororities, what percentage of the students belong to them and what percentage live in them? Is there freshman rushing? What is the college's official attitude toward them? Is there a stated policy on possible fraternity and sorority discrimination?
3. What are the social opportunities if you choose not to join a fraternity or club? What facilities are available for parties, dances, and intramural athletics?
4. What activities, such as concerts, speakers, informal athletics, and tours does the college sponsor? Do most students remain on campus on weekends or is it a "suitcase" college?
5. What is the makeup of the student body in terms of geographical origin, and what are their academic interests? What are the most popular majors? How many students go on to graduate school?
6. How good is campus security? Is there drug taking?
7. Is there much political activism? Is there pressure to conform, or can you "do your own thing"?
8. What control do students have over campus social and academic life? Do students sit on judicial committees, or help affect policies?
9. How much religious diversity is there? Are the facilities for various religious groups adequate? If the college is church-affiliated, how do students of differing faiths fit in?
10. How are ethnic minorities accommodated? Are there special programs and facilities for minority members who want them?
11. Are jobs available to those not on financial aid? What services are there for job placement in summer or after graduating?
12. What is the ratio of men to women? (Note: when there are many more men than women, some women find the situation uncomfortable socially and academically.) Is there any evidence of sexism? (This is a question women must ask other women on campus.)
13. For sex-segregated colleges: what arrangements are there for dating? What are the social activities?
14. Before leaving any campus, make sure that you have been provided with all relevant statistical data about the college, especially the most recent freshman class profile, with its breakdown of SAT scores, alumni children admitted, minority members in the class, etcetera.

THE ACADEMIC CONCERNS

1. What departments are considered outstanding, average, or weak? (Admissions officers and faculty members can be surprisingly candid about this.) Is there more academic opportunity than is listed in the catalogue (special research projects, field trips, and so on)?
2. Can you create your own interdepartmental major?
3. Do you have to do independent work? Are there off-campus reading periods? What would be your chances of getting into an honors program?
4. What is the student/faculty ratio? (Make sure the figure is based on faculty members available to students and does not include nonteaching research personnel with faculty appointments.)
5. Are classes large or small? How many lecture courses will you take? In courses with large enrollments, are there small sections?
6. Is the faculty available to students after class? (Ask students this one.) Is there diversity in faculty background: that is, do most of the members come from different regions or from one region; have most of them been educated at one kind of university or at many different kinds of universities?
7. Are most course requirements cut-and-dried, with two hour exams, one paper, and a final examination? Or is there individuality in the way different professors grade?
8. Are introductory courses taught by professors or by graduate assistants? Are freshmen taught by top members of the faculty?
9. What recognition is there for advanced courses taken in high school?
10. How good is faculty counseling? Are there remedial or tutorial services?
11. How good is the career counseling and placement office in helping students plan for jobs or graduate schools?

THE FACILITIES

1. What health care arrangements are there?
2. Does the library have most of the research materials you will need in your field?
3. How good is the bookstore?
4. Are there enough parking spaces? Will you need a car?
5. Are laboratories kept up to date? Are art studios available? How good is the theater? Are there music practice facilities?
6. Are athletic facilities taken up mostly by varsity sports, or will you be able to use the gymnasium, pool, or tennis courts on a regular basis?

CAMPUS COMPARISONS

Here are two campuses compared by a student.

Country Campus	Urban Campus

Student Body

Country Campus	Urban Campus
Informally dressed, friendly, kind of suburban, laid back, very athletic, rah-rah, frat parties big deal, few blacks. Weekly paper, good literary magazine. Strong theater.	Much high fashion, rush-rush, involved in politics, downtown stores, rock concerts. Much beer, no drugs. Many minorities, foreign students. Daily paper, top radio station.

Academic Factors

Country Campus	Urban Campus
Small classes, library cubicles for seniors, big computer center, new micro bio lab, few government courses, profs accessible, writing course obligatory.	Exciting lecture on Truman Doctrine — 500 in hall. PC required for accounting. Library jammed. Grad students teach many courses.

Campus Facilities and Social Life

Country Campus	Urban Campus
Dorms have suites, common room, social programs, lectures. Dining hall self-serve, fair food. Social life determined by fraternities. Sororities very quiet, have housemothers! Six squash courts.	Skyscraper dorms, huge cafeterias, beer/wine with fancy meals. Mass protest on S. Africa followed by torchlight parade. No squash courts. Frisbee big.

Overall Impressions

Country Campus	Urban Campus
Very comfortable feeling here. Many students are like me. The two profs I met urged me to apply. Said their pre-med program is tops. Is there enough challenge here?	I felt I was in another world, a very exciting but unsettling place. Not sure some students aren't loafing. More like the real world. Not gentle.

Rating

Country Campus	Urban Campus
2 — Might apply to this college.	4 — Not for me. Too unstructured.

7. What commercial outlets are nearby? Are town-gown relations tense? Are there restaurants and motels nearby for visiting relatives and friends?

THE USES OF COLLEGE GUIDEBOOKS

As you visit campuses you will probably be looking at one or two campus "inside" guidebooks based on the observations of undergraduates or recent graduates. Some are obviously amusing and deliberately vulgar. Others pronounce on institutions summary judgments that are only the opinion of one person, or perhaps a few self-appointed critics. So long as you do not take their pronunciamentos as gospel, such books are harmless and may even stimulate you to look more closely at an institution, to question students and others about assertions such as the impersonality of the professors or the animal house character of fraternity life.

There appear to be sufficient errors and prejudices in some guides to have brought a warning from forty-one members of the Eastern Group of Admissions Directors. In a resolution of February 15, 1985, it was resolved "that the Eastern Group of Admissions Directors discourages current and would-be journalists and authors, as well as publishers, from exploiting the legitimate needs of college-bound students and their parents by writing and publishing inaccurate, misleading and highly subjective information that purports to be correct and authoritative."

We might add that it is always useful to check any opinion about a college with other sources.

THE OPTIONAL INTERVIEW

You will know from catalogues and other sources that some colleges require an interview, but the policy of most colleges is to make the interview optional. You should be aware there is disagreement about the importance of the interview. When a college tells you that the admissions office interview, or an interview with a member of an alumni schools committee working as a volunteer for the college, will not affect your admissions chances one way or the other, can you believe this? We believe you can.

At Dartmouth we were told, "We can't make definitive judgments on the basis of twenty minutes or half an hour with the student." At Wellesley we learned that no student has ever been turned down on the basis of an interview. "A good student can have a bad day. We look at the overall record," an admissions staff member said.

If the interview is crucial, how can it be optional? One explanation is that with so many applicants from all over the country, it is impossible to interview all of them. To which we say, this is precisely why the interview does not weigh heavily in the folder. As an admissions officer, Howard Greene interviewed hundreds of students for Princeton, and he always enjoyed the candidates who challenged him with sharp questions about the college. Never was an interview a deciding factor in accepting or rejecting a candidate. In the admissions process a report on an interview is largely useful to confirm and support other evidence about a candidate.

It should be remembered that admissions decisions are arrived at by a committee. You will recall from Step One that decisions about the weakest and best candidates are arrived at quickly, usually prior to any interview, so the interview can have no bearing on these decisions. The remaining candidates compete for places on the basis of their accomplishments. If an interviewer in a committee makes a case for a candidate who has made a very favorable impression in the interview, others can challenge the interviewer by pointing to candidates they think are stronger — candidates who may never have been interviewed.

We queried eighty selective colleges about factors that determined their admission judgments for the class of 1997, and did not receive one word about the importance of the interview. However, remember what Colgate said: "Don't worry about the interview or trying to second-guess what admissions is looking for. All we look for — beyond the customary qualities of intelligence, curiosity, sense of humor, motivation, sensitivity, and appreciation of others (tolerance) — is what the student *is*."

Your questions should be genuinely probing and should *never* concern information easily obtained in the catalogue, viewbook, or other publications. Nothing irritates an admissions officer more than a candidate who wastes interview time with such questions as How many students do you have? or Do you give credits for AP tests?

In short, we urge that you keep the interview in perspective and use it constructively to ask serious questions that will help you decide (a) whether you would be happy at the college and (b) whether your candidacy will be strong or weak.

THE OBLIGATORY INTERVIEW

Admissions information in college catalogues will tell you whether an interview is required before any decision can be made on an application for admission. And in most cases, Early Decision candidates are encouraged to interview. However, even obligatory interviews are not a major factor in admission decisions. Their main purpose is not to learn more about the candidate, but to help the candidate learn more about the college and about the admissions process. The interviewer may ask why you are applying to the college, but this is to make sure that you have a sound understanding of the nature of the college, and to try to determine if you would enroll if admitted.

All Early Decision candidates should interview because of the conclusiveness of the result when a candidate is admitted. Each college wants to make sure that Early Decision candidates realize that they are making the college their first choice, and that, if admitted, they must not apply elsewhere. The college also would like those for whom an admission decision is deferred until spring to accept in spring if admission is offered. The interview is a selling tool the college uses to assure itself of as many acceptances of top students as possible.

"We want to sell our college to applicants," an admissions staff person at a prestigious women's college confided to us. Because the candidate is in a position to turn down an offer to enroll, selective colleges want to improve their "yield" of acceptances; they want to enroll a higher percentage of candidates whom they admit. Selective colleges also have a public relations problem: when they reject a candidate, they may arouse lasting hostility in the candidate, in the candidate's family, and in the candidate's school. They would like to emulate Abraham Lincoln, who was said to be able to get a smile out of someone whose request he denied.

THE MYTH ABOUT BLOWING THE INTERVIEW

A successful businesswoman graduate of a Pennsylvania liberal arts college told us that she was turned down by Bowdoin because she was so rattled during the interview that she made a poor impression. No college will tell any candidate why he or she was turned down. If a candidate chooses to believe that the interview was the reason, what can we say? By now you should be convinced that admissions decisions ride on no single factor.

In plain English, YOU CANNOT BLOW YOUR ADMISSIONS CHANCES IN AN INTERVIEW. The worst that can happen is that an interview will confirm what the folder already is telling a college: this candidate is not for us. Conversely, a very successful interview will not convert an unlikely candidate into one likely to be accepted.

The person interviewing you wants to know why you are interested in the college, and what you think the college has to offer you in particular. It is never the intention of an interviewer to grill you or intimidate you, though you may feel that this was the case. You cannot blow an interview.

WHAT IF YOU ARE NOT INTERVIEWED?

Since at most colleges interviews are optional unless you are applying for Early Decision, the lack of a note of an interview in your folder will have no bearing on your admission. It would be a pity for you to decide not to apply to a college because you were not interviewed. Information you lack can be obtained by a telephone call to someone in the college.

Almost the total benefits of an interview are the information you gather from it and the impression you take away from the interview about the college.

THE GOLDEN RULES FOR INTERVIEWS

A typical *good* interview was Tim's at Middlebury. He told us he arrived on a cool July day wearing a seersucker jacket, button-down shirt without a tie, chino pants, and loafers. The admissions officer began by asking him about his trip, what his impressions of Vermont were, what other colleges he was visiting, and then asked why he was considering an application to Middlebury.

Tim said, "I've heard about your language program from my French teacher, who got his master's here." The admissions officer immediately pointed out that the summer graduate program is independent of the undergraduate program, and that majoring in French at Middlebury would be no different from such a major at any good small selective college. This candor Tim found refreshing.

The next topic was skiing. As a Rochester boy he skied either in New York State or Canada, was on his school ski team, and hoped he might be good enough to ski for Middlebury. He was told that from his record this looked like a reasonable ambition. The interviewer then asked Tim if he was considering applying for Early Decision. Tim said no. The interviewer said that he should ask his college advisor's opinion, but from what Tim said about his academic record, he looked like a very promising candidate.

Tim came away from Middlebury with a strong feeling about the college, but did not apply for Early Decision there because he preferred Colgate. In his notebook he wrote: "Apply here if Colgate does not accept me ED."

Theodora's interview at Wellesley was not satisfying. She found herself drawn into a discussion of her rural Massachusetts high school and her somewhat uneven grades. It was a mediocre school sending fewer than half the students to college, and so there was no incentive to do well, she explained. Politely the interviewer asked if Theodora was a self-starter. Did she need others to inspire her, or would she in a very competitive environment be able to keep up? Her response was overly defensive, she realized later. She said she was a very competitive person. Her basketball coach, she said, considered her one of the most aggressive players she had ever coached. Was this a compliment? the interviewer asked with a laugh. Theodora slumped in her seat, she recalled, and mumbled something about the coach playing favorites.

The interviewer said nothing for a moment. Then she said kindly that this did not seem to be Theodora's day, and invited her to return when she felt more sure of herself. Back at school when she complained to her college advisor about the "cold" interview, her advisor asked her to put herself in the admissions officer's place and give an impression of Theodora. It took several months to get her to see that her negative attitude was holding her back. Her advisor taught her little interview tricks, like putting one foot in front as she sat, so that she would be thrust forward and prevented from slouching. In time Theodora learned not to overestimate herself (she was not qualified for Wellesley), and subsequent interviews at other colleges were more satisfactory.

Be yourself. Do not try to be what you think the interviewer wants or expects of all applicants. Be natural. The interviewer knows that students are often nervous, and he or she will help to put you at ease. As the interview progresses and you reveal your true self, the interviewer can help you decide if this college is appropriate for you.

Ask questions. Coming prepared with one or two questions is the easiest way to overcome your own nervousness. Here are three examples of questions asked by applicants with different interests:

1. I am interested very much in theater productions. In school I enjoyed designing sets. Can I get involved in drama here without majoring in your Theater Arts Department? I am thinking of majoring in history.
2. In school I took four years of French and three social studies courses. Is it possible to combine a major in French and political science, and realistically spend a semester or a year abroad?
3. I have a mild language disability, which I am proud to say I have not let stand in my way. I have worked hard in all my courses, and have taken several honors courses. The only subject to give me problems is Spanish. Is it possible to have a language requirement waived or fulfilled in some other academic way?

Find out where you stand. Before leaving an interview, you should have an idea of what your admissions chances look like on the basis of information you give the interviewer about yourself. No selective college can promise that you will be admitted, but you will be given a frank answer to your question. Here is the range of answers you can expect:

"You will be a strong candidate. We hope you will apply."

"On the basis of what we know about you, you will face stiff competition. Please apply here, but be sure to apply to some other colleges."

"Frankly, you would not be a strong candidate. You, of course, may apply. Conditions do change. But as of now you probably would not be admitted."

The third answer leaves an opening for the college to react to a sudden surge in your grades, a brilliant achievement in athletics, the arts, or some other field. Unless such change occurs, you would be advised not to apply to this college.

IF YOU CANNOT VISIT SOME CAMPUSES

Usually students are interviewed at the college, by someone in the admissions office. But when this is not possible, students may be interviewed by an alumnus or alumna who is a member of the committee of volunteers helping the admissions office. The Fairfield County Harvard Club in Connecticut interviews more than 150 candidates every year.

Alumni interviews do not put you at any disadvantage, even for obligatory interviews. In fact, an alumnus interview gives you the opportunity to ask the interviewer why he or she is glad to have attended the institution. Looking back, what made it special; would he go there again in its present form? If the interviewer cannot answer a particular question, the information can be obtained for you by a phone call.

You can certainly get into a selective college without visiting the campus. You may find it impossible to visit far-off places, and may have to rely on what you know about them from catalogues, friends, and alumni enthusiasts. A New Jersey girl decided that the University of Michigan was her first choice. After enrolling there, sight unseen, she observed wryly, "It's like Paris. You don't have to see it to know you want to go there."

So while we highly recommend a number of campus visits, we know that there are reasons why you may never get to the campuses of some colleges of great interest to you. If you do enroll somewhere you have never visited, you will have other campus visits as a basis of comparison.

AFTER CAMPUS VISITS

A thank-you letter to the admissions office for having seen you is a nice gesture. It will go in your folder and be a sign of your interest in the college. Such letters should be relatively noncommittal unless you have already made a decision to apply. Your saying to an admissions office that a college is your first choice is taken with a grain of salt. The experience of admissions committees is that there are so many variables between the time you visit and the time you might enroll, that the sincerest statements of intention become meaningless. Your letter, then, is a courtesy, not a persuader. The essays and personal statements that go with applications are powerful persuaders. Save your efforts to make a strong impact for these important creative statements.

Trying to butter up admissions officers is counterproductive. Admissions directors and their staffs are amused by such obvious attempts to win their favor as "I love your tie!" The applicant who appeared for his interview at Columbia in tails got nothing but scorn for his flamboyance. A wordy letter after an interview is worse than no letter. Polishing the apple does not go over in admissions.

USE YOUR SUMMARY SHEET

When all your campus visits are completed, you will have your College Visit Summary Sheet to consult for each college. Some you will file and forget, having decided that you will not apply to colleges that do not suit you. You wondered what a college would be like. It looked beautiful in the literature, but you have found it too remote, or too dedicated to the arts and without enough science emphasis. You are surprised to learn about a college that you had not considered, and now you feel very strongly that it is your first choice. Another college has reacted so favorably to you that you feel almost certain that it will admit you. It may become your second choice. A state college you considered somewhat less selective than you felt worthy of you turned out to be one of the most exciting places you visited. You will apply there.

The rating you give each college will not necessarily correspond to the order of your choices. You may have visited Stanford just to see what it is like, and you may rate it higher than the colleges you will apply to. Or you can be surprised by a phone call from the alumnus of a college you have not visited, asking you to consider his college. A brilliant mathematician had made Rensselaer her first choice after visiting the campus, but when a Princeton alumnus in her New England town asked her to consider applying to Princeton, she made that her first choice and was admitted.

As you go over your College Visit Summary Sheets you will begin to arrive at important decisions about where to apply, so you want to be careful to avoid snap judgments and impulsiveness. Now is the time for discussion with counselors, teachers, friends, and family. Get their reactions to your reactions. You say you want to apply for Early Decision at the Wharton School of Finance at the University of Pennsylvania. Your counselor thinks you will be almost certainly deferred. But the university has not discouraged you. So you decide to apply in the hope that being deferred will result in your being admitted to the University of Pennsylvania in April as a liberal arts rather than a business school candidate. Your counselor will remind you that you should file perhaps three other applications.

KNOWING WHAT'S IMPORTANT TO YOU

They say that every choice is a sacrifice, that there are trade-offs required in decision-making. In winter you long for summer, but then come the mosquitoes. So it is with colleges. You look at Columbia's rich curriculum and you look at the urban campus. You can't have one without the other, and you may not want the excitement New York offers. In visiting campuses it is useful to set up characteristics that clash, and to ask yourself what means more to you.

Here are some dichotomies we use in helping students reach decisions about specific colleges:

Quality of reputation and programs vs. location
Quality of reputation and programs vs. size
Quality of reputation and programs vs. sex segregation
Quality of reputation and programs vs. distance from home
Academic prestige vs. appropriate curricular interests
Academic pressure vs. participating in extracurricular activities and
   sports

Bear these conflicting characteristics in mind as you talk to people on campus; ask how others have resolved them. You may find that a high school football star at an Exceedingly Demanding college has decided to drop his sport because he is not going to be a professional football player but an accountant, so he has chosen to put academics first. You may say, I have a chance to be on the tennis circuit, so I would rather attend a college that allows me time to play lots of tennis.

CONSIDERING A MAJOR SUBJECT

During a campus visit the question of majoring in a subject may come up. Some high school students know already that they will major in chemical engineering or history or fine arts. Most freshmen enter college with no clearly defined academic program in mind. In your discussions with students and faculty members, you should realize that college is an exploratory process for most students.

Liberal arts colleges do not put pressure on freshmen to make up their minds about a field of concentration. Their curriculum is like a pyramid, with the base laid in the freshman year in survey courses in the arts, humanities, sciences, mathematics, and the social sciences. In the sophomore year the choice of electives narrows somewhat as you take courses with possible majors in mind. Then in your junior year you concentrate on one major subject, or on a combination of subjects like French language and French history or biology and chemistry. By the senior year the narrowing of interest requires more concentration in your major field, plus a thesis, project, fieldwork, or some special research.

Jesse enrolled at Lewis and Clark, for instance, with no idea of what his major might be. At his private day school in Seattle he had got an A in an honors biology course, and he had been assigned a biology professor as his advisor. The advisor steered him to several biology courses during his first four terms. Jesse found it impossible to get an A in any of them for all the work he did, while he got A's in economics, geography, and social ethics. By the end of his sophomore year he had decided to major in business administration, and minor in social ethics. His ambition was to work for a corporation with a large program of community service. It was pointed out to him that his biology courses were not wasted and that they might help him if he should work for a drug company or go into agribusiness. Thus the pyramid's base undergirded the subsequent structuring of his college program.

Test this pyramid concept, as you meet faculty members or graduates of a college, to see how their undergraduate programs worked out. You will find much similarity in undergraduate programs, yet each college will have particular academic strengths that may appeal to you. This kind of investigation may have the effect of changing your senior high school course choices to allow you to take a college-level course in economics, for example, instead of studying a language.

REVISITING CAMPUSES

Revisiting the campus of a college you consider your first or second choice may be advisable for a number of reasons. We mentioned the case of the summer visit. You would be wise to see the campus when students are there, and to stay overnight. You may want to return to see faculty members, coaches, and others who have shown willingness to put in a good word about you at the admissions office. Or a particular theater production, athletic event, or special occasion might draw you back.

Such second or third visits should be made only to colleges you believe will probably admit you. It makes no sense to go back to a college you like, but that has given you no encouragement that you will be admitted.

In returning to a campus, do not seek out the admissions staff. If you run into someone from the admissions office, be cordial but do not bring up the subject of your application. Say why you are back on campus. You will be understood. Admissions personnel are under enormous pressure to give every applicant as much attention as his or her folder justifies. You have had your turn and will be considered on your merits. If you are pleasantly surprised by an encouraging word, just let it go at that. Keep your cool. Being on campus shows your intense interest in the college and suggests that, if admitted, you will enroll there and not somewhere else.

CONSIDERING YOUR OPTIONS

Your campus visits will have the effect of sharpening the focus of your selective college admissions process. When the visits are over, you will have a much clearer understanding of which colleges are right for you. The number to which you might apply can be reduced to a reasonable few. Which of these might admit you? Some have more or less assured you that you would be a strong candidate. Others you thought might be a possibility for you now look doubtful, and you wonder whether to apply to them. You begin to draw up a list of your preferred colleges and you discuss them with your counselor. What chance do I have for Vanderbilt, what about Washington and Lee? you ask. At this point you know you are ready to calculate your chances for admission to those colleges where you feel you would love to spend a happy four years. This you will learn to do in Step Eight — Find Your Place in the Class Pie Charts.

Step Seven Checklist

1. Plan your visits to college campuses. Phone for interviews several weeks ahead. Get directions, road maps, plane or train schedules, and line up your lodgings.

2. Prepare for the visit by reviewing the material you've collected in your notebook about each school you will visit. Formulate questions you want to ask.

3. Prepare your parents for the visit, to allay their (and your) anxieties and enlist their support.

4. Try to stay overnight in a dormitory for the "10:30 test."

5. Remember that interviews are useful primarily as opportunities to learn more about a college. They are not important in admissions decisions.

6. Review the Golden Rules for Interviews to make the most of each interview you have.

7. Ask many questions — of students, faculty members, admissions officers, staff members — and note your impressions for the College Visit Summary Sheet.

8. Refer to the questions in this chapter in considering the character of the student body, the nature of academic work you may do, the quality of the facilities. Give each college an overall rating, from 1 down to 5.

9. Revisit campuses (a) if you have visited in summer when no students were there; (b) to talk to faculty, coaches, and others who may have a direct interest in your admission. Do not call at the admissions office a second time.

10. Use your campus visit notes to help you decide where to apply and possibly to inspire you to improve academically and intensify your extracurricular commitments.

Find Your Place in the Class Pie Charts

GRAPHING YOUR POSITION

*I*f you don't have fun with this exercise, we'll be surprised. It's a chance to use the skill in graphing you learned in math classes. You see pie charts all the time in textbooks and in the media to illustrate percentages, revenue sources, ethnic distribution, and so on. Now you can start drawing circles and figuring out what your chances of admission to various colleges look like graphically, in terms of pie slices! By studying characteristics of previous classes at a college, you can quickly see the nature of the competition you face from other applicants.

For example, here's a simple pie chart that shows the regional diversity of alumni children applicants. An applicant from California could reasonably conclude from this that his or her chances are better than those of someone from New Jersey. Read on.

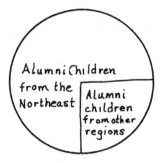

FINDING THE COMPETITIVE EDGE

You know all about admissions requirements and procedures; you know your academic and nonacademic strengths; you have visited most of the colleges of interest to you. But you also know how much competition there is for places in selective colleges, and you want to apply where you have the best chance of acceptance. You hate the idea of applying to a nonselective "safety." So you ask yourself, Where do I have a competitive edge? What are the conditions that narrow the competition?

With your understanding of the diversity that selective colleges seek, you can gauge your chances of acceptance at any college by dividing the freshman class's composition into a number of categories, and matching them against your own personal profile. In Step One, you learned about the admissions factor known as "rounds," in which students classified in general categories are considered together. Now let's take a closer look at these seven categories, and see how they influence your chances for admission at the colleges you're considering.

SEVEN ADMISSIONS CATEGORIES

ALUMNI CONNECTIONS

Each college has its own rules about admitting alumni-related applicants, and the admissions office is the only reliable source of this information. Applicants ought to ask for these rules. Here are the possibilities the college considers in a separate applicant round:

- only the children of alumni
- both children and grandchildren of alumni
- candidates recommended by alumni who have played an active role in helping the college
- applicants related to, but not children of, alumni

No selective college considers separately the children of alumni who have made substantial gifts to the college but have not been actively engaged in some alumni work, such as serving on the board of trustees or on a fund-raising committee or admissions committee. In other words, selective colleges do not raise money by promising wealthy people admission of their children whether or not they would otherwise be admitted.

Most colleges say that alumni-related applicants have about a two-to-one better chance of admission than that of non-alumni-related applicants. Nonetheless, as many as 50 percent of such applicants are turned down because of the competition. You may consider yourself a probable candidate for admission because your father or mother went to Duke, but you can't be sure unless you are admitted by Early Decision or until you get an Early Action report that lists you as a probable candidate.

It will be hard to justify ignoring a selective college where you have such a connection. Such a college is one of your best possibilities for admission. If you are admitted and decide to go elsewhere, nothing is lost except perhaps some momentary domestic harmony. This college should definitely be among those you visit.

Those familiar with modern investment practices will see in what we propose a similarity to diversifying your portfolio. Mutual funds function this way. Invest in a number of different sectors to avoid being hurt by a business downturn in one sector, like high-tech stocks. Apply to a sufficient number of colleges to insure a successful acceptance rate. Alumni connections are simply good insurance.

FACULTY CONNECTIONS

An applicant who has a parent on the faculty or administration of a selective college has two things going for him or her: probable admission to the institution and a partial or free ride as far as college tuition goes. Some colleges pay for faculty children's college education wherever they choose to go. Those in this position need no advice from us. We simply want all applicants to know that this is one small applicant category reserved for the few who qualify. Some applicants with faculty relatives are turned down, because the competition in this category is keen.

MINORITIES

Members of minority groups who apply to selective colleges compete against each other and not against the total applicant pool. More minority members apply than are accepted. This should be understood, lest anyone think that minorities are privileged and accorded a right to admission. Need it be said today that the concept of a minority implies a social disadvantage, which takes many forms, sometimes including an educational handicap? Yet probably a high percentage of minority applicants applying to selective colleges could be admitted without so identifying themselves. The ultimate criterion of minority admissions is the ability to do the academic work of the college.

But why a separate consideration of minorities if those who apply really belong in the selective admissions pool? Because of the accepted concept of the balanced class. In a society where minority tensions exist, higher education has taken a leadership role in making sure that minority students are sufficiently represented on campus and, eventually, in positions of leadership and responsibility after graduation.

Minorities are now defined as including African-Americans, Hispanics, Native Americans, disadvantaged Asians, disadvantaged whites. They do not include most Americans of Japanese, Chinese, Korean, or Southeast Asian extraction. They do not include the physically handicapped.

WHAT ABOUT LEGACIES?

If your father or mother attended a college you are applying to, you are considered a "legacy" that entitles your application to be reviewed in a separate round of selection by the admissions committee. All selective colleges admit a significantly higher *percentage* of alumni sons and daughters than the candidate pool at large. A British observer of the educational and social scene has compared this special status and the American prestigious-university pecking order to England's class system, which is based on bloodlines and inheritance, and finds it to be just as elitist and unfair. For hundreds of years the only opportunity for being admitted to Oxford and Cambridge universities was to attend one of the old-boy private boarding schools like Eton, Harrow, and Rugby that admitted students on the basis of family history and standing.

We beg to disagree that the U.S. system is as elitist. For one thing, American democracy, we all know, is riddled with contradictions. Americans are all equal before the law and entitled to the same opportunities to strive, to excel, to succeed. But some individuals are more equal than others, some have more opportunity to demonstrate their talents, and some inherit specific advantages such as a family history of attending an Ivy college. These richly endowed institutions became such in large part because of the generosity of their grateful alumni over many generations; and the admissions officers are asked by their trustees and presidents to perpetuate this tradition for the benefit of the institution at large and the extraordinarily diverse population of students they can afford to attract and educate today and in the future.

The result of this policy is that applicants with legacy status may well be admitted ahead of other equally qualified candidates, although there is no guarantee that all legacies will be offered a precious place in the incoming class. It is common practice for Ivy League institutions to target 15 to 20 percent of the freshman class for the daughters and sons of their graduates.

Unfair? Perhaps, but unlike the British educational system (which, interestingly, is becoming more like the American one in terms of more types and levels of universities and scholarship opportunities for needy students), the U.S. system has always had a much broader range of excellent institutions a talented student can attend. Rejected by Yale but accepted by Vanderbilt, Davidson, Pomona, or the University of Michigan, he or she will receive an excellent education and go on to a successful and satisfying life. Perhaps the most wonderful element in this legacy tradition is that every year thousands of exceptional young men and women from all walks and stations of life graduate from supposedly elite institutions and thus create legacy status for the children they will raise in future years!

Minority-group applications are considered in a special round because many minority-group students have the disadvantage of weaker schooling and poor testing preparation. If you are an applicant from one of the groups listed above, you may or may not be contacted by an admissions officer who belongs to a minority group. You probably will meet minority-group students when you visit campuses.

You should certainly draw up a list of many colleges and see if there are other categories in which you fit. Are you an athlete; have you a talent? At what college will you most likely have an added edge? Minority-group applicants wind up like other applicants, winning some, losing some, with admissions offers from one or two of four to seven colleges where they apply.

ATHLETES

"Over the years, I have been persuaded that the school athlete is a reliable model for determining leadership capacity for a broad range of roles within society," David T. McLaughlin, former president of Dartmouth, said in a 1984 banquet talk. Selective colleges love good athletes for their talents, perseverance, courage, and popularity. Athletes are usually wonderful role models for nonathletes. But colleges insist that athletes be serious students, prepared to do the work, get a degree, and go on to something else besides athletics on graduation. True, there are Ivy Leaguers playing professional football and basketball, but former college stars are more likely to be businessmen, doctors, lawyers, and journalists than they are to be players, coaches, or recreational directors. They often continue their sports interests by supporting amateur athletics, refereeing, raising funds for athletics: former Princeton basketball players raised enough to endow a coach's "chair," really a bench, to allow a kind of economic security not attached to the number of games he wins. A Yale alumnus endowed the varsity football coach's position for the same reason.

Few selective colleges provide athletic scholarships as such. But most make sure that good athletes who need aid get it in the form of scholarships, loans, and jobs, like others who are not athletes. In general, the selective colleges are not cursed by professionalism. Athletes on campus are not in effect salaried as they really are where athletics are big time and colleges are farm clubs for professional teams. Selective college athletes do not major in "phys ed" and get credit for courses without reading lists. Selective college athletes do not usually leave the campus without a degree.

So why the edge in admissions for varsity athletes? Because selective colleges like to have a good percentage of winning teams. President Pusey of Harvard is said to have told an assistant after Yale beat Harvard 54–0 in 1953: "Don't let this happen again!" To get good scholar-athletes selective colleges must recruit them. This means that in the athletic round, when only the folders of athletes are under consideration, admissions committees are under pressure from coaches to take applicants who might not be admitted without their star quality. A potential All-American in the middle of the class may get a call from a selective college he never even considered.

But athletes applying to selective colleges have to reckon with competition, too. Coaches have no power to admit anyone, and a coach's assurance that "we want you" should not be interpreted as an admission. Coaches lose battles with admissions committees. They can let admissions officers know what they think of an applicant's chances to play varsity, but they can't demand the admission of anyone.

Athletes who decide to go to selective colleges may sacrifice lucrative offers from colleges with big budgets for more than an athlete's college expenses — spending money, a car. Selective college athletes consider a quality education worth giving up these temporary perquisites.

TALENT

Talent is a broad term that goes beyond creativity. You may have a talent for languages that is attractive to selective colleges, which will give you special admissions consideration. Howard Greene, for example, encouraged Marcia, a slightly above-average student, to apply to an Ivy League college because she had studied Russian (she is an American). She was accepted as the only student fluent in the language that year.

Are you talented? Playing in the band, singing in the church choir, having the lead in the senior play: these do not in themselves constitute talent. Such activities can impress those examining your folder, but they will not consider you in a special round of talented applicants. Professional assessment of talent is what impresses admissions offices. When a voice teacher says her pupil should make a career in singing, colleges take notice.

But to what colleges should talented students apply? We encourage talented applicants who stand high academically to include selective colleges among those they are considering. Professional schools have an obvious allure, but they ought to be considered *after* receiving a liberal education. We say "considered." Some talented students may lack the patience to do selective college work and should not attempt it, any more than intelligent professional tennis players whose minds are so riveted on the tennis court and their bank accounts that they soon leave a selective place that recruited them.

Some talents should be developed in a selective college — writing, for example. And one college may be a better place than another for a talented writer. Talking to faculty members is most helpful in sorting out such considerations as how much time is devoted to creative writing, or whether fiction or poetry is emphasized.

For the right talents, selective colleges provide an opportunity to broaden interests that may otherwise be narrowed by an overconcentration on talent development.

INTERNATIONAL STUDENTS

Nationals of other countries are of great interest to selective colleges because of the diversity foreign students add to the selective campus. We distinguish noncitizens from American students living abroad who apply to selective colleges. (International applicants should read our section on their particular situation at page 269.) They are considered as a group usually because one staff member is responsible for the initial evaluation of their credentials, which are quite varied.

The number of enrolled international students in American higher education is approaching 415,000. But usually their numbers on any selective college campus are small. A strong foreign candidate has little competition in the foreign-applicant category.

REGIONAL DIVERSITY

Many selective colleges now admit that geography can influence admissions decisions. Achieving diversity in a class involves reaching out for students from faraway places.

A selective admissions office may not tell you that where you come from is a plus in your folder, but you can tell that it may well be by examining the college's annual published list of students and seeing where they live. If your locality turns up infrequently, you can consider your chances improved, a good reason to apply to colleges outside your region. We have had very good results bringing to selective admissions offices' attention good applicants from schools that have never sent graduates to such colleges. We have done this only for strong candidates, however. Counselors less familiar with the selective admissions process may have to be persuaded. A girl in a rural Tennessee school whose parents were both Brown graduates was told by her counselor that she ought to attend a local state college and forget about any selective college applications. She carried on with applications to several selective colleges and eventually went to Brown. The counselor now keeps an eye out for exceptional students she thinks ought to consider applying to some selective colleges.

GO EAST, YOUNG APPLICANT!

East Coast colleges welcome West Coast applicants. A heavy marketing effort has made California and the Northwest the second- and third-largest regional sources of applicants to eastern colleges, which at one time predominantly received applications from east of the Mississippi. This is a consideration when you are pie-charting.

CHURNING THE APPLICANT POOL

In the interest of diversifying their student bodies, the selective colleges of the East are deliberately cutting back on the numbers they will admit from high-density areas, particularly metropolitan New York. Conversations with admissions officers of Yale, Brown, University of Pennsylvania, Columbia, Duke, and Tufts, for example, reveal their sensitivity to becoming parochial, "too New Yorky," one admissions director said. Another said she was hearing complaints that their student body was getting too "liberal," a code word in the West for easterners. They hasten to add that the limitation will be random and is not aimed at any group: racial, prep school, wealthy, or those needing aid.

"We worry about a critical mass of one type of student," another said.

To take these eastern places, the eastern colleges will be looking for good students from other sections of the country, including rural areas. They want more undergraduates from the South, the Southwest, and the Far West; the Middle West has long been well represented at eastern colleges and will continue to be.

Colleges in the South, Southwest, and Far West, in their turn, are conscious of the regional dominance of their student bodies and are eager to have applications from top eastern students.

This new situation suggests that many strong applicants in the metropolitan East will not be admitted to their preferred eastern colleges. While you can never be sure of an acceptance anywhere, your chances, if you are turned down in the East, are very good at the selective colleges on our list in other regions, with the exception of those in the Exceedingly Demanding category like Duke, Stanford, Cal Tech, and Berkeley. The best application strategy for many eastern applicants will be to include among their colleges one or two in these regions.

In developing a strategy for selective state universities like the University of Virginia, William and Mary, California, Vermont, and North Carolina, you should pay special attention to the issue of quotas on out-of-state enrollment. Most public universities limit the number of places available to "nontaxpayers," thus creating greater competition for admission. Because of the large number of applications to be processed, the admissions committees normally set cutoff scores on the SAT or ACT and class rank. For example, Virginia insists on a 1200 combined score on the SAT verbal and math. If you do not have those and a class standing in the top 20 percent of your high school class, then you need to find a special category to be considered for admission. For some students, identified talent as a future varsity athlete will work; for others, applying to the school of architecture or performing arts, an audition or submission of a portfolio will convince the committee; and for others it may be minority status that enables consideration under the affirmative action program.

Almost no private college or university has set cutoff figures on test scores and class rank and consequently will look at the total dossier of every applicant. For the state institutions, however, you need to find your special category if you are to circumvent the statistical hurdles.

YOUR PIE CHART ANALYSIS

The seven applicant categories can be approximately quantified in percentages that vary from one institution to another. One college may enroll 20 percent alumni relatives in its freshman classes, and another only 15 percent. An eastern college may enroll 75 percent of its freshmen from east of the Mississippi; a southern college may enroll 50 percent of its freshmen from below the Mason-Dixon line.

These percentages provide you with a means for estimating the intensity of your competition for admission at different selective colleges, all of which, as we know, seek a diverse student body.

It's much easier to visualize these percentages with the aid of a device long favored by marketing experts, accountants, and statisticians: the pie chart.

INDEPENDENT SCHOOLS AND COLLEGE ADMISSION

A generation ago the quality of suburban high schools began to put "prep schools" in the shade. These famous old places were deemed too elitist. Gradually the private schools have recovered their allure. They have abandoned the term "private" for the more appropriate term "independent." Through huge financial aid programs they have broadened the composition of their student bodies racially, ethnically, and geographically to such an extent that some independent schools have a more diverse group of students than some public schools.

Applicants from the better independent schools are now perceived by admissions deans as often wonderfully prepared for rigorous college work. In a very real sense the hard-to-get-into schools have done some of the identification and recruitment work for the selective colleges.

An amazing fact: although nonsectarian independent boarding and day schools represent only 1 percent of the U.S. school population, their representation on the most selective campuses, especially in the East, can be between 30 and 40 percent of the student body. While their cost is prohibitive to most families, they do have financial aid programs. And some schools will allow a student to enroll for a year or two. The intensive reading and writing programs often prove to be worth a financial sacrifice.

MAKING A HARVARD PIE

In 1977 a Harvard faculty report on Harvard College admissions found that male applicants were coded by "personality types" as follows:

S — First-rate scholar in Harvard departmental terms

D — Candidate's primary strength is his academic talent, but it doesn't look strong enough to qualify as an S

A — All-American — healthy uncomplicated athletic strengths (though not necessarily a varsity prospect here) and style; perhaps some extra-curricular participation, but not combined with top academic credentials

K — Krunch — main strength is athletic; prospective varsity athlete

P — PBH style — real social concern and action [PBH stands for Phillips Brooks House, a service organization at Harvard]

B — Boondocker — unsophisticated rural background

C — Creative — in music, art, writing and so forth

T — Taconic — from culturally depressed background, usually includes low income

L — Lineage — candidate probably could not be admitted without the extra plus of being a Harvard son, a faculty son, or a local boy with ties to the university community

SOURCE: Robert Klitgaard, *Choosing Elites* (New York: Basic Books, 1985).

THEY DON'T COME HARDER THAN STANFORD

More than 1,300 of the 2,841 applicants admitted to Stanford's Class of 1993 had a perfect 4.0 grade point average! And as many straight-A students were turned down. Almost a third of the applicants scored 1400 or higher on their SATs.

You could have fun pie-charting the following statistics: 37.2% of the admitted students were Californians, 6% were Texans, 5.5% were New Yorkers, 3.4% were from Washington State, 3.4% were from Illinois, and 2.9% were from New Jersey.

Racially, 9.3% were African-American, 24.7% were Asian-American, 9.9% were Mexican-American/Chicano, and 1.3% were Native Americans. All fifty states were represented and foreign applicants included students from Ukraine, Bosnia, Jordan, Ethiopia, Peru, and Thailand.

You can convert data from the freshman class profiles of the colleges that interest you into pie charts representing each of the appropriate admissions categories. Then you can locate your own place in those charts to see how you compare with the competition. You'll be able to see from the size of the "pie slices" where the competition is great and where it is slight.

As an example, let's take the class profile of Wesleyan University, in Middletown, Connecticut. In an interview with the *New York Times* on December 9, 1985, Karl M. Furstenburg, dean of admissions, gave this information on the approximate composition of the class of 1990 as he foresaw the enrollment.

- 75 percent will be from the Northeast (New England, New Jersey, New York, Pennsylvania, Delaware, and Maryland)
- 23 percent will be residents of New York State
- 50 percent each will be men and women
- 33 percent will be admitted on Early Decision
- 5 percent will be alumni sons and daughters
- 63 percent will be in the top 10 percent of their school classes
- 70 percent will be admitted on their academic record

(A call to any college will provide you with similar percentages, if these are not available from the published class profile or other printed material.)

It should be noted that Dean Furstenburg makes no distinction between applicants and enrolled freshmen; the regional composition of the applicant pool is considered more or less identical to admitted freshmen and to those who accept Wesleyan's offer of admission.

On the basis of this information, a "regional diversity" pie chart for the class of 1990 would look like this:

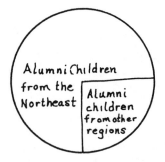

You can see that there are far fewer applicants to compete against if you come from outside the Northeast. In other words, if you fit in the "other regions" pie slice, you compete against only one fourth of the applicant pool. The chart shows, for example, that a student from Chicago stands a three times better chance of being accepted at Wesleyan than a competing candidate whose profile is similar and who lives in Connecticut.

Let's say that you are from Connecticut. A call to Wesleyan informs you that 16 percent of applicants live in your state, and you know from Dean Furstenburg's breakdown that 23 percent live in New York State. We can represent these percentages on the "regional diversity" pie chart this way:

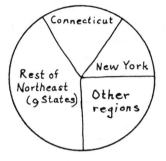

An applicant from Connecticut competes against a much smaller applicant pool, and therefore stands a much better chance of being admitted than does a candidate from New York.

Let's see how you would fare as a Wesleyan applicant whose father is a Wesleyan alumnus. Your pie chart for this situation illustrates your advantage:

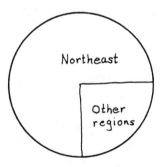

Alumni children compete for admission against one another. Chances for admission are much stronger for such children if they live outside the Northeast, because fewer students apply from other regions.

In discussing the diversity that characterizes the student body of this Exceedingly Demanding college, the former Dean of Admissions said: "Everyone knows there are certain categories of applicants you watch out for. We don't have many kids from Montana applying, so maybe we'll take somebody from Montana. Or maybe we'll take somebody from a blue-collar background who doesn't have all the stuff in terms of high numbers."

Now, if you live in Montana and are interested in applying to Wesleyan, you know at once that you will compete against 25 percent of the applicants, whereas if you live in New Jersey, you will compete against 75 percent of the applicants. Other things being equal, your chances of being admitted from Montana are three times better than those of the New Jersey applicant to Wesleyan.

You can quantify a pie chart by putting numbers into the slices. Wesleyan had about 4,500 applicants for the class of 1990. Of these, 3,375 were from the Northeast and 1,125 were from the rest of the United States and abroad. For Montana you draw a line that makes a mere sliver, thus:

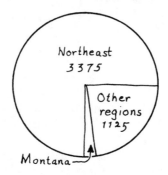

The slice from Montana, among other regions, has no number in it. The probability is that few if any applicants will apply from that state. If you are a good student, your chances of acceptance from Montana are very, very high at Wesleyan.

Wesleyan is not the only selective college that seeks geographic diversity for its well-rounded classes. A former member of the Wellesley admissions staff told us: "The dean would say something like 'We haven't taken anyone from Alabama in five years.' So the staffer responsible for Alabama would scout for candidates. Alumnae in Alabama would be asked for names of any good students they knew."

Clearly, regional diversity or any other such factor works to the advantage only of applicants who fit into the small slices of this kind of class pie chart. You need to examine your standing within a number of such categories, for each college you're considering, to see where your advantages are greatest.

Continue the pie chart analysis until you have exhausted all the categories you can fit yourself into. Are you an athlete, a talent, a pre-med candidate? You can discover what the competition is in each category at each school where you're considering applying.

Your aim is to identify the colleges where you fit into the most slices of the pie. Therefore, when you have finished charting your prospects at one college on your list, turn to the next, and so on until you have a series of pie charts that represent your admission chances.

A further word about pie-charting. It is not an exact science; it is a tool to guide you in estimating probabilities of college admission. There are a few general rules you can follow in determining the approximate size of pie slices. At most colleges alumni relatives represent 15 to 25 percent of freshman classes, athletes represent 20 to 25 percent, minorities represent 5 to 15 percent. Furthermore, without knowing exact percentages, you know that when you apply to a college in a different region from your own, you belong in a regional diversity slice of the pie, for all colleges except state universities get fewer applicants from afar than they would like. In general, when you apply to a state college in another state, it makes little difference where you live; what matters most is how you score on your SAT.

College profiles may give you some clues about the composition of freshman classes, but not all colleges provide full information, such as the percentage of varsity athletes enrolled. Two other sources of use to applicants who know what they would like to major in are the *College Board Handbook* and your college advisor in school. These sources can show you where opportunities lie. For example, if you are interested in studying for a career in diplomacy, you will have a better chance of admission to Johns Hopkins than to Georgetown, because Georgetown attracts so many more foreign-studies majors. Your college advisor is in a position to know from contacts with admissions offices what the colleges are actively seeking in the way of applicants committed to certain majors.

Pie charts are for your own use and can be drawn freehand, as they have been for this step. We can tell you from most recent experience that pie-charting has made the difference for many of the applicants counseled by Howard Greene. Students in despair because they focused on colleges where their chances were poor were convinced by pie charts to broaden their application base. One who had limited himself to Amherst, Williams, and the University of Connecticut wound up with eight acceptances, ranging from Middlebury to Vanderbilt. Wisely, he applied to neither Amherst nor Williams.

TWO EXAMPLES

Here are pie charts copied from those of two students, Audrey and Jim. Audrey, in the upper 15 percent of her regional Illinois high school, was vice president of the senior class and captain of field hockey. Her mother is a Smith graduate. Audrey was particularly interested in applying to Smith, Northwestern, and Colorado College. She drew these three pie charts.

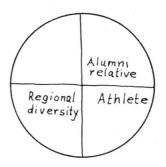

Audrey drew her Smith pie chart first in a schematic way, cutting the pie into four equal slices and finding herself in three of them, as opposed to only two at Colorado College and one at Northwestern.

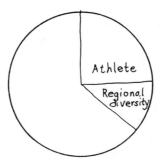

At Colorado College Audrey felt that she would be considered in the athletic round and that coming from Illinois gave her some regional diversity, though not as much as someone from the East or South would have.

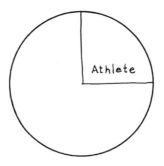

At Northwestern, Audrey felt after looking at this pie chart, her chances were not as good as at Colorado, since she would be offering only her field hockey as a special qualification. Her chances were strongest at Smith.

Jim, a minority-group student in a Newark, New Jersey, high school, was in the upper 10 percent of his class and an all-state hurdler on the varsity track team. He drew pie charts for Princeton, the University of Chicago, and Tufts.

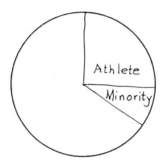

At Princeton, his pie chart showed, he would be considered in both the athletic and the minority rounds.

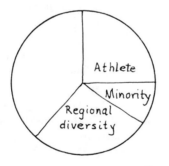

Jim's Tufts pie chart showed that in addition to his status as an athlete and minority candidate, he would be attractive as a candidate from New Jersey.

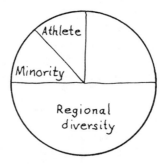

Drawing his pie chart for the University of Chicago, Jim made the regional-diversity slice much larger than for Tufts, since midwestern universities have far fewer eastern applicants than eastern colleges have. He rated his chances best at Chicago and least good at Princeton.

EMPHASIZE YOUR UNIQUENESS

Pie-charting is tailoring admissions to your size. Within each category there are literally thousands of variations, and these can provide opportunities for you to emphasize your own uniqueness. You've been considering your strengths, academic and nonacademic, to identify your distinctive characteristics. Now consider the possible categories where these very features will place you within small slices of the pie.

Every student has a unique profile, and every selective college its unique diversity. Bringing the two together will reveal the institutions most likely to respond favorably to your application.

Kenyon and Vanderbilt have a long literary tradition, so a student who shows promise as a poet will have better chances at these two colleges than at NYU, which has no such tradition.

Do you write poetry? At Kenyon and Vanderbilt, for instance, you'd look like this in the talent pie chart:

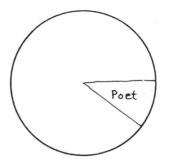

Kenyon has long been a poetry center and encourages applicants of talent to apply. Vanderbilt's poetry tradition dates back to the 1920s. Your chances for admission to either are excellent if you see yourself in the poets' pie slice.

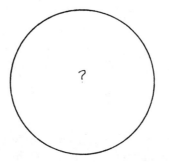

New York University has no particular poetry tradition, so you could not make any slice for your talent in your pie chart of that college.

Are you a rower? The athletes' pie chart at the University of Pennsylvania would place you like this:

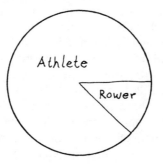

A rower applying to the University of Pennsylvania can always find a particular slice in the athletes' pie chart, whereas at Reed College, which has no crew, a rower would not be considered in the athletic round, and no pie slice can be drawn:

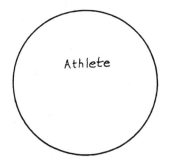

It is of course understood that you apply only to colleges that you sense are right for you. There may be many reasons why you would prefer to enroll in a large urban university despite some academic lack. A graduate of NYU can develop a poetry talent in a Master of Fine Arts program at a number of institutions like the University of Iowa or the University of Massachusetts. Only you can know where your own preferences lie.

Pie-charting opens your eyes to admission possibilities. It is up to you to decide where you really want to go. In studying pie charts you have two general situations: either you fit into a number of categories and therefore have extra competitive chances, or you are unique and are competing against few applicants. For example, an admissions committee, noting that you are both an alumnus's child and an athlete will be more inclined to admit you than another applicant with your profile minus the athletic gift.

On the other hand, a college seeking students for certain programs will look closely at applicants for those programs. While pie-charting is not an exact science, we can tell you from experience that it has proved to be one of the most reassuring tools an applicant can use to sort out admissions chances.

Milton was a kind of whiz kid in his private high school in New Hampshire, so much so that the school allowed him credit in his senior year for building a computer-controlled robot. His math SAT score was 700, his verbal 500, reflecting high grades in math and science and average grades in English. Checking on colleges where computer science is strong — Dartmouth, MIT, and Cornell — he learned that the competition for places at any of them would be too strong for him. He asked us how we might find the best college for his unusual talents.

Working with pie charts, Milton found that he had no extracurricular accomplishments that fitted into those slices, but he did have his robot, which was unique. What he needed was a selective college just beginning a major computer science program and looking for students from good-quality New England high schools. Duke proved to be the perfect answer for Milton, where he is now at work building robots and studying the field of artificial intelligence.

Milton drew four pie charts to visualize his competition. At MIT it was enormous.

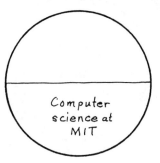

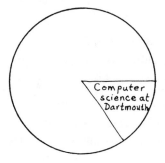

The Dartmouth computer science program is larger than Cornell's.

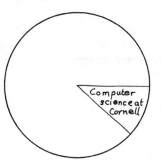

Cornell, Milton could see, attracts more computer science majors than Duke University does.

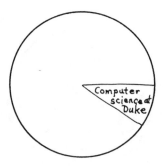

Duke's computer science students are fewer in number than Cornell's. Milton saw that his chances for admission would be greatest at Duke and really minimal at MIT.

Milton's case also illustrates how you can use your pie charts as a basis for exploring college programs where you may have a competitive edge. Arnold did exactly this.

Arnold had it all — SATs in the 700s, Subject Tests likewise. He was a school leader in a large suburban high school on Long Island. He had been an intern with a congressman. A natural for Harvard? Not when twenty others in his class were applying to Harvard. Yale, Princeton, or Brown was a good possibility. But Dartmouth seemed to offer an even better chance, for two reasons: geography and its new Nelson Rockefeller Institute for Political Studies. Dartmouth gets so many applications from Massachusetts and Connecticut that a Long Island application is attractive to admissions. And Arnold's work in the Model UN and in Congress led him to want to study political science. Dartmouth accepted Arnold on Early Decision.

Tamir, a Lebanese whose family lives in New Jersey, is trilingual, with combined SATs of 1300 and Subjects in the 600s. He was number two in a small boarding school. He was obviously an attractive candidate and would have no trouble getting into a selective college. But which one? After visiting several New England colleges, including Yale, he visited Georgetown. There he learned for the first time about Georgetown's School of Foreign Service. His fluency in Arabic and French was unique. He might have used it at other colleges for language studies or Middle East studies, but he was not interested in these subjects. He wanted to work in some department of government. His enthusiastic response to Georgetown's program for future diplomats matched Georgetown's need for students with Tamir's qualifications. His pie charts showed that the competition would probably be too tough at Harvard, that he would have little competition for a place at Tufts, that Yale might want him for his French, and that Georgetown would be eager to admit him. Result: Tamir was turned down by Harvard, accepted by Tufts, wait-listed by Yale, and accepted by Georgetown, where he enrolled.

You may find an academic interest that puts you in a class by yourself. Vivienne knew from early in her high school career that she would like to be a high school teacher. During the summers, she worked with children in day camps that included optional French courses. She did extra reading in history, so that she could combine language teaching with the history of France.

Her mother had gone to Smith, but Vivienne wanted a coed college. The Five College Consortium — Amherst, University of Massachusetts, Smith, Mount Holyoke, and Hampshire College — in Massachusetts attracted her attention. She knew that she probably would be accepted by Smith, but Amherst was the college of her choice. It offered courses in education as well as history and French, and if she went there she could enrich her program with courses in education at the University of Massachusetts. Her advisor pointed out that her record was below that of the average applicant admitted there. Vivienne therefore contacted the education department at Amherst, which was delighted by her interest in teaching. Vivienne was admitted to Amherst.

What unusual academic interest or combination of interests do you have that might look like a special slice on a class pie chart? Here are some that have proved to be strong factors in selective college admissions.

Combined interest in Russian and child psychology
Mathematics and biology research
Architecture and ceramics
Lasers and photography
Penology and journalism
American literature and Civil War history
Astronomy and chemistry
Robotics and engineering
Software and education
Film-making and Native American culture
Polish literature
Marketing and Latin American culture
Food chemistry
Political science and traffic control
Geriatrics
Poetry and environmental management
Playwriting
Population control
Cartooning and art history
Land use and economics
Balkan history

Consider the case of Travis, an intellectual in a Westchester County, New York, high school. He knew by his senior year that he was going to study philosophy and religion as an undergraduate, and then go on for a Ph.D. One of the Exceedingly Demanding colleges would be the logical place to do undergraduate work in philosophy. But Travis did not test well on the SAT, for all his intellectual depth. He made the mistake of lingering long on questions that intrigued him, turning them over in his mind like a good philosopher. This is a fatal test procedure, and it put him in the 1100 category for combined SAT scores, when he probably could have made 1300 with long training in test-taking to break him of his ruminating habits.

After counseling, Travis began looking at selective colleges noted for sending a high percentage of their graduates on for doctorates. He found that both Carleton and Kenyon offered little competition in the way of applicants already committed to a philosophy major and a plan to earn a Ph.D. So the academic pie slices were favorable at both places. Also going for him were the geographic slices. These small midwestern liberal arts colleges are very interested in attracting eastern students to give diversity to a predominantly midwestern constituency. He found another little slice in the reputation of his school for academic excellence.

A third factor for Travis in applying to these colleges was financial; they are less expensive than the Ivies, and they have substantial scholarship programs. Both colleges accepted Travis and offered generous financial aid packages. He chose to go to Carleton.

Will it help your admissions chances if you know as an applicant what you want to major in in college? Yes, but only to the extent to which you realize what the competition is in your field. For example, only the very strongest candidate now has a chance for admission in MIT's electronics program. Rensselaer Polytechnic Institute and Carnegie-Mellon are overwhelmed with applicants wishing to major in chemistry, electronics, and computer science. The competition for pre-medical places is heavy at all the Ivies as well as at Johns Hopkins, Rochester, Emory, Washington University, Franklin and Marshall, Haverford, and others.

Future lawyers believe their best chances for admission to top law schools lies in a degree from an Ivy League college, or from Williams, Amherst, Wesleyan, Tufts, Stanford, Chicago, Duke, and the better state universities. You therefore can expect the toughest competition at such places if the law is your career choice.

So to draw a pie chart relating to specific academic disciplines, you will have to contact the colleges themselves, the admissions office or departmental offices, to get an idea about the competition. You must realize that even admission to a selective college is no guarantee that you can get into upperclass programs such as the Woodrow Wilson School of Public and International Affairs at Princeton or the McIntyre School of Commerce at the University of Virginia.

The fact is that the majority of freshmen arrive without a clear idea of what their major will be, so not knowing what you want to study is the norm and is not a hindrance to admission. The glory of the liberal arts colleges is that they offer you a chance to explore their offerings in order to discover where your interests lie, so we urge you not to try to fit into a piece of the pie by arbitrarily deciding you will opt for a specific academic program. Some years ago applicants would apply and be admitted as engineers because selective colleges with engineering programs were short of students. The result was that some students who had no business being engineers would enroll and after a year transfer out of engineering and into liberal arts. They had found a way of getting into selective colleges that would otherwise have rejected them. It did not take long for the colleges to eliminate such unqualified applicants to their engineering schools.

There are some colleges that will admit you more readily because of your race or religion. Yes, we know that colleges deny no one admission on such grounds, but they can go out of their way to seek a particular group. Dartmouth will give a full-blooded American Indian a full scholarship if he or she can qualify for admission. If you are a Quaker and a good student, you probably know that Swarthmore and Haverford, Quaker institutions, are eager for your application, although neither can assure you automatic admission; among the 250,000 Quakers in the United States, though, your competitors will be few in number. Virtually every selective college gives special consideration to racial minorities.

Review the notes you took on your campus visits to discover how your uniqueness can be fitted into a slice of the freshman pie chart where the competition is not overwhelming. If you need further information, go after it. Phone the college and talk to your contacts. Here are some questions colleges get from applicants:

Would my gymnastics be of value in your cheerleading activity?

I have never rowed, but I am six feet tall and too light for college football. Would the rowing coach be interested in me?

In my father's software company I help answer phone queries. Could I start a software hotline at your college?

If I make up for my foreign language deficiency with a summer in Mexico perfecting my Spanish, would you waive the language requirement?

How could my folk singing fit into your campus activities?

Is there any way I can be a stringer on your campus for a metropolitan paper?

To earn money I plan to start a pizza agency selling pizzas and subs in the dorms at night. Would your college allow this?

How would you feel about my bringing my live snake collection on campus? None is poisonous.

The French call such questions *l'esprit de l'escalier,* things you do not think to mention until you are on your way downstairs after a meeting. Visiting a number of campuses, some students do not think of these questions until they are back home. Colleges understand this and welcome queries, which they try to answer frankly. "No, we have more than enough experienced rowers for our small rowing program. . . . Yes, you could help our cheerleaders with some acrobatics."

DRAWING PIE CHARTS IN YOUR JUNIOR YEAR (OR EARLIER)

Usually applicants need not calculate their chances for admission until they are getting ready to apply to selective colleges. There are cases, however, when a student will benefit by drawing some pie charts late in junior year. Leroy, for example, was under the impression that his grades were good enough for an Ivy League college until he began making a few pie charts after some college visits. What he discovered was that his competition had already taken honors courses. His suburban Washington high school counselor had urged him to take honors courses, but he had to find out for himself what a pickle he was in. How could he catch up? He went to Cornell summer school and took enrichment courses in history and political science. In his senior year he took advanced placement courses in history, English, and economics, plus a fourth-year French honors course. He was captain of his tennis team and was in the Model UN. He was admitted to an Ivy League college. But this would not have happened had he not charted his course, so to speak, in his junior year.

More unusual is the case of Janice, a student in the top 5 percent of her class in a rural high school just beyond the Boston suburbs. Janice decided as a sophomore that she wanted to go to Harvard/Radcliffe. Her father, a successful businessman, wanted her to attend a day school noted for its success in sending graduates on to very selective colleges. But Janice's counselor told her that no one from her high school had applied to Harvard/Radcliffe in years, and he calculated that if she finished near the top of her class, she would have a better chance of being admitted to Harvard/Radcliffe from public school than from private school, where she probably would not have finished as high in her class and would be competing against all the other candidates in the Boston area.

This is the pie chart for Janice's situation vis-à-vis Harvard/Radcliffe:

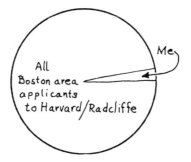

Janice drew her pie chart this way to show how slight her competition was. Had she applied from a private school, she would have been competing against many others with similar profiles. In a rural high school, she was the only Harvard/Radcliffe candidate, and this fact greatly improved her chances.

Janice realized that in a sense she was competing only against herself. True, she had to be a qualified candidate along with all the others in the Boston area, but she would not be pitted directly against a comparable number of applicants. She stood out as a loner, attracting attention because of her high school.

Janice was admitted to Harvard/Radcliffe as well as to Vassar (where her mother had gone) and Tufts. Yale wait-listed her.

PRIVATE SCHOOL PIE-CHARTING

The great boarding schools like Exeter, Groton, and Choate (now Choate–Rosemary Hall) are no longer the automatic high road to the Ivies. How does a girl like Melissa with a B average and 1100 combined SAT scores estimate her chances for admission to Dartmouth, Williams, and Harvard/Radcliffe after four years at such a boarding school? In the academic slices of the pie charts of Exceedingly Demanding colleges the competition was overwhelming. In what slice of the pie charts of their upcoming freshman classes might Melissa encounter fewer opponents for place?

Melissa was a wonderful squash player, captain of her team, and ranked nationally. The three colleges named happened to have very active squash programs. Her pie-charting showed that she was virtually alone in this slice of the pie charts at each college. Would this fact be sufficient to gain admission to one of them? Academically she was below average by their admission standards. But in satisfying the test of diversity, their classes do include such students. With the squash coaches of all the colleges in her corner, she could not miss, was admitted to all three, and accepted Harvard/Radcliffe.

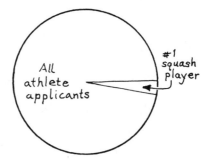

Melissa drew one pie chart for Dartmouth, then realized that the same two charts could be drawn for Williams and Harvard/Radcliffe. There was no applicant like her in any of the three athletic rounds (admission committee sessions devoted only to athletes' applications). The size of the slice is much too large for the circumstance of absolutely no competition at all.

LIST YOUR COMPETITIVE ADVANTAGES

With your pie charts spread out in front of you, you are ready to list the colleges and the pie slice or slices that give you an advantage at each. For instance, you could list them this way:

Colleges	My Slice of the Pie
1.	Computer science
2.	Legacy
3.	Track
4.	Geography
5.	Disk jockey
6.	Math

You may have several slices at some schools, or none at all for one or two. Next, you can qualify the college admissions situations at each as Most Likely, Likely, Possible. "Impossible" situations you simply avoid!

You will get an astonishing psychological lift from such rational strategic planning. You'll find yourself thinking, "I know that I can certainly enroll at College X, and very likely at College Y too. College Z looks chancy, while at College Alpha I really face overwhelming competition!" Instead of worrying, you'll face the future with increasing assurance.

DECIDE WHERE YOU WILL APPLY

You are now ready to narrow your list of colleges to between four and seven where you will apply. Your choices will reflect the range of your possibilities, based on everything you've learned thus far in the Twelve-Step Plan.

Consult with your counselor, and select one school where you have rated your admissions chances "Most Likely." Next, choose a college where you judge your chances to be "Possible," say, fifty-fifty. Between these extremes, you will also choose two or more colleges where your chances are reasonably good — the "Likely" category from your pie-chart ratings. (Be sure that your list is not clustered!)

When your list is completed, you are ready to write to these colleges for application forms.

This kind of rational selection process that you are undertaking parallels what the colleges are doing as they examine folders. The more exacting and honest you are in your calculations, the more satisfying the admissions results. Selective colleges very much appreciate the candidate who has taken the trouble to shape the choice of colleges to match their needs with his or hers. They anticipate a symbiotic relationship with such candidates and try to admit as many "comfortable fits" as they can.

Step Eight Checklist

1. Consider the general categories of diversity, and identify those that apply to you.

2. Create pie charts to represent your standing within each category, for each college you're considering. Use published class profiles, your notes on the colleges, and printed materials as sources of data. Phone the colleges for information not available elsewhere.

3. Review your strengths and unique characteristics, and identify the variations on the general categories where your uniqueness will be emphasized. Explore college programs where your uniqueness gives you a competitive edge. Use unusual academic interests, definite career goals, even race and religion to find your possible niches.

4. List the colleges you're considering and the "slices of pie" that give you an advantage at each. Rate the colleges as "Most Likely," "Likely," and "Possible" places that will admit you.

5. In consultation with your counselor, select between four and seven colleges where you will apply. Make sure your choices span your admissions possibilities at the schools you have considered, from "Most Likely" to "Likely" to "Possible."

6. Send for the application forms from these colleges.

Write an Exciting Essay

APPLICATION TIME

Applications involve writing — answering questions lucidly and imaginatively and, above all, writing an essay, or personal statements, that will inspire an admissions committee to admit you. Later in this step, we will discuss how to fill out an application form to the satisfaction of an admissions office. Because your writing skills are so crucial to your application, you will begin working on your essay, practicing your writing, at least six to eight weeks before you actually file your applications. (For those applying for Early Decision, this means starting your essays and questions in early September, and for the rest, in mid-October.)

A SPARKLING ESSAY

Your essay is your opportunity to influence an admissions committee directly, in your own words. A lively, bright, and absorbing essay, whatever your topic, can set you apart from the crowd of selective college applicants. The following essay is by Adelaide, who was admitted to several very selective colleges, on the basis of the quality of her essay and the personal qualities reflected in it. After you read it you will understand why.

> Standing in my front yard one day this summer, I watched a car creep up and down the road past my house four times before it finally turned into my driveway. Roads in New Canaan are thin and winding, and all the trees look the same, so my parents and I are used to giving directions to travelers who have taken wrong turns. However, this driver was not lost or looking for help, but rather returning at a slow speed deliberately, to a territory whose every bump and twist he knew perfectly. When the man stepped out of his car, he introduced himself to me as the boy who had grown up in the house that I live in now. And though I did not

recognize the stranger standing in front of me, I felt I already knew the boy of whom he spoke.

For seventeen years I have collected old glass marbles and matchbox cars as they have surfaced from an abandoned sandpile in my backyard. I connected quickly that the man in my driveway was the child responsible for their burial, and I told him of my collection. He laughed as he remembered his pile of toys in the sand, and when I asked him why he had left them there when he moved, he answered, "I used to play with them every day, and when I was finished playing at the end of each afternoon I would just leave everything there until the next morning."

His explanation sounded simple. When he was young, he would play with his toys when he wanted to, go inside when he wanted to, and return to his sandpile again the next day. However, the fact that the marbles and matchbox cars are still buried today suggests that there was one morning when the boy woke up and decided not to play. There was one exact moment in time when something changed, when he did not return to his sandpile, and he has not been there since.

The idea that there are singular, unpredictable moments in time that divide one stage of life from another has greatly affected my life. I am conscious that something I am active in today may become part of a past stage without my realizing it, and so I commit myself to each project with the belief that I will never do that particular activity in just the same way again.

For example, if I want to publish a short story today, I am not going to worry that I would have a better vocabulary to write it with in ten years. And when I volunteer to teach illiterate adults, I do not question whether I would be more effective after a few more years of my own education. For today I can pursue both of these activities with the capabilities of a seventeen-year-old, and although the story I write and the class I assist may not be as successful as they would be if I tried them again in ten years, they will invariably be a reflection of my best effort at this point in my life. For as long as I believe that my life comes in stages whose beginnings and endings are invisible, *this* moment is always the right time to write and to work, and I am never too young to try anything.

Wouldn't you like to meet the person who wrote that essay? If you were a teacher, wouldn't you think: this student has the potential to learn and grow? That is all an essay need do: make an admissions committee believe in you as someone their college can benefit.

"When in doubt about an applicant," Watson Corliss, former Director of Admissions for Middlebury College, told us, "the admissions committee always takes a second look at the personal statement and the essay. It can tell things that no teacher or counselor can express so convincingly about the character and inner light that shines in a person."

Adelaide switched on her inner light to reveal her character, and she did it artfully and without false modesty, but not without practicing her essay writing, and then rewriting her essay before submitting it. Rarely can even the best students dash off a convincing essay that conveys something about their character, let alone lets any inner light shine in them. Good students polish their writing.

Whether you are applying to the most competitive selective college or not, you must practice, practice, practice writing short essays to show to teachers, counselors, your parents for their comments. Their remarks may make you wince — *boring, pretentious, unconvincing, bragging, vague,* and *confused* are some of the adjectives that can be scribbled on your manuscript. Like Adelaide, though, you are capable of swallowing your pride and learning to write a good essay just as you have learned to handle quadratic equations or translate Balzac, Silone, or Cervantes.

COLLEGE STUDENTS NEED WRITING HELP, TOO

Freshmen in selective colleges are often brought up short when informed that their writing leaves something to be desired and that they must therefore take a freshman writing course. Wasn't the essay with my application terrific? the freshman may wonder. Perhaps it was, as far as it went, but now that papers have to be written for college, some intensive writing practice may be needed to bring the college student's prose to a more sophisticated level.

Harvard has an extensive faculty in its Expository Writing Program. Brown, Swarthmore, and the University of Pennsylvania offer courses in writing improvement, as do many other selective colleges. At Georgetown there is peer-teaching by students with well-developed writing skills.

One of the chief disciplines instilled is rewriting, which is not a punishment but professional necessity. Elaborate and pretentious phrasing is discouraged. Poetic prose is not acceptable.

As you work on your writing, do not be discouraged by the difficulty of getting your prose right. Many of the brightest freshmen have to do "remedial" writing.

YOU ARE THE TOPIC

The word *essay* suggests a paper written for a course, a formal piece of prose on a subject you have researched. This is not what admissions committees ask you to write. They are giving you the opportunity you should eagerly welcome, the opportunity to write about yourself, for two to three double-spaced typed pages. If you write in legible longhand, the word count should not exceed five hundred. Here is how Isabella began her essay:

"I am purely and simply the shortest person I know!" She is laughing at what she considers a handicap, her height. Continuing in this light vein, she manages in one punch line to let the reader know she is a very serious person. "I will be the first child therapist who can see eye-to-eye with her patients." Isabella will be a child therapist with a wonderful sense of humor. Her essay helped get her into Harvard/Radcliffe.

Oliver, an applicant admitted to Princeton, opened his essay with this dramatic paragraph:

> A middle-aged man out jogging suddenly stops, grabs his chest, then falls to the ground — unconscious. A crowd of onlookers gathers, yet no one knows what to do. Four to six minutes later the man is dead of the leading cause of death in the U.S. — heart attack. The tragedy is that this man could have been saved. As a Red Cross instructor I have been deeply involved in teaching people how to react to this and other emergency situations.

Your essay need not be clever or dramatic. It can be matter-of-fact, like this first sentence, which sets the tone for Karen's entire essay:

> My tour of the Soviet Union this past December has sharpened my interest in a culture that I have had a growing curiosity about for several years, and fostered a desire for greater understanding of what I saw and experienced.

This serious statement suggests strong convictions, and a desire to do something about them: in this case study Soviet culture and Russian language at Yale, which accepted Karen.

BE SINCERE, BE CLEAR, BE SPIRITED, BE PERSONAL

Be sincere, be clear, be spirited, be personal in your writing. These are the qualities we ask students to put into their essays written for practice and for submission to colleges. Paste this exhortation on your typewriter or your desk, and test your prose against it. We offer the following guidelines.

KNOW YOURSELF

We come back to a necessity we stressed in Step Two — Determine Your Strengths. In filling out the Student Questionnaire, you learned things about yourself by responding to questions concerning your college interests. Now the field of interest broadens to encompass anything about yourself that you would like an admissions committee to know. The sky is the limit. You are not confined to a consideration of yourself as a student, as a candidate for a selective college. You are free to consider everything from a love of animals to a dislike of junk mail. How you look, what you wear, what your voice sounds like, where you live, how tidy or untidy you are, what magazines you read, where you have traveled, who your friends are, why you jog, what your family means to you, who your favorite teacher is and why — you could spill your personal inventory into a tape recorder and possibly find an essay topic very quickly.

Example by Isabella, who is now at Harvard/Radcliffe:

I am purely and simply the shortest person I know! So much of my life has been colored by this fact that in matters of direct personal importance it ranks very close to the top of my list. When I was three years old the pediatrician thought perhaps I was a dwarf — but no such luck. (Dwarfism, I figured, would definitely qualify me for minority-group status and make me a shoo-in at Harvard.) Today I can reach the 4'11½" mark, thanks to years and years of ballet lessons, where I learned to stretch my neck and hyperextend my legs through the hip sockets. But that's it — unless I am "en pointe" — and walking around in toe shoes all day is positively hazardous to one's health (not to mention one's toes).

And so I've learned to cope with, take advantage of, and compensate for my shortcoming (pun intended). I grin and bear it when the middle-aged crowd coos and gurgles and says, "How cute — how old is this little one?" I also know to answer with a single-digit number lest they go into cardiac arrest on learning I'm practically old enough to vote. I try to have my social life revolve around activities other than large parties and dances because other people's belt buckles do not make interesting conversation. I have talked my mother out of sending me on errands to butcher shops, bakeries, and delicatessens, because no way can I reach the little machine that gives out the numbers that allot you your turn.

The advantages: I consider myself an honest and law-abiding citizen, but when the chips are down and allowance runs short and baby-sitting prospects are dim, I am not above letting ticket-takers at museums, theaters, and ski-lifts assume that I am in the "12-and-under" category. I have more clothes than anyone else I know; I get "hand-me-ups" from my younger sisters as well as "hand-me-downs" from the older one. Traveling is easy because one can pack many more small-size clothes in a suitcase than average ones.

Finally, the compensating. I've wanted to be an actress ever since I played a Munchkin in my fourth-grade production of *The Wizard of Oz*. But my dreams were dashed when I subsequently read an article in the *New York Times* which quoted a famous director as saying that being a commanding stage presence has a great deal to do with having a large and imposing physique. So I substituted a career in psychology. Aside from a very real interest in the subject, I figure I will be the first child therapist who can see eye-to-eye, literally as well as figuratively, with her patients.

Other compensations: my very loud voice, my larger-than-life enthusiasms, and my determination to be the smartest and the best — because I'm never going to be the biggest!

Lewis Carroll's Alice (of Wonderland fame), when drinking her potion and shrinking to subnormal size, said, "Why, there's hardly enough of me to make *one* respectable person!" Nonsense, Alice, take it from one who's lived it that size has nothing to do with respectability — or brains or talent or determination. And besides, there are ways to add inches emotionally and mentally, if not physically. I know that becoming one of the 10,000 of Harvard (and the only Munchkin), for example, would do that for me.

But do not stop at the first inspiration. Keep thinking about who you are, warmly, appreciatively; focus on what you would like to be or on what you desire in life; recall what you have done up to now, and try to interpret your accomplishments. Admissions committees have your folder full of records of your academic and nonacademic performance. You must help to put flesh and bones on grades and awards, on lists of activities. Think of the thousands of high school students whose records resemble yours. Colleges want to know what distinguishes one good applicant from another. The essay is one of the places where they look for those qualities that set you apart from the crowd.

Ask yourself: how do I differ from my friends? What are my strengths? What weaknesses or handicaps have I overcome? Who is my most interesting relative, and why? Who has had an important influence on me? Who are my heroes and heroines? What famous person, living or dead, would I like to meet? What impossible dreams do I have?

In this expanded self-knowledge you will find much to work into your essay, and you will be giving admissions committees the benefit of your introspection. Avoid a mere recital of what you have achieved; that information is already in your folder. You are the fastest person on your track team? So are hundreds of other applicants on theirs, but maybe you will be the only one with the imagination to capture in your essay the torture of running the mile.

LIST TEN ESSAY TOPICS

Listing ten essay topics will loosen you up and give you confidence that there are many essays to be written. You can discard many of the topics, then practice on those you prefer. Take a list like this:

Possible Essay Topics

1. Lessons learned from work
2. This summer's experience
3. Political Incorrectness
4. Why I read the comics
5. Cultural differences
6. On not mowing the lawn
7. Peace is not impossible
8. Teaching my parents to use the computer
9. The bilingual trap
10. What I hope to gain from college experience

Any of these topics can be developed into an essay, providing you relate it to yourself and shine a light on an aspect of your personality. In driver's education you clashed with the instructor or backed into a wall, or you learned the importance of safety. You love your shopping mall or you do not. What is different about your reaction? You hate political correctness but this is politically incorrect at your school. You read the comics not for laughs but for insights. Bilingualism, you think, is un-American. The "soaps" are feeding the public silly fantasies. Strike a new note. Harold brought his personal experience into this sensitive essay.

My sister is three and one half years older than I, but I have always been her big brother. Laurie is communication handicapped and neurologically impaired. Because of these disabilities, she did not even start to speak until age six. Many tasks are difficult for her. I seemed to sense her needs when I was quite young, and I became her helper and protector. Living with Laurie all these years has helped to make me knowledgeable about life, more caring, and, above all, patient.

I accompanied Laurie to speech therapy, occupational and physical therapy, and tutoring. These took place at special education schools, a Cerebral Palsy Center, and a hospital for brain-injured children. During these visits I was able to see tragedy firsthand; children who couldn't walk, speak, or even feed themselves. I interacted with the other children, participated in the actual therapy, or at other times just watched and listened. I even became part of a Brownie troop for learning-disabled children. What a feeling — to see children whose greatest desire was to be like me.

It has become a natural instinct for me to keep one eye out for my sister. There was always fifteen minutes to play catch with Laurie before a Wiffle ball game with my friends. When Laurie wanted to go for a walk "all by myself," I would have a sudden impulse to go for a bike ride on the same route. I was probably the only teenager playing house with his sister. Playing with me was better than playing with our parents because I filled the void left by the friends she never had. As I accomplish tasks that Laurie never will, but wants to, such as driving, I always keep her feelings in mind. I praise even her smallest accomplishments while downplaying my own. I get more than my share of praise. I try to show similar concern for others. Although they may not need the degree of attention that Laurie does, I try to look for the good in people and help whenever and wherever I can.

One of the most important attributes that one needs to develop when dealing with others is patience. With Laurie it is a necessity, and a definite challenge. I rapidly learned to throw a ball softer, speak a little slower, and patiently wait for a thought to be finished. Many tasks require a great deal of repeated explanation. Although it would be easier to do many things myself, I have learned to lead and guide her toward a goal while enabling her to accomplish the task independently.

Every day is a learning experience with Laurie, and I still have much to learn. I get frustrated, aggravated, and even embarrassed at times. I just cannot always react perfectly, but I have many years to continue learning. I will always be there for her. It is a lifetime commitment. My desire to go into the medical field stems, in part, from all that I have experienced during my years with Laurie. So many have helped her in so many ways, but there are so many more people who need help and guidance. Perhaps what I learn in the future can, in some way, help me to help Laurie. After all, think of all she has already taught me. In the face of every adversity she has shown me how to face a problem, smile, and try, try again.

Harold was admitted to six selective colleges.

Choose a topic that will not overwhelm you. Your solution for the Middle East conflict is liable to be pretentious. But if you spent a summer in Israel, your observations will have personal authority.

Here is one essay that reflects very personal feelings.

The human mind is very powerful. It controls, analyzes, and creates various thoughts and emotions. When I brood alone in my room, my mind lets images and ideas race wildly. My room is my isolation tank, because it is the only place where I can really be left alone to dream and think. I slowly lose touch with the real world around me and focus only on my inner world. I close my eyes and start to contemplate. Thoughts start racing in my mind and a battle begins. It is as though several people with differing views are arguing about these abstract ideas. Very rarely does any one person win the battle. The explanation is usually never reached and I am left confused. Certain disturbing thoughts, like death or life after death, are most mystifying; they dance chaotically in my mind without my control. These thoughts are so powerful that whenever I try to dismiss them they reappear. Subconsciously I probably want to brood over these ideas because I want to discover a comforting explanation. Life and death are issues that really scare me. I sometimes lie awake at night thinking about whether I am living my life the right way and to the fullest. I also try to analyze the meaning of death and try to find a solution that I feel comfortable with. Death is a frightening concept because it is something that humans cannot understand. Death, for all we know, could be the paradise and happiness that all humans look for and life could be the hell that humans suffer. I always try to look within myself to see if what I stand for as a person, and what my beliefs are, are good. The more I think of myself, the more I torment myself. As if listening to a scratched record, I hear the same arguments repeated.

This year in my Shakespearean-tragedy course we read and analyzed the play *Hamlet*. I felt a strange yet comforting connection between Hamlet's thoughts and queries and my own. He is a tragic prince who thinks and worries too much and therefore torments himself mentally. He has lost all faith in mankind and believes that most of us are dishonest and "seemers": that people are not what they seem on the outside.

Hamlet expresses this after he finds out that his uncle is a murderer. He notes in his "tables" that "one may smile and smile, and be a villain." He cannot figure out whether his life is worth living. He is disillusioned about the whole concept of life. Many people today have these doubts. Like Hamlet, they come to the conclusion that life is not worth living and therefore commit suicide. Most people, however, including me, have thought, "To be, or not to be . . . ," but have had enough love for life to survive the doubts.

Books are mirrors of human actions and nature. They tell the story of our thoughts and emotions. Even writings from ancient times such as *The Epic of Gilgamesh* describe human worries and fear of death. Gilgamesh sees the death of his best friend and tries desperately to find the solution to prevent his own. Literature and Shakespeare, in particular, have allowed me to understand the world and human nature a little bit more. By studying Shakespeare's characters, I have developed the capability to see the connection between human emotions and values on one hand and the lack of understanding between human beings on the other. Like actual people, these characters are tormented by disturbing thoughts and also have a hard time understanding their own true selves. Human beings throughout the ages have developed considerably but their tormenting, unanswerable thoughts have continued unchanged.

The following essay is more notable for its sincerity than for its writing. The applicant, who was admitted to a fine university, was stronger in mathematics than in verbal skills (720 math, 556 verbal SATs). We include the essay simply to show the range of quality in writing submitted by successful candidates.

A long time ago I heard somebody say — "Your liability becomes your greatest asset." I did not understand those words then.

I do now.

It was a crisp autumn day — the kind they call "perfect football weather." And I was ready. Although I am not very big, by football standards, my head coach said during practice — "You're starting. You've worked hard. You like to hit. We want you in the middle at inside linebacker. In fact, you've been doing such a great job, next week we will probably put you in on offense, too."

I *had* worked hard — 7 long years, in fact: 3 years of Pop Warner, then the Freshman team, Junior Varsity and now, finally, as a senior, the ultimate goal — Varsity Football.

Pre-game drills went quickly, more so than usual and before I knew it, it was time for the opening kickoff. We lost the coin-toss and were to go on defense first. As I stood out on the field waiting for the national anthem to be completed, I was laughing along with a teammate of mine because our band was torturing America's Song. They need more practice, I thought. They're not ready. But I am.

Then we lined up for the ensuing kickoff. Big deal. I had never been seriously injured so my "up" and relaxed mood continued.

But 7 seconds later, as I was making the tackle on the man with the ball, everything came to a sudden halt. Somebody jumped on the pile after the play and, as I looked down, I saw my knee straight and the rest of my leg jutting out at a 90 degree angle. I knew it was broken.

They tell me I tried to straighten my leg and stand on it, but the intense pain has blurred most of my memory of that moment of denial. I was rushed to the hospital by ambulance and immediately given demerol and valium while we awaited an orthopedic surgeon. The x-rays, in the meantime, indicated a broken tibia and fibula with tremendous displacement. When the doctor arrived he put my leg in a cast, but a subsequent x-ray revealed a mis-alignment so I had to go to surgery and receive anesthesia while he re-did the job.

What followed was a week in the hospital in a cast up to my hip, excruciating pain which alternated with drugged slumber and incredible depression. When I was finally discharged from the hospital, I was confined to a wheelchair for a few weeks because I was too weak to support myself on crutches. Initially the length of recovery was estimated at 15 weeks in a cast followed by extensive physical therapy. There was even some doubt as to whether I would be able to play baseball (my best sport) in the spring. The thought of this was mind-boggling, to say the least.

However, my loyal friends and family pulled me through this terrible ordeal with their visits, phone calls, gifts and aid. The community, as well, was extremely supportive in helping me deal with my situation and all the football articles in the local papers wrote about me and wished me a speedy recovery. Even a coach from an opposing team called me several times.

Although I have had to endure a great deal of pain and mental anguish, I have been able to put this experience into its proper perspective; in other words, I know it could have been a lot worse. For instance, I recently entered one of our games in my wheelchair, only to encounter another former player from the opposing team in his wheelchair. He asked me about my injury and then told me his story. He had a blood clot and when they operated on him, they discovered he had a cancerous tumor.

Suddenly, my leg didn't hurt quite as much. Suddenly, my problems didn't seem so bad.

In conclusion, I've learned a good deal from this experience. As I write, I am still in a cast (only to the knee now) and will remain so for several more weeks. But I put my crutches aside and use a walking boot for short periods and my leg is healing just great. I feel very positive about the future. I've had a lot of extra time for school work and my grades have been excellent so far. I've also had a lot of extra time to think and I've learned that I can surmount any obstacle because I have the support of my friends, family, and community. With this in mind and some hard work ahead, I have no doubt that I will be in perfect health for the baseball season.

I found these lines by Shakespeare in a book of quotations under the section labeled adversity. I thought this an appropriate way to end my essay.

> *Sweet are the uses of adversity;*
> *Which, like the toad, ugly and venomous,*
> *Wears yet a precious jewel in his head;*
> *And this our life, exempt from public haunt,*
> *Finds tongues in trees, books in the running brooks,*
> *Sermons in stones, and good in everything.*

> William Shakespeare
> *As You Like It*

WORK ON THE LEAD

The late Farnham Warriner, a wonderful English teacher at Saint Paul's School in Baltimore, used to make his eighth graders memorize the opening lines of great novels. "All happy families resemble one another; every unhappy family is unhappy in its own fashion." So begins Tolstoy's *War and Peace.* Journalists, particularly, struggle over the opening lines they call the lead. Often the text flows easily from a satisfying lead.

It is much easier to learn to write a good lead than to figure out that infernal topic sentence the writing textbooks ask you to find. Topic sentences are not in the vocabulary of newspapermen. As you read newspapers and magazines, underline leads like these:

Hijackings, accidents and even hurricanes have created a downdraft on airline traffic — and, perhaps, on fares too.

The camera rolls. A teacher in the economics department at Carnegie-Mellon University strolls into class, puts down his briefcase and begins. "I think babies ought to be put on the free market."

Providing an extraordinarily frank glimpse of struggles in the government to stabilize the economy, the Finance Minister directed criticism tonight at his Cabinet colleagues and at the persistence of "financial tourism" by Western businessmen who visit but do not invest in Russia.

He was a King when he was 18, a prisoner at 20, an exile at 31, a Prime Minister at 32, a chief of state again at 38, a prisoner again at 54, an exile again at 69.

Against the backdrop of opulent residences and elegant restaurants, Boulevard Georges Pompidou, a scenic roadway overlooking the West African coast, could easily be mistaken for a glittering stretch along the French Riviera.

World politics is entering a new phase in which the fundamental source of conflict will be neither ideological nor economic. The great divisions among mankind and the dominating source of conflict will be cultural.

A *Newsweek* editor used to urge his writers to "get the suckers into the tent" — get the reader hooked. Notice the wordplay in the first lead. Puns are risky, even deplorable, but they bring a wry smile. The second lead is an updating of Swift's famous "modest proposal" to solve Ireland's hunger problem by eating babies.

Leads do not have to be funny, clever, or witty.

> With the TWA hijacking last month the American public's estimate of Greece reached a new low.

> Citizens of totalitarian countries enjoy certain benefits. The forces of order offer effective protection against terrorism (except the kind that comes from above), and there is little espionage in these parts.

Helena, now at Georgetown, emulated journalists with this sharp lead: "At the age of seventeen, I have had a range of experiences, political, military, cultural, linguistic, that have shaped my life and thoughts to a considerable extent. I was born in Beirut, Lebanon, of an American mother and Lebanese father."

It makes you want to know what this mixed marriage produced. Your family can be an excellent source of essay topics. Alicia, applying to Bowdoin and several other small liberal arts colleges, chose to tell in her essay how the separation and reconciliation of her parents affected her life, beginning: "When my Mother told me that Daddy had left her, I felt a sense of relief. Their fighting was interfering with my studying."

Write some leads for the fun of it. "As I started to back up, the rearview mirror turned black. A UPS truck had come down the driveway when I wasn't looking. Thud!" Or "I badly wanted to have my own telephone number at home until I was elected president of the student council. It rang off the hook, so I bought a cheap answering machine and taped a message: 'If you are calling about council business, please leave a message in my box in the principal's office.' "

LEARN TO WRITE ABOUT YOURSELF

A brief essay should make a central point, supported by illustration of what the point is. A candidate who plans to study medicine may write about what brought about this important decision — observing the dedication of a parent who is an M.D. It would be a mistake to list the doctor's routine, or to recall several episodes in a long career. One or two striking characteristics of healing, diagnosis, or research will make the point. The structure of such an essay might begin with the candidate's first memory of the father as a doctor — say, when the desire to study medicine became strong as a result of something the father did — and conclude with a statement about what the candidate would do in a medical career and how it would differ from the father's.

A more lighthearted essay need have no more structure than a series of statements related to the central point. Suppose you wrote an essay on why

BOOKS ON WRITING

Applicants are not expected to have all the writing skills at this stage of their education. From their writing experience in school, they ought to know how to spell correctly and write grammatically. A good dictionary and careful proofreading will reduce the number of careless errors. And the best applicants can use a little help from a friend; that friend we recommend is *The Elements of Style* by William Strunk, Jr., and the late *New Yorker* essayist most students know from *Charlotte's Web:* E. B. White. It is only seventy-one pages long and is available in paperback. The publisher is Macmillan.

The booklet is best used after you have written a first draft. It can be read in an hour or so. You can then go over your copy with its rules and advice fresh in your mind. On second and third drafts it becomes extremely helpful and you will probably want to use the book the rest of your life.

Take Rule 13: "Omit needless words." In two parallel columns, Strunk and White show how you can be more concise:

Instead of	Use
the question as to whether	whether (the question whether)
there is no doubt but that	no doubt (doubtless)
used for fuel purposes	used for fuel
he is a man who	he
in a hasty manner	hastily
this is a subject that	this subject
His story is a strange one.	His story is strange.

Or take their presentation of the warning about a word as commonly used as *anybody:*

> **Anybody.** In the sense of *any person* not to be written as two words. "Any body" means *any corpse,* or *any human form,* or *any group.* The rule holds equally for *everybody, nobody,* and *somebody.*

Another excellent book, now out of print, you may be able to find in a library is *The Reader over Your Shoulder* by Robert Graves and Alan Hodge (1943). This, however, is not a book that can be read quickly. Should you have the good fortune to find it and study it during a vacation, you will find that your writing will improve in clarity and possibly in style, too. It is made up of examples of how not to write — unless you are deliberately trying to put one over on the reader.

you prefer sailboats to motorboats. If you had a motorboat that constantly conked out, ran out of gas, and lost propellers on shoals, all you would need to do would be to recount your progressive disappointment, climaxing with the relief of getting rid of the motorboat and acquiring a sailboat. Or perhaps the climax is the rescue in your sailboat of a friend whose motorboat has broken down. The point of such a story might be to tell an admissions committee that you love the water, that you know what you like, and know how to get it.

Practice will help you find the balance between bragging and an "aw shucks, ma'am" approach to your personal subject. Show what you write about yourself to others, and ask them whether your writing is both revealing and genuine. Take their reactions to heart. Then rewrite your writing sample.

"What can I do?" I asked Keith, the playroom director, as I walked in and noticed how quiet the room was. "Well, it's a slow day," he replied, as he checked the list of patients he held in his hand. "You can go and sit with Melissa, a three-year-old girl, in her room. She cannot speak, but she does, on occasion, moan. She also likes to be held, but give her some time to get used to you. Then she will be receptive."

"Okay, that's great," I said, as I headed for the door.

When I found her room, I saw from the doorway a little girl lying curled up in a fetal position on the bed. Upon entering, I quickly realized that Keith had failed to tell me how sick Melissa really was, and that there was physical evidence to prove it. I came closer and sat on a chair next to her bed. I held out my hand, which she willingly grasped and then squeezed. I wanted her to become familiar with me before I attempted to hold her.

As I looked at this poor child, I saw that her head was completely shaved and that she had deep incisions in her head from surgery. Her legs were so thin I thought they would break at the touch. I could fit my hand around her thigh, she was so frail. I saw her untouched meal tray on the table beside her bed and realized that the only form of nutrition she was getting was from the I.V. needle in her arm. She looked so withdrawn, sitting there, shaking and alone. Every once in a while she would emit a moan, the only sound that she could utter, as Keith had told me. I wondered what she felt, what she was thinking. Did she know where she was and what was happening to her?

After ten minutes or so, she started grabbing on to my entire arm, which indicated her willingness and desire to get closer to me. At that point, I climbed onto the bed and placed her in my lap. I held her close, giving her warmth and support, to which she seemed to respond. The more I enclosed her in my arms, the more she wanted that comfort and security.

We sat there for three hours, in the same position. There was a radio on softly in the background, but besides that we only had each other. I held her close to my body, rocking her back and forth, wishing that somehow I could transfer through osmosis some of my good health to her tiny frame, and tell her that everything would be all right. I was afraid she was dying; she would never have the chance to live out her life, never have a chance to see outside the dreary hospital walls. I, a young woman with a multitude of opportunities ahead, and she, a child stricken with a fatal illness, connected during these three hours, as the thought of our unfortunate differences brought tears to my eyes. I wanted to tell her that the security she felt while in my arms would last forever, but I knew I couldn't make good on such a grandiose promise. It was so unfair that she had to endure such misery, and I wished that I could just help alleviate her suffering and help her to recover.

This is only one of many experiences I have had at Memorial Sloan-Kettering Cancer Center, where I have dedicated my time and energy each week for the past three years. Although I worked with elderly patients during my first year, I later transferred to the children's playroom. At first, it was hard to see kids my own age and even younger afflicted with what is, in most cases, a life-threatening disease. I often felt guilty about my own sound health; did I deserve to be robust when they couldn't be, too? I also wasn't sure how I should act; should I be sympathetic or just pretend that their illness wasn't there?

Questions like these were answered after my first few weeks in the children's playroom. I knew from my many job experiences with children that they are usually fun-loving and innocent, without a care in the world. However, these children had missed all those fun, carefree years, having been forced to mature way before their time. Therefore, each time I enter the hospital, I try to replace the pain I see with a little cheer and joy. My job is hard yet fulfilling — particularly those times when I can evoke a smile or a giggle and know that I have left the children with some happy memories. That is why I return to the hospital, week after week; the smiles I see on the children's faces and the fun we create during our time together is what renders my service all the more rewarding.

My experiences at Memorial Sloan-Kettering have created in me a desire to help put a stop to cancer and other diseases. I have seen firsthand the devastating effects of cancer, both within my family and in the hospital. I have seen diseased bodies, weak and distorted from illness and medication, sometimes even missing limbs. I have seen suffering, both physical and emotional, the likes of which I could never have imagined. I have even seen death, which is, for some, the unavoidable end to a long battle.

The strong feelings I have developed about the patients and the disease they fight have solidified my decision to pursue a career in medicine. The pain must be stopped, and I want to help stop it. I truly believe the United States has both the resources and the intellect needed to beat this illness and others. We have made remarkable progress in other biological areas, such as genetic disorders and the composition of DNA, and I feel we have the power to discover possible cures for other diseases. I want to dedicate my professional life to finding these answers. Through the biological sciences, I hope to help people by relieving their suffering and restoring their health. No one deserves to endure the pain I have seen at Sloan-Kettering; there are solutions, and I am committed to finding them.

REWRITE, REWRITE, REWRITE!

When Winston Churchill had finished a manuscript, he went to work on galley proofs. Maddeningly, he would return to the publisher thousands of words of corrections, costing thousands of dollars to reset, for which Churchill, naturally, had no intention of paying. The publisher recovered this expense in the sale of the great Englishman's best-sellers. Churchill believed in what he preached. He offered his countrymen "blood, toil, tears and sweat," and he asked it of himself at his writing desk.

Looking at a text over and over, you will find ways to improve it — by adding or cutting, by rewording, reparagraphing, changing punctuation. You may find your lead in the last paragraph, and the lead you have may become the final punch line. You will spot bad taste, exaggeration, inaccuracy, clumsy phrasing, flowery words. You will get rid of clichés like *hit the nail on the head; throw out the baby with the bathwater; awesome, man!* Percy Cowan, a well-known English teacher at Morristown High School in New Jersey, forbade his students ever to use the word *interesting,* because it says nothing — certainly nothing interesting.

Reading favorite authors before and after you practice writing will help you in rewriting to achieve the clarity and grace of practitioners of good prose. Whether it's McPhee, Hemingway, Vonnegut, Annie Dillard, Sue Miller, or Alice Walker, look at their work to see what makes it distinctive. Then turn back to your copy with a good soft pencil the way editors do, and mark it up until it's hardly legible. There is nothing sacred about a first, second, or third draft.

PROOFREAD YOUR COPY

Proofreading is your responsibility. Your teacher or counselor may like your essay, but it is up to you to rid it of typing errors and grammatical faults. Retype it, double-spaced, on white paper. Doing this should take only a half-hour. Handwritten copy should be clean and easy to read. Photocopies are perfectly acceptable, but be careful not to leave pages out when submitting copies to different colleges. Put your name on your essay in case it gets mixed in with other essays in the admissions office.

Be sure to give yourself plenty of time to show your essay to your busy counselor, so that you will have a final copy ready before you begin to fill out your applications. It may take a month to six weeks to get them all ready for mailing. Since deadlines are usually between January 1 and February 1, you should have the essay done by mid-November. Here is one more writing sample, by a student who was admitted to several Ivy colleges.

The Image and Role of Women

In her novel *The Color Purple,* Alice Walker portrays the South and the African continent during and around the Great Depression. In this world during this era, it is the female, more intensely the black female, who is discriminated against. These women are denied many of their basic freedoms and treated as the possessions of their menfolk, husbands, fathers, brothers, and cousins. These females are brutalized and cast down, except for a few who have the strength and will to fight back, such as Shug Avery, Sofia, and eventually Celie. The role of the women portrayed in the novel is one of mother, housekeeper, farmer, and sex partner. And very often the females are the true emotional strengths behind their men. For those who do not stand up for their rights, it is a life of constant denial and subservience. For those who do fight back, it is a long, rough road to freedom from their men.

The males in this novel dominate the women, or at least most believe that this is the way they should treat the females. The males think that they are supposed to keep their women in line by physically beating them and mentally making them feel like dirt. One gets an image of the female forced into this life of servitude but feeling internally strong, or at least having deep inside her the power to be independent. The view is that according to the males, women are worthless without a man. The goal of many women is to fend for themselves and do without a torturing husband.

Two women in the book do not fit the mold of the model black female because they fight back: Shug and Sofia. These females are seen as unwomanly, with manly traits. Celie says of Shug, "That when I notice how Shug talk and act sometimes like a man. Men say stuff like that to women, Girl, you look like a good time. Women always talk bout hair and health. How many babies living or dead, or got teef. Not bout how some woman they hugging on look like a good time."(p. 82) Shug is unfeminine because she does not talk about trivial things like vanity or motherhood. She seems interested in sex, which is odd, for women are not supposed to enjoy it like Shug does. Women are also viewed as weak and cowardly. Sofia is not either of these, as is evidenced by her attack on the mayor and her response to Squeak's slap: "Sofia don't even deal in little ladyish things such as slaps. She ball up her fist, draw back, and knock two of Squeak's side teef out."(p. 83)

Harpo, Sofia's husband, wants to treat his wife as his father treats Celie, with beatings and orders. Unfortunately for him, Sofia is bigger than he, has a strong will, and fights him back, physically. This quote not only shows Harpo's relationship with Sofia, but Celie's uncaring marriage and life with her husband Albert, Harpo's father: "You still bothering Sofia? I ast. She my wife, he say. That don't mean you got to keep on bothering her, I (Celie) say. Sofia love you, she a good wife . . ." Here Celie lists the expectations of a good wife. ". . . Good to the children and good looking. Hardworking. Godfearing and clean. I don't know what more you want. Harpo sniffle. I want her to do what I say, like you do for Pa. Oh, lord, I say. When Pa tell you to do something, you do it, he say. When he say not to, you don't. You don't do what he say, he beat you. Sometime beat me anyhow, I say, whether I do what he say or not. That's right, say Harpo. But not Sofia. She do what she want, don't pay me no mind at all . . ." As a woman, this is supposedly wrong of Sofia. ". . . I try to beat her, she black my eyes . . . Some womens can't be beat, I say. Sofia one of Them. Besides, Sofia love you. She probably be happy to do most of what you say if you ast her right . . ." But this does not matter to Harpo, who feels things are not right (and they Are not) if he does not have to force his wife to comply with his demands. ". . . Harpo, I say, giving him a shake, Sofia Love you. You love Sofia . . . Mr. —— marry me to take care of his children. I marry him cause my daddy made me. I don't love Mr. —— and he don't love me . . ." This is such a life of compliance for Celie. She has literally grown up to this point without a thing to say about what has been happening to her. ". . . But you his wife, he say, just like Sofia mine. The wife spose to mind. Do Shug Avery mind Mr. ——? I ast. She the woman he wanted to marry . . . Little as he is, when she git her weight back she can sit on him if he try to bother her."(pp. 65, 66) But of course it is only right that Celie follow the woman's tragic course of marriage without consent.

Yet Celie admires Sofia and Shug. This is evidenced by her eventual liberation from her patterned life of a beaten woman. "But peoples use to men doing this sort of thing. Women weaker, he say. People think they weaker, say they weaker, anyhow. Women spose to take it easy. Cry if you want to. Not try to take over."(p. 195) Men here see women as the more fragile sex. Why, then, do they abuse them when they should be protecting them with their false pretenses? Evidently, men are weaker emotionally. Physical abuse is their way of expressing power, while the real strength lies in the woman's mind. Men need to abuse the women in order to feel powerful. Women need only their own inner strength.

Celie is unhappy as a man's slave, so she fights back in the end and becomes independent and content. Celie's sister Nettie, on the other hand, finds happiness in acceptance of the men. The reason for this, however, is that she fortunately ends up with a good man, Samuel, a missionary who treats her almost as an equal, when they go to Africa together. It seems rare that two passive souls meet and find happiness together in this world.

Alice Walker certainly feels that a woman's most important trait is her will. From her will stem her strength, pride, and intelligence. A woman needs this will to free herself, both spiritually and physically, from any form of unhappy submission. It is true that a woman can play a valuable and rewarding role as a mother, housewife, laborer, or lover, but she should do so voluntarily and on her own terms. Walker encourages her women to liberate themselves and lead their own lives.

OTHER WRITING MAY BE REQUESTED

Many colleges allow your essay to be on a topic of your own choice, with the proviso that it should give the admissions committee some insight into your character, personality, and interests. Typically the college suggests that you discuss some personal experience or your goals, values, and ideals. But other colleges may ask you to respond briefly to a provocative question. Stanford has asked such questions as:

> Given the authority to establish a holiday, what would you choose to commemorate? Briefly explain.
> Suppose you had the opportunity to spend the day with anyone, with whom would it be, and how would you spend your time?

Boston College offered applicants a choice of two questions:

> You have just been appointed editor of a major news publication. Write an editorial on a controversial issue (its scope can be of personal, local, national, or global importance), in which you effectively defend your position.
> You have been selected to spend an evening with any one person living, historical or fictional. Whom would you choose and why? What would you do that evening, what would you discuss, and what would you hope to learn from this unique opportunity?

These are not trick questions. Unlike questions on an exam, these are untimed. You can take weeks to think about them, write drafts, rewrite until you are satisfied with what you have written. What you must remember, though, is that the questions are trying to get at you, your feelings, your ideas, your imagination. To say you would like to spend a day with Hillary Clinton or Martin Luther King or Hamlet does not call for a review of that person's life. How would you interact with the person? What impact has this person made on you?

You might feel, for example, that Hamlet is a rather self-righteous individual, and you would like to engage him in a dialogue in which you point out that what a person does is more important than what he thinks. You have brought along your tape recorder and your essay is a transcript of the conversation. Such a device would allow you to show an admissions committee how you have behaved when confronted with alternatives.

To write an essay in response to this kind of question is really no more restrictive than an open-ended request by a college to "tell us something about yourself." In fact, your imagination may be more stimulated by your having to frame your writing within certain limits.

From the point of view of the admissions committee, these questions make it possible to compare candidates more readily. Here, then, is an opportunity for candidates to display writing talent, imagination, and some aspect of their lives. Students planning careers in science or engineering are sometimes more at ease with figures and diagrams than with words. They have an opportunity in such essays to discuss the world of science, the famous pioneers, environmental problems, the exhaustion of mineral resources, and control of traffic, and to quantify their statements if they so choose.

It will be worth your while to work on these question essays if you are asked for them on an application. One of the most inquisitive colleges is Dartmouth, which has asked the following questions:

Which academic subject in school is most meaningful to you?

Briefly elaborate on the activity or activities you find most meaningful.

How did you spend last summer?

Choose to answer one of the following questions:
  What is the best advice you have ever received?
  Describe the greatest challenge you have faced or expect to face.

What have you read that has had a special significance for you?

You have answered many questions on this form, all asked by someone else. If you yourself were in a position to ask a provocative and revealing question of college applicants, what would that question be?

Now that you have asked your ideal question, answer it.

Tanya's response was this:

If you could enter the mind of a human being as a thought, what kind of thought would you be and what would you hope to accomplish?

Within the intricate and perplexing mind of a human being, millions of thoughts compete for survival. Fortunately, I happen to be one of the luckier ones; I am a Mandatory Warning Thought. As such a thought, I am often pushed aside and even ignored, but unlike other thoughts, I can never be totally eliminated. In my role as a warning thought, I automatically enter the mind of every human being in order to counterbalance its desire to prejudge others.

Unfortunately, as a young mind develops, it is traditionally influenced by the mannerisms of its society. It never has a fair chance to decide whether or not it wants to accept or reject individuals for what they truly are rather than what they appear to be. Every time the mind starts to prejudge an individual, I act as a warning signal to force it to recognize this disparaging thought. At this point, the mind may ignore me and continue to prejudge, but I will come back again like a smoke alarm whenever another derogatory thought emerges.

I know that I will never be able to do away with all prejudicial thinking. However, by reminding human beings every time they prejudge others I ultimately hope to condition their minds to be more tolerant.

We know that you will have your own way of writing a good essay and your own answers to questions put to you on admissions applications. You can insure your admission to one or even two selective colleges by writing with conviction and self-knowledge. By telling an admissions committee what you want them to know about you rather than telling them what you think they are looking for in an applicant, you will be showing the committee your uniqueness. Selective colleges are not looking for clones of those already enrolled. They are looking for you. So go to work on your writing.

They warned me about him. All of the baseball players who had played under him told me that he was very strict and nearly impossible to please. I had also heard, however, that Coach Jim Dolan was one of the best coaches in the area.

When I entered my sophomore year at Joel Barlow, I was very sensitive and insecure. However, I was very eager to play varsity baseball after playing well for the junior varsity team in my freshman year. My eagerness was somewhat dulled when I first saw how Coach Dolan handled the varsity tryouts in the spring of 1991. I realized that he was very strict, very critical, and very quick-tempered. I had no idea how much he would change my life over the next two years.

Coach Dolan had a reputation for picking out one rookie who he felt had good potential and making that player the scapegoat for the entire season. I had heard stories from a player who was the coach's target the previous year, and being one of only three sophomores on the team, I knew I was bound to be Dolan's 1991 choice for scapegoat.

I was right. I was the victim of Dolan's wrath for the year. If anything went wrong, if anyone made a mistake, it seemed that somehow I was always to blame. Everyone on the team acknowledged my unique plight and frequently told me they were glad that they were not in my position. The criticism did not affect my playing time, however, as I played every inning of every game in the number-five batting position and in right field.

There were times when I felt I could not deal with Coach Dolan anymore. In one incident, he gave the batter the bunt sign while I was on first base. Normally in that circumstance the runner on first should wait until the bunted ball is on the ground before leaving for second base. However, being a nervous rookie, I ran to second as the ball was pitched and I was thrown out by the catcher. Dolan literally dragged me off the field and yelled at me in front of a rather large audience. Meanwhile, the batter, who coincidentally was the Coach's scapegoat the year before, got away with missing the bunt sign completely and swinging at the pitch, an offense much worse than mine. But Dolan saw my mistake and immediately yelled at me, no matter that a more serious mistake was made on the same play.

There were times when I felt the Coach was unfair, times when I wanted to say something back to him, and even times when I wanted to quit. I quickly grew tired of Coach Dolan yelling: "Roth! Wipe off that poopey-face and play like a man" whenever he thought I was getting down on myself. I continued to play simply because I loved the game and I loved the team.

What I could not see was how this man was changing my life. By the end of my sophomore year I felt I had matured a great deal. I had learned to accept constructive criticism as well as a bit of beneficial yelling.

Coach Dolan helped me change my behavior outside of baseball as well. During my junior year, I had a very difficult course load, including five honors classes. If Coach Dolan had not helped me mature, I seriously question whether I could have handled my junior year as well as I did. He helped me overcome my insecurity and oversensitivity, which allowed me to set reasonable athletic and academic goals and to know how to accomplish them. By the end of the 1992 baseball season, during which I endured some criticism (but not nearly as much as I had during my sophomore year), I felt as if I had matured five years instead of two.

Coach Jim Dolan has coached his final baseball team for Joel Barlow High School. He decided to retire at the end of the 1992 season because he wanted to watch his seven-year-old son play Little League baseball. As a good-bye present, the 1992 varsity baseball team won the Western Connecticut Conference championship and advanced to the quarterfinals in the state tournament. We sent Coach Dolan off with a bang.

His influence will not easily be forgotten by me or anyone else who has ever played for him. As I talk to the upcoming freshmen and sophomores who want to try out for the varsity team, I think of Coach Dolan and tell them something like: "Well, if you put out 110 percent, and no less, and you never show any 'poopey-face,' then maybe, just maybe, you will have a shot."

THE FEE WAIVER OPTION

All selective colleges will waive the fee for admissions applications for financially needy candidates. Your high school college counselor can write a statement of support for the fee waivers. So do not feel that you cannot afford to apply to a number of selective colleges. Despite the large numbers of applications they are receiving, these colleges do not wish anyone who feels qualified to apply for admission to fail to do so because of the fee. Admissions offices have ample funds to cover fee waivers.

GET AN A IN APPLICATIONS

An application is deceptively simple looking. It asks for the following:

- Basic information about yourself, school, family
- A nonacademic profile
- A personal statement or essay
- An academic transcript to be submitted by your school — also in some instances a midterm report
- Two or more recommendations to be submitted by teachers or your counselor
- If you are going to study engineering, a statement about your motivation and aptitude
- If you plan to be a varsity athlete, a form describing your sports record (not all colleges ask for this with the application for admissions)

You will find that selective college applications vary widely in format. Brown has seven separate forms; Princeton's application is eighteen pages long, and it asks you to sign a pledge that the essay is entirely your own; Dartmouth goes farther, asking for your assurance that the entire application is truthful.

Care in completing an application is essential. It does become somewhat routine and even tedious to fill out half a dozen applications, so you must determine to devote as much care to the last as to the first. It is quite possible to turn off an admissions committee by submitting an application that appears to have been tossed off without enough thought.

You will note on the application form that each college asks why you have chosen to apply to this particular school. Why Smith and not Wellesley? Why Duke and not Columbia? The college is looking for your assessment of its educational character — not an assurance that you will enroll if you are admitted.

"I am applying to Oberlin because of its strong commitment to modern languages, and because of its rich research resources."

"Boston University's urban location would let me combine business courses with practical part-time work in a brokerage firm."

All colleges realize they are competing for qualified students. No applicant is given preference on the basis of a promise to enroll if admitted.

Each application should be letter-perfect, without typing errors, smudges, erasures, or spelling mistakes. Whatever your grades in school, you should get an A in completing college applications. The colleges expect this. The volume of applications puts an enormous burden on their staffs. If an application is not clear, if it has mistakes in it, the reader's enthusiasm for the applicant diminishes. If you submit seven applications, make every one of them perfect.

You can assure yourself of this by proofreading each of them. If a member of your family will let you read each application aloud, errors will be more

---

THE COMMON APPLICATION

One hundred twenty-one colleges and universities have agreed to accept a common application. The selective ones among them are Barnard College, Bates College, Boston University, Bowdoin College, Brandeis University, Bryn Mawr College, Bucknell University, Carleton College, Colgate University, Connecticut College, Denison University, Dickinson College, Duke University, Emory University, Franklin and Marshall College, Hamilton College, Harvard University Haverford College, Johns Hopkins University, Kenyon College, Lafayette College, Lawrence University, Lehigh University, Lewis and Clark College, Mount Holyoke College, Oberlin College, Pomona College, Reed College, Rensselaer Polytechnic Institute, Rice University, University of Rochester, Saint Lawrence University, Sarah Lawrence College, Smith College, Swarthmore College, Trinity College, Union College, Vanderbilt University, Vassar College, Wake Forest University, Washington and Lee University, Wesleyan University, Williams College, and Worcester Polytechnic Institute.

The application is sent to all schools by the National Association of Secondary School Principals. It has the virtue of cutting down the time devoted to completing applications when you apply to more than one of the 121 colleges.

---

easily caught than if you yourself go over the same copy a number of times, for we tend to see what we want to see and not what should be on the page. Having helped many students get into selective colleges, we can assure you that the best students took the most care in completing their applications. You do not have to be an A student to get an A in application writing. You do have to be diligent.

ABOUT RECOMMENDATIONS

Usually two teachers' recommendations are requested, to be mailed by the teachers to the college. Your counselor's recommendations and those of the principal or headmaster or headmistress are added to the official school transcript. Before approaching any teacher for a recommendation, think about it. You want to make sure the teacher is going to give you an unreserved recommendation, such as the following:

> This is a letter of recommendation for Maria. Maria was a student of mine in tenth grade Regents Biology and is currently enrolled in my Advanced Biology class. Maria is an excellent student. She fully accepts her personal responsibilities; shows genuine interest and is actively

involved in classroom discussions: is considerate of others' rights and feelings; and shows an excellent depth of understanding. She is currently involved in a thirty-week Drosophila research project which entails extensive independent work. . . . Her acceptance to your school will be of mutual benefit.

What you want to avoid is a bland endorsement that refers largely to your character and says little about your academic qualifications for college. Admissions committees are quick to read between the lines of a recommendation that lacks substantiation of assertions, such as "I feel certain that Jack will make his contribution to your college." What reassures admissions committees is a forthright statement like "Michael's sensitivity, commitment, intellect and idealism make him one of this year's outstanding graduates," a recommendation from a teacher in a competitive New York school.

HOW TO GET A GOOD RECOMMENDATION

Recognize that your teachers will say no more about you to an admissions committee than they have already reported to you or your parents. If you

---

THE OPTIONAL WAIVER OF ACCESS

Under the Family Educational Rights and Privacy Act of 1974 (the Buckley Amendment), every applicant has the right of access to the files containing his or her recommendations. Many colleges offer candidates the option of waiving their right of access — in other words, waiving their right to see the recommendations in their file. The option is exercised by checking a box next to a waiver statement on the application form.

Waiving your right of access is a gesture of confidence in the integrity of your teachers and others whom you've asked to supply recommendations. You are free, of course, not to grant this waiver. However, admissions committees consider that anyone giving a recommendation is likely to be less candid knowing that the student will see the evaluation. Furthermore, it is only natural for anyone reading your application to wonder whether you doubt the judgment or fairness of those whom you've asked to recommend you. (And what recourse will you have if in fact you are not satisfied with a recommendation?)

As a selective college applicant, you have surely earned favorable recommendations from the appropriate teachers, counselors, and others. If you follow the guidelines in this step for obtaining your recommendations, you should have no anxieties about the evaluations in your files.

are not one of the year's outstanding graduates, what can a teacher say in a recommendation? Assume that you are in the upper quarter of your class, and have a B average. The colleges know this and are not looking for recommendations that contradict the record. They want statements that will help them decide whether to admit you in preference to someone else with a similar record. Here is how to get useful recommendations.

You pick two teachers for whom you have performed well, teachers who have praised you for a paper, an exam, a project. Acquaint them with your college objectives on a single sheet of paper, preferably typed double-spaced. List the colleges you are applying to, say why, and tell these teachers your tentative college plans. At the end of this memorandum ask the simple question: "Do you think you can write a strong recommendation for me to any or all of these colleges?" Include in your memo the fact that you have consulted closely with your advisor, have visited a number of colleges, and have taken all the necessary steps for college admission.

A sympathetic teacher will certainly not write a noncommittal recommendation merely saying what a fine outstanding person you are. Teachers want their rewards like anyone else, and nothing gives teachers more pleasure than the knowledge that they are helping a good student get into a good college. They will respond positively in most instances, and you can feel sure that what they say in their recommendations will be warm and substantive. "Susan is diligent, completes all assignments, has a positive attitude that your college will value. Her contributions to class discussion were always thoughtful and stimulating. Marked improvement in her work occurred during the year."

In writing to a teacher, you are not being manipulative, you are not polishing the apple, you are making a reasonable request. Be sure when you do this to send a copy of this request to your advisor, whom the teachers may consult before replying to you.

After you know which teachers will write your recommendations, make it easier for them by attaching a stamped envelope addressed to each college to the recommendation sheet that is part of the application. When they let you know they have mailed off their recommendations, which they will not show you, thank them personally.

You are not limited to two teacher recommendations. Anyone in your school or community who will write briefly about you should be asked to do so: principal, head of school, counselor, music director, clergyman, government official, camp director. For Cicely, now at Bowdoin, her college advisor wrote: "Cicely is passionate, committed, mature, willing to take intellectual risks, eloquent, opinionated, forceful, active and optimistic." For Harriet he wrote: "Harriet has the brains, the training, and the determination to be successful at Duke." Harriet was put on Duke's waiting list. When she was taken off and admitted, she enrolled in January (Duke admits a few freshmen in January to fill vacant places in the college left by students taking a semester off campus).

ENCLOSURES AND OTHER DOCUMENTS

Use your notebook to list the enclosures needed for each application — essays, answers to questions if on separate sheets, and the check made out to each college. Allow yourself enough time so you are not rushed getting the applications out all in one evening when you are tired. It is very easy to put the wrong check in the envelope, or to put into a Harvey Mudd envelope a statement intended for Colorado. We would not mention such mundane things if it were not for the fact that they happen all the time, and mixups do not improve admissions chances.

Your transcript and recommendations are mailed by your school to the colleges you designate. Usually, your counselor is responsible for mailing the transcript, and the individual teachers are responsible for mailing the recommendations. However, it is up to you to make sure that in every case this is actually done. A little tact is called for in checking up on the counselor and teachers, who are doing the same thing for many other students. This is why you should allow them enough time to meet application deadlines.

You will recall that the College Entrance Examination Board sends each college to which you apply your SAT and Subject Test scores, so each admissions office gets these mailings:

1. Your application — mailed by you
2. Your transcript — mailed by the school (usually your counselor)
3. Your recommendations — mailed by teachers
4. SAT and Subject Test scores — mailed by the College Board

Keep a record of your obligations in your notebook, checking off what has been done, so that you can see at a glance what tasks remain. Such a record might look like this:

College	Deadline	Transcript Mailed	Recommendations Mailed	Application Mailed
Yale	Jan. 1	Dec. 12	Dec. 6 (Cohen) Dec. 9 (Tate)	Dec. 4

(Teachers' names — Tate, Cohen — distinguish each recommendation.)

The college will contact you if for some reason any material is missing from your folder, and you will have an opportunity to track down the necessary records or paperwork.

Make a note of the date when each application is mailed. If within two weeks you get no acknowledgment that it has been received, phone the admissions office — not the director or the dean — and ask politely if your application has been received. No? Explain that you mailed it in time, and send a copy at once.

Of course you have copies of everything you send out. Keep them in a file where you can quickly lay hands on them.

Is that all? Not quite. We have said nothing about applying for financial aid, which is the subject of the next step. If you are going to apply for financial aid — and as many as 80 percent of applicants do apply now — you need only check a box that lets the college know your application form is being filed separately.

CONTINUE TO ACHIEVE

Once all your applications are in the mail, you have completed the major tasks for successful admissions to a selective college. What remains is follow-up, which we call marketing yourself, and finally deciding where you want to enroll if you are admitted to more than one college.

But you still have to complete the rest of your senior year. One of the requirements of selective colleges is that you perform in your remaining months at your usual level. A senior year letdown can be fatal. Though it rarely happens among selective college candidates, colleges can of course withdraw their offers of admission late in spring if they are convinced that a candidate has not satisfied their requirements. You will continue to be the person you know yourself to be. You will study and remain active. You will stretch. The senior year is your hardest year of secondary school. But your freshman year in college will be harder. Keep your study skills honed!

Step Nine Checklist

1. Take an inventory of your attitudes, expectations, and achievements as you search for essay topics that will allow you to reveal your personality.
2. Be sincere, be clear, be spirited, be personal in your writing.
3. Practice, write drafts, then polish your writing.
4. Proofread your writing. Get an A in applications — no errors, please.
5. Write a one-page memo to two teachers explaining your college admissions plans and ask for recommendations. Give your college advisor a copy.
6. Watch your deadlines, and keep a record of all documentation that is part of your application.
7. Keep a copy of all applications and enclosures, in case you have to supply a backup if an application is lost.
8. Work as hard during the rest of your senior year as you ever have. Your record counts right up to graduation.

Plan Your Selective College Finances

FINANCIAL AID PROBLEMS HAVE THEIR SOLUTIONS

With the cost of a selective private college education approaching $30,000 per year by the year 2000, financial aid becomes an almost universal consideration for candidates. Even the selective public universities charge a premium for out-of-state students. Scholarship resources are shrinking. This means that more and more students will be borrowing and working their way through, even postponing enrollment to build savings.

This, however, is not the first time in American history that lack of sufficient means has been an obstacle to a college education. During the Depression of the 1930s the selective colleges still managed to attract students whose families were suddenly almost penniless. We know that if you want to attend a selective college badly enough you can find the money to pay for it, if not now, then in the future, after graduation.

It is therefore crucial that you resist the temptation to lower your expectations to attend a selective college for purely financial reasons. Certainly there are low-cost options, but you get what you pay for. In the long run the benefits of a selective college education far outweigh the difficulties encountered in paying for it. Strategies for meeting the costs will require sacrifice and self-discipline.

Just as there is academic and nonacademic competition, so too there is competition for financial aid. In this Tenth Step we want to acquaint you with the problems and how to overcome them as others have and will continue to do.

THE NEW TRENDS

The new trends, as we noted in our introduction, are (1) the disappearance of need-blind admissions policies at all but the most heavily endowed colleges, both public and private; (2) an increasing number of financial aid packages in which academic achievement is rewarded; (3) a larger dependence on borrowing to pay for undergraduate as well as graduate education; and (4) new federal loan programs.

Selective colleges, with their large endowments, are in a better position to help undergraduates financially than institutions dependent on tuition for much of their income. (See the box on page 12 for a list of institutions in order of the size of their endowments.)

Financial aid can influence your choice of college, of course. Many applicants and their families will shop around for the best bargains among selective colleges. There are colleges — including some of the most expensive in the

---

FINANCIAL AID AT BRANDEIS

Lynda S. Watson, Director of Financial Aid at Brandeis University, says, "We never turn down a request for aid when there is demonstrated financial need. Brandeis students received more than $15 million in grant and scholarship funds in 1992–93. Thirteen million dollars was from university funds. About 45 percent of our students are awarded university grants and scholarships, and another 40 percent receive subsidized loans."

She is concerned by the lack of understanding about private college costs that is causing some students to apply only to places they think they can afford, mostly public institutions. Colleges and universities with strong financial aid programs, like Brandeis, can help families with even modest resources to meet the costs of attending such high-priced institutions.

Ms. Watson provided us with four examples of aid for families with incomes over $70,000. Total annual billed costs at Brandeis were $24,230 at the time.

Case 1. $70,554 parental income, family of 4 with 2 in college — $12,740 university scholarship, $1,000 university loan, $3,200 Federal Family Educational Loan, $1,800 campus job (12–15 hrs./wk.).

Case 2. $79,367 parental income, family of 5 with 3 in college — $11,640 university scholarship, $1,000 federal Supplemental Educational Opportunity Grant (SEOG), $800 state grant, $2,500 federal loans, $1,400 campus job.

Case 3. $88,855 parental income, family of 6 with 2 in college — $4,120 university scholarship, $1,400 university loan, $2,620 federal loan, $1,500 campus job.

Case 4. $91,861 parental income, family of 4 with 2 in college — $3,620 university scholarship, $1,400 university loan, $2,620 federal loan, $1,700 campus job.

COLLEGE COSTS RISING FASTER
THAN THE INFLATION RATE

Although tuition increases are no longer going up by 20 percent a year as they did in the early 1980s, the rate of increase is averaging more than twice the inflation rate. Most tuitions for the year 1993–94 are 6 to 8 percent higher than the previous year. The Consumer Price Index is rising about 3 percent a year.

Tuitions at most selective private colleges now are more than $18,000 a year. Princeton's tuition is $18,940; Harvard's is $18,745; Yale's is $18,630. With room and board Yale's total charges come to $25,110. By contrast, total charges at the University of Connecticut for an in-state resident are $8,780.

The main reason why college tuition continues to rise at such a pace is to meet the pressure for faculty salary increases. The American Association of University Professors reports that during the 1970s purchasing power of the average faculty member fell by about 21 percent, and colleges are still trying to help their teachers catch up with the rest of the population. Another development facing colleges is the increased cost of liability insurance.

Despite the higher cost of selective colleges, there has been no drop in the number of applicants for admission. On the contrary, applications continue to rise.

country — that offer large scholarships to the very best applicants, and there are selective state institutions where tuition is roughly half that of private selective colleges. The military academies are selective and they cost a family nothing. ROTC scholarships provide a four-year all-expenses-paid college education. There are other options, too, which we will discuss.

HOW FINANCIAL AID WORKS

Financial aid comes in a "package" consisting of three elements: scholarship, loan, and campus job. Aid packages vary because of college policies and available funds. It is possible for a candidate to receive an admit-deny notice, meaning that the candidate is admitted but is denied scholarship aid, on the grounds of not needing it. Such a candidate can still borrow at low interest and work on campus, and the parents can still participate in tuition plans that save money, or borrow at favorable interest rates.

If you qualify for financial aid, you will be expected to meet your share of costs from your savings and jobs, and you will pay back any loans in installments, usually after graduation. Your parents and you will be responsible for paying the difference between the financial aid package (which includes sums

FINANCIAL AID AT PRINCETON, CLASS OF 1997

CASE 1

Annual income: $19,000
Two parents, 3 children, modest family savings. Student has $700 in savings.
   Parent contribution $500. Student contribution $240 from savings, $1,420 from summer employment.

Need	$24,655

Work study	1,745
Student loan	1,880
University scholarship	21,030

If she gets $1,000 outside scholarship, $750 goes to reducing the loan, and $250 reduces the Princeton scholarship.

CASE 2

Annual income: $52,000
One student in college. Money market fund $15,000. Home equity $60,000. Student has $400 in savings.
   Parent contribution $7,300. Student contribution $140 from savings, $1,520 from summer work.

Need	$17,855

Work study	1,745
Student loan	3,380
University scholarship	12,730

CASE 3

Annual income: 90,000
Two children in college. Home equity $100,000, savings $65,000. (Of $165,000 in assets, only $15,400 is added to adjusted available income.) Student savings $2,000. Travel expenses of $600.
   Total parent contribution $24,000 or $12,000 each student. Student contribution $700 from savings, $1,520 summer earnings.

Need	$13,195

Work study	1,745
Student loan	3,380
University scholarship	8,070

CASE 4 (Without Need)

Annual income: $110,000
Assets $250,000. No need, but $3,500 Princeton student loan and
$2,000 merit-based scholarship from hometown.
    Parents to finance remaining $16,550 with a Princeton parent loan.
Four-year total $66,000. Monthly payments $615 for fourteen years.

SCHOLARSHIP AND LOAN OPPORTUNITIES ABOUND

College Bound, a newsletter for high school counselors on issues and
trends in college admissions, publishes lists of unusual scholarship opportunities. If your school does not presently subscribe, ask the guidance
office staff to invest $59 for an annual subscription by writing to College
Bound, 7658 North Rogers, Chicago, IL 60626.
    While some wealthy private colleges continue to offer good financial
aid packages, less selective institutions are coming up with enticing
programs to attract good students. You should take a look at any of the
following for interesting deals: Hartwick College, Antioch College, Saint
Norbert College, Dominican College, Drew University, University of
the Pacific. Programs include tuition discounts and loan conversions to
grants for academic achievement.
    New College of the University of South Florida is possibly the best
buy among selective colleges. It is part of the state system, turns down
66 percent of all applicants, and tuition is only $9,293 for out-of-staters.
Average SAT scores: 1243!

you contribute from savings and job earnings) and the total annual cost of
your education. (If you are independent, of course, all the financial responsibility is yours.) Your parents are not strangers to meeting their financial
obligations. Yet the college years may impose the most strains yet encountered
on the family purse. An appreciation of their willingness to help you at this
time will strengthen family bonds.

APPLY IF YOU NEED AID!

Every financial aid official of the colleges we are in contact with has urged
us to get this message across: APPLY FOR AID IF YOU NEED IT! Let the *college*
determine whether you are eligible for aid.
    The College Scholarship Service says: "The only way to know for sure if
you're eligible for financial aid is to apply for financial aid."

FINANCIAL AID AT PRINCETON

The tabular analysis of aid applications for Princeton's Class of 1997 reveals that the largest category of those applying for aid had family incomes of under $35,000.

ADMITTED STUDENTS IN THE CLASS OF 1996
WHO APPLIED FOR FINANCIAL AID

Family Income Level (Dollars)	Applying for Aid	Percentage with Financial Need	Average Need of Those Eligible (Dollars)
$0–34,999	197	97	$22,000
35,000–44,999	91	99	19,400
45,000–54,999	83	99	18,100
55,000–64,999	102	96	16,900
65,000–74,999	90	93	14,800
75,000–84,999	98	94	11,500
85,000–94,999	81	76	9,900
95,000–104,999	66	76	8,500
105,000–114,999	56	68	8,300
115,000–124,999	41	37	9,500
Over $125,000	165	25	7,000

SOURCE: *Princeton University Admission Information 1992–93.*

Those qualifying for aid were well taken care of by Princeton, among the most expensive of all colleges. Its official brochure states: "The University believes that, by taking advantage of a variety of available resources, any admitted student will find a Princeton education within reach."

The booklet *How to Put Your Children through College without Going Broke,* by the Research Institute of America, says, "Even if you're not sure you'll qualify, you should apply" for financial aid.

What happens when a family decides it is ineligible for aid, and therefore does not apply for it? The cost of college becomes the chief consideration in deciding what college you want to attend. This is reversing the sound procedure of deciding what colleges you really like, and then taking the necessary, and sometimes difficult, steps to meet the bills.

So the rule is: if your family says that an expensive selective college is beyond their means, persuade them to apply for aid. The worst that can happen is that you will be turned down for a scholarship. Aid, remember, includes tuition payment plans, low interest loans, and possible job opportunities for you. Just because you are not considered eligible for aid does not mean that the college will not help at all.

Anthony M. Cummings, Princeton's director of financial aid, says, "Don't fail to apply for financial reasons. Don't opt yourself out of the applicant pool."

SCHOLARSHIPS BASED ON MERIT

Most selective college applicants will be familiar with Merit Scholarships, which are awarded to 16,000 students a year now on the basis of performance on the Preliminary Scholastic Aptitude Test, and National Merit Scholarship Awards (PSAT/NMSA). The criterion for the awards is scholastic excellence among competitors. Financial need is not a consideration. These awards are a testimony to the students' capacities and studiousness.

The NMSA, the most widely distributed merit scholarship, is modest by comparison with merit scholarships offered by a number of selective universities. For example, applicants to Johns Hopkins may compete for one of twenty Beneficial-Hodson Scholarships, which cover three fifths of the tuition. Winners must have outstanding scholastic and extracurricular records, but "financial status is not a factor in the decision process," according to a university brochure. A survey by the National Association of Independent Colleges and Universities showed that between 1981 and 1983 aid *not* based on need rose 154 percent to $341 million.

The old-fashioned tradition of helping deserving students by giving them scholarships has largely yielded to government provision of grants based solely on financial need. To be deserving no longer means to be among the top students, but simply to be a student who cannot meet all the costs of college. There is resistance by some donors to private colleges, who insist that scholarships be a reward for academic performance.

Cindy, among the top three Merit Scholarship finalists in her large urban New England high school, applied to several Ivy League colleges and was admitted to all of them, as well as to Vanderbilt. Her family can be described as middle income, and they felt that considerable scholarship money would be necessary to carry Cindy through four years of a selective college.

The Ivy colleges offered Cindy similar aid packages, for it is their custom not to compete for students by outbidding each other with larger scholarships. They confer in the spring to compare aid packages of students admitted to two or more of these colleges and adjust packages that are out of line. The scholarships were all about $5,000, give or take a few dollars.

Vanderbilt, however, offered her a $9,000 scholarship. In fact, this situation had been anticipated when Cindy first discussed admissions with us and mentioned the family concern about paying for college. She was told that the Ivies are generous, but that there are colleges and universities anxious to attract top applicants away from them. Among such fine well-endowed institutions

COLLEGES WITH MOST FRESHMAN MERIT SCHOLARS, 1992

This table shows, in rank order, the top colleges and universities attended by freshman Merit Scholars named in 1992.

The first column lists the total number of Merit Scholarship winners, while the second lists the number of those whose scholarships were paid for by the institution, and not by the National Merit Scholarship Corporation or other corporate sponsors.

	Number of Scholars	Number Sponsored by Institution
Harvard/Radcliffe	383	0
Rice University	227	135
University of Texas at Austin	212	165
Stanford University	152	0
Texas A&M University	140	108
Yale University	139	0
Princeton University	137	0
University of Florida	130	105
Massachusetts Institute of Technology	121	0
University of Oklahoma	118	92
Brigham Young University	110	79
Georgia Institute of Technology	104	76
Ohio State University	100	73
Carleton College	98	80
Northwestern University	97	57
University of Chicago	97	71
Duke University	87	0
University of California at Los Angeles	78	63
Vanderbilt University	73	45
University of Houston	68	54
Cornell University	62	0
George Washington University	58	45
Washington University	58	34
Harvey Mudd College	57	43
Johns Hopkins University	57	36
Michigan State University	56	45
Virginia Polytechnic Institute and State University	56	43
Baylor University	55	50
University of California at San Diego	55	38
Case Western Reserve University	54	37
Oberlin College	53	38
University of Southern California	52	34
Macalester College	50	42

University of California at Berkeley	50	0
Brown University	48	0
University of Michigan	46	0
Williams College	46	0
Bradley University	44	38
Tulane University	44	30
University of Kentucky	44	37
Trinity University	43	33
University of Arizona	43	35

SOURCE: National Merit Scholarship Corporation, as cited in *The Chronicle of Higher Education.*

A DISSENTING VIEW ON MERIT SCHOLARSHIPS

Twenty-five selective colleges have joined others in a statement critical of the practice of awarding merit scholarships without consideration of the student's ability to pay for the cost of college. In part the statement says:

"We oppose the concept of non-need (merit) scholarships. If we awarded financial aid on the basis of merit, virtually everyone enrolled in our institutions would receive financial assistance. Students are admitted to our institutions on merit; financial aid is given only to those with demonstrated need."

The selective colleges making this statement are Amherst, Barnard, Bates, Bowdoin, Brown, Bryn Mawr, Bucknell, Carnegie-Mellon, Clark, Colby, Colgate, Connecticut, Franklin and Marshall, Harvard/Radcliffe, Lafayette, Middlebury, Mount Holyoke, Smith, Trinity, Tufts, Union, University of Pennsylvania, Vassar, Wellesley, and Williams.

Vanderbilt is building a reputation for strong academic programs preparing half the student body for graduate school, which might have been difficult at an Ivy college where she would have had to work at a job to pay her bills.

Cindy's case is not unique. There are 5,000 National Merit Scholars each year with scholarships of up to $2,000. Most get further scholarship offers from outstanding institutions. Some Merit Scholars require no aid, yet their education is largely paid for by the colleges and the government.

The Ivies are not complacent about losing students like Cindy, and they do not lose all the National Merit Scholars. They are proud of the fact that they reserve their largest scholarships for those with the greatest need. Princeton's very detailed admissions brochure reports an example of an applicant from a lower-income family receiving a $21,030 scholarship. A $12,730 scholarship was part of the aid package of an applicant whose family is described as middle income.

Other selective colleges that give scholarships to the very brightest students regardless of need are the University of North Carolina, Virginia, Lehigh, Carnegie-Mellon, Johns Hopkins, Michigan, Duke, Emory, Washington University, Northwestern, and the University of Rochester. It is good fiscal strategy to apply to one or two of these colleges when money is a concern.

SCHOLARSHIPS BY THE HUNDREDS

It used to be said that there were so many scholarships that some went begging for lack of applications for them. This is no longer the case, thanks to computerization of scholarship data.

We have provided a bibliography of sources that will lead you to scholarships for which you may be eligible. What kinds of scholarships? Here is a random sample.

Education Communications Scholarship Program — Awards about 50 scholarships of $1,000 each to top students who submit an essay on the topic "What has been the most rewarding experience in your life? How has it influenced you, your goals, and aspirations?" Write to: Educational Communications Scholarship Foundation, 721 North McKinley Road, Lake Forest, IL 60045.

Jostens Foundation National Scholarship Program — Awards 200 scholarships of $500 to students who have excelled in school and community activities. Write to: Jostens Foundation National Scholarship Program, Citizens Scholarship Foundation of America, P.O. Box 297, St. Peter, MN 56082.

National Society of Professional Engineers — Engineering Scholarships — Awards about 150 scholarships of $1,000 and $2,000 to qualified applicants who write essays on engineering. You must score at least 600 on the SAT math test to be eligible. Write to: NSPE Educational Foundation, 2029 K Street, N.W., Washington, DC 20006.

Be sure to ask your counselor for the latest news about scholarships you may be eligible for in your region.

THE STATE UNIVERSITY OPTION

Our list of selective colleges includes seventeen state universities (Table 1, page 8). You may decide to apply to one or more of them for other than financial reasons, but certainly their lower costs make them attractive, too. For the very brightest students, some like Chapel Hill (North Carolina) and Berkeley (University of California) have financial aid packages that lure students from the private selectives. Chapel Hill's Morehead Scholars receive a four-year "free ride," the academic equivalent of athletic scholarships.

The University of Michigan had a 17 percent increase in out-of-state applications for the class of 1990, and most of them were from selective college candidates. Michigan's financial aid office says many of these applicants are applying for financial aid and believe that they will get a fine education at a great university for far less than it would cost at a private college, even if they do not receive aid.

If you are admitted to a selective state university, though, before you enroll at what you and your family consider an excellent "bargain," visit the campus if you have not already done so, and make sure that you really like the college and not just the money. Some students and their families ignore the state university option until the last minute, then apply "just in case." Then, almost on a whim, they get out the pocket calculator and on the basis of comparative figures decide that, after all, the state university is best. The first time the student sees the campus is registration day. The educational experience may be great, or the student after a year finds the institution unsuitable and transfers elsewhere. A campus visit is worth the travel expense.

GROWING NONRESIDENT TUITIONS IN STATE COLLEGES

In their quest for money, state legislatures are turning to out-of-state college students. The California state system is not just highly selective: for nonresidents the tuition is $10,185, almost four times what a resident pays. But little University of Vermont charges nonresidents the biggest tuition among public colleges, $14,750.

MILITARY OPTIONS

All the military academies are selective. Appointments, arranged through your Congressman or Senator, are given only to good students. Once you are accepted, though, your expenses for four years are covered. You, of course, agree to join one of the five military services — army, navy, marines, air force, coast guard, or merchant marine.

Selective colleges with ROTC programs admit applicants who then apply for admission into the Reserve Officer Training Corps on the various scholarship programs. Acceptance can mean an all-expense-paid college education in a civilian setting, and an agreement to serve a term as an officer in the armed services after graduation.

SAVING TIME AND MONEY

If you can complete your undergraduate education in three years instead of four, you save one year's college costs. This may be possible by taking in school several advanced placement courses that allow you to enter as a sophomore. If you can get credit for college courses taken elsewhere, doing this can shorten your time in college. The three-year program is not popular because part of the selective college experience is the four years you spend with your professors and classmates. This consideration helps explain why the year-abroad programs attract fewer students these days.

SPLITTING YOUR COLLEGES

Some students attend public institutions for a year or two years, then transfer to a private selective college, or to a selective state university that originally turned them down. This certainly saves tuition money, but we have to warn you that the most selective colleges take very few transfer students. Transferring into a college puts you at a social disadvantage, because friendships have developed and it is not easy to break into circles that are frequently rather closed. But if financing your education is a primary consideration, this is a strategy to consider seriously.

FEDERAL STUDENT AID PROGRAMS

There are seven federal student financial aid programs, which presently amount to over $16 billion a year.

Pell Grants. Named after their sponsor, Senator Claiborne Pell, the grants are distributed essentially on the basis of need to students from lower-income families in varying amounts.

Federal Family Educational Loans (FFEL), formerly called Stafford Loans. Low-interest need-based loans made through a bank, credit union, or savings and loan association ranging from $2,625 to $4,000. Non-subsidized loans for families without need are also available. Both programs have a cap of 9 percent on the interest charged.

Perkins Loans. Low-interest, need-based loans up to $9,000 over a four-year period.

Supplemental Educational Opportunity Grants (SEOG). Federal funds distributed by the colleges to a few students in relatively small amounts.

College Work Study (CWS). Work study funds are allotted to colleges, which then employ students directly on campus jobs in cafeterias, libraries, and other facilities for no more than 15 hours a week.

Perkins Loans. Banks administer these loans, which are interest-free until 6 months after graduation. Then interest is modest — 5 percent. Repayment is made in 5 to 10 years, depending on the amount.

Parent Loans for Undergraduate Study (PLUS). Largely for parents, these bank-administered loans are also available to graduate students and independent undergraduates. Interest at about 10 percent begins 60 days after the loan is issued, but repayment is deferred until after graduation.

Via the Federal Aid Form, you can request a Student Aid Report from the U.S. Department of Education, telling you whether you and your family qualify for one or more of these programs. For information on receiving this report, see the discussion of the FAFSA on page 220.

LOW-INTEREST LOANS

As part of their financial aid packages, many colleges make low-interest loans available to their students. In addition, there are several independent companies that provide various financing plans. As examples: The Tuition Plan, Concord, NH; Richard C. Knight Insurance Agency, Boston, MA; Academic Management Service, Pawtucket, RI. These are established firms that will prepay the college tuition and arrange a payment schedule to fit the family's financial circumstances. A life insurance rider is available to cover the full cost of the student's education in the event of the parents' death.

THE $100,000 QUESTION

There's no denying that metropolitan Boston is a selective college center — Harvard, MIT, BC, Tufts, Brandeis, Wellesley, BU, to name the obvious. But when the *Boston Globe Magazine* runs an article under the heading "As the cost of a college education hits six figures, students and their tapped-out parents wonder if they're getting their money's worth," you might think the writer, John Powers, is questioning the value of these institutions.

On the contrary, he found it is just such places that *are* worth the sacrifice, and points to the steady increase in applications for admission to these schools.

Powers quotes Marcie Schorr Hirsch, Executive Director for External Programs at Wellesley College: "A liberal arts degree is perceived as less valuable than it once was, but the reality is, it's more valuable." What makes it so is that at the right college you learn to think clearly and develop the ability to size up changing circumstances. This is what employers are looking for. Hence the student "flight to quality."

JOBS

Today, almost all students earn money in college and on vacation, whatever the family income. Students who earn money as part of their aid packages are assigned jobs by the college's financial aid officer. For those students who are not eligible for aid, there may be employment opportunities on campus. If not, a student employment agency lists jobs off campus with reliable employers. Job markets, of course, vary. A student not receiving aid who nonetheless is expected by the family to earn money while in college will do well to determine how much work will be available. Another point to remember is that colleges today recommend no more than fifteen hours' work on a job in a week. Longer hours result in a weaker academic performance, and that is counterproductive.

The colleges use the Preliminary Estimated Contribution as a *guideline* in working out their aid packages, hence the description as preliminary. In the end the colleges themselves administer student aid, so they are the final arbiters of what a student and family must pay. Colleges are therefore free to provide more aid or less than the Preliminary Estimated Contribution.

YOUR COUNSELOR CAN HELP

Your college counselor will probably not claim to be a financial expert, but counselors are a good source of information on the student aid distributed by your state, and on scholarships in your community or region. You should tell your counselor that you are filing for aid. Information you have on college costs, aid policies, scholarships, and the like will become a resource for others in your school.

WHEN AND HOW TO APPLY
FOR FINANCIAL AID

Ideally, planning college finances should begin in your junior year, or sooner. Some prudent people begin planning for college costs while their children are still in the cradle. The impact of inflation on family finances may call for a review of the family financial situation in your junior year. Starting early is necessary, particularly if you are going to need federal grants. Some federal grant money is in such demand that it runs out before all who need it can be satisfied.

It is essential to begin financial planning in your junior year if you are strong enough academically to consider applying for Early Decision in the fall of your senior year. Such candidates must file for financial aid by November 1, so that the financial aid packages can be announced when the students are admitted in December.

If you are not applying for Early Decision, you will file your Financial Aid Forms early in January. Colleges that require you to file an application for financial aid in addition to the Free Application for Federal Student Aid (FAFSA) and the FAF have varying deadlines that you should be aware of. Once enrolled, you will be asked to file a shorter form each year you renew your request for financial aid. Unless your academic record is unsatisfactory, you can expect to receive your aid package each year, with adjustments for inflation. (However, it is uncertain how much money the federal government will continue to allot to student aid.)

Be aware, if you aren't already, that family finances are more often than not a sensitive area among family members. In our experience, most parents prefer not to divulge the particulars of the income, taxes, and so forth to their children. Most of the necessary financial planning will fall to your parents (unless you are personally independent). They will rely on professional help from a financial advisor, be it a bank, a lawyer, or a tax accountant.

Financial planning is a sophisticated field, calling for a knowledge of investments, insurance, and taxes. But financial advisors may know less than you do about aid packages, tuition payment plans, and sources of scholarship funds. The information you have been gathering will be extremely helpful to your parents when they talk to bankers, brokers, or investment counselors about your college costs.

Every family has its own way of doing things. We believe that you should be as involved in planning your college finances as is consistent with family harmony. He who pays the piper calls the tune. Parents are used to being responsible for giving you the best, and they will tend to be senior partners in this expensive college venture of yours. But they will be grateful for your help.

You can provide them with a copy of *Meeting College Costs,* a pamphlet sent to your school by the College Scholarship Service. You should do this during your junior year if possible. It would be well to study it first, go over any questions with your counselor, and then hand it to your parents. This will put you in a position to discuss financial aid knowledgeably.

You can also contribute to the planning process by providing information about different college costs, tuition payment plans, and other information that may already be in your notebook from your campus visits, such as:

The costs of each college under consideration
Payment plans available at each college
What the College Scholarship Service requires on its Financial Aid Form
What kinds of aid packages are typically worked out at the colleges
What scholarships you might be able to get
What loan programs you should consider
What government programs may offer you

Make out a sheet like the following for your parents. (There's a copy in the Appendix.)

FINANCIAL WORKSHEET

Colleges	1. _____	2. _____	3. _____	4. _____
Tuition				
Room and board				
Fees				
Books and supplies				
Travel				
Personal expenses				
Total one-year budget				

KINDS OF AID AVAILABLE

Tuition payment plans Monthly payments				
4 years payable in advance				
Scholarships				
Student loans from the college				
Family loans from the college				
Government aid plans administered by the college				
Campus jobs available				
Hours per week				
Noncampus jobs available				
Summer job leads				
Financial counseling				

Be mindful of the need to file the FAFSA and possibly the FAF early in January of your senior year. If the college requires an application for financial aid in addition to the FAF, send for it. Most colleges publish thorough information on financial aid in their admissions brochures. A financial aid office works closely with admissions personnel at each college, and it is quite appropriate for parents to contact this office for information. The colleges understand that many applicants may never enroll, but they value goodwill and are prepared to discuss patiently the complexities of financial aid.

COMPLETING THE
FINANCIAL AID FORMS

In applying for financial aid from the federal government, you should file the Free Application for Federal Student Aid (FAFSA). These programs include Pell Grants, Federal Family Educational Loans, Supplemental Educational Opportunity Grants (SEOG), Perkins Loans, PLUS Loans, and College Work Study. Many individual colleges also require a filing of the College Board's Financial Aid Form (FAF) completed by your parents. However, for some state and private aid programs you will have to fill out other forms. To find out more about which form you should use, contact your high school counselor, the financial aid office at the colleges of interest to you, or your state scholarship agency.

Selective college applicants who take the tests of the American College Testing (ACT) program will probably use the Family Financial Statement, ACT's financial-need-analysis form, instead of the College Board's FAF. Most colleges accept either form. Remember that in either case you may also have to fill out an application for financial aid on the colleges' own forms.

Careful reading of *Meeting College Costs* will answer many questions about financial aid, but the estimated parent's contribution figures could lead to the erroneous conclusion that families with assets of more than $10,000 and income of more than $90,000 are disqualified for financial aid. This is not necessarily so. We strongly urge no family to draw conclusions about aid eligibility until they have applied for aid.

While there is a fee for each college when filing the FAF, an applicant can request a fee waiver based on need. There is no fee for filing the FAFSA.

The FAFSA and Financial Aid Forms call for information on your parents' finances, such as information from last year's Internal Revenue Service tax return filed by your parents. Because, as we have said, of the sensitive nature of family finances, we strongly advise you *not* to ask your parents about their finances! Instead, let your parents fill in the financial data after you have answered all the questions that pertain to you. You will almost certainly avoid a raw nerve if you hand your parents the forms with the assurance "I'll fill in my part and sign the form. You can fill in your part — that's your business." Your parents can do so and mail in the form. If they choose to share financial information with you, nothing has been lost. Our experience is that the financial aid forms infuriate many parents with their bureaucratic insensitivity.

YOU CAN MAKE ENDS MEET

In concluding this discussion of a sensitive issue, the high cost of college and how to pay for it, we assure you that if you concentrate on doing what you must do to be admitted to a selective college, you will find the necessary money. No selective college wants to lose an applicant because of insufficient funds, and it will go out of its way to work with you and your parents on a reasonable aid package.

Financial aid can influence your choice of college. But you may well wish to persuade your family that it means more to you to attend Columbia than anywhere else that may cost them less; they may be willing to take out a second mortgage and sacrifice several thousand dollars in scholarship money. There are many good reasons to enroll where the out-of-pocket family cost is greater than it is at other colleges. If the most selective colleges were not considered premium institutions, why would anyone be willing to spend what they cost?

Every college will give you a hearing if you are dissatisfied with its offer. You may not get a bigger scholarship, but the loan and job components of your package may be improved. We know this from years of observation. So never say die where money for college is concerned. Plan ahead and ask the selective colleges how to make ends meet. You will be pleasantly surprised by the positive answers you will get.

Step Ten Checklist

1. Plan your college finances as a junior partner with your parents. Start by bringing home *Meeting College Costs* in your junior year, if possible.

2. From the colleges, obtain information about their costs and financial aid policies.

3. Look into scholarship opportunities for top students at well-endowed colleges and at state universities. Use your school's reference sources for lists of scholarships.

4. Complete and sign your part of the financial aid form, then let your parents complete theirs and mail it to the College Scholarship Service early in January of your senior year. Remember that you may have to fill out an application for financial aid on the colleges' own forms as well.

5. Do not fail to apply if you need aid; do not opt out of the admissions pool. There is no penalty if colleges determine you do not meet aid criteria, and there are other loans and jobs that can help.

6. Never give up on selective colleges because of cost. If you are admitted to a selective college, ways can be found to fund your higher education.

STEP ELEVEN

Market Your Strengths

HOW ONE STUDENT MARKETED HIS STRENGTHS

*D*avid, a senior in a rigorous Pennsylvania private school, seemed to be an average student who was overestimating his possibilities of being admitted to a Very Demanding selective college. Nonetheless, he was eventually admitted to two of them, because he discovered his strengths and successfully marketed them at colleges seeking just his kind of student. David was fortunate in having a college advisor who helped to bring together the marketing ingredients: the product (applicant) and the buyer (college).

David's combined SAT I scores of 1170 and English Subject Test of 490 were unexceptional, but he had scored 620 on his American History Subject Test and 4 out of 5 on his Advanced Placement test in the same subject. His grade point average was B−. Not engaged in extracurricular activities, he was active in a church program for the homeless.

In his senior year David got permission not to take a fourth year of French, in which his work was mediocre, and to take a beginning course in Greek, with the objective of eventually reading Plato in the original when he majored in philosophy in college. Unfortunately, he did no better in Greek than he had done in French.

In discussing his difficulty with this course, he told his advisor for the first time that he had been reading philosophy on his own. This explained the observation of his teachers that David had an inquiring mind, but he often went off on a tangent in class discussions by introducing irrelevant speculation about the existence of God, the problem of evil, and the limits of knowledge. Now in his senior year he was taking his first philosophy course, ethics, and his teacher was impressed by the breadth of David's knowledge, which ranged from Plato to Jean-Paul Sartre. He would do very well in this course. The Greek, though, was giving him trouble. He was a C Greek student, his teacher said.

The first bit of advice David received from his advisor was not to worry about his course in Greek. Admissions officers are aware that seniors often do poorly in a class of freshmen, and a C would not make that much difference if, instead of dwelling on a weakness he was not likely to overcome, he paid more attention to his strengths. Once they were identified, he would be able to market them at colleges looking for his kind of student.

What were his strengths? David ranked just below the middle of his class, and his SAT scores were both 100 points below the class median. Yet his teachers maintained that David had considerable academic promise. He had earned A's in computer science and in reading. His one Subject Test score of 620 was a clear signal that David could do strong academic work under the right circumstances. He had done well enough, too, in an Advanced Placement history exam without having taken an AP course.

David's advisor recognized from experience what David himself was unable to perceive: that his interest in philosophy was his chief strength. For his wide reading, however, he had received no recognition, no grades to give him confidence in his interest. Like many adolescents, he had not yet found his way. It was crucial, therefore, that he begin to think of himself as an academic winner. Pointing to his A's and his Subject Test score of 620, his advisor said to David, "You have a chance to show some excellent colleges that you are capable of improving your grades this first term of senior year." David responded positively.

By mid-term he had an A+ in a psychology course, three B's, and a C in Greek. Meanwhile, in addition to other colleges, David began to consider seriously two that his advisor recommended for their philosophy departments: Johns Hopkins and Boston College (David is a Catholic). During the fall he visited both places and conferred with members of their philosophy departments. He also spent time with philosophy majors on both campuses, some of whom seemed impressed by how much he already knew about philosophy.

Admissions offices in both colleges were rather neutral about his prospects for admission. They each wondered about his academic drive and commitment. He would have to show them what he could do during his senior year. During the winter, David kept in touch with philosophy faculty members at both places, sending them papers in which he had received A's in English, psychology, and philosophy.

His application essay was devoted to a cogent and passionate statement about the importance of philosophy today, all the more convincing because he related it to his experience at church helping homeless men.

He wrote to each admissions office that in June he would retake the English Subject Test and take the Subject Test in Literature. Although these scores were reported after he was admitted to both colleges, the fact that he was stretching, challenging himself, went into his folders. Scores of 600 on these two tests justified all the expectations of his advisor.

David took care to get teacher recommendations to strengthen his case: "He is as familiar with prominent writers in philosophy as any student I know." "Tremendous potential for growth." "David is going to blossom in college as he more carefully defines his focus of study." Such ringing accolades contrasted with David's far from brilliant four-year record. What they said was that David had come alive in his senior year, and that he would be an unusual philosophy major. Philosophy does not attract many students as a major, despite the excellence of the philosophy departments at Johns Hopkins and Boston College.

Academic departments are under constant pressure to justify the cost of paying outstanding professors to teach a handful of students, and furthermore, when the number of majors in a department drops too low, faculty members start looking around for opportunities to teach elsewhere. Conversely, when departments can show that they are attracting good students like David, the word gets around, and it becomes easier to hold the faculty and to attract the best of the new group of professors.

So by identifying his academic strengths, with his advisor's help, David was able to market them at colleges that, he was told, would probably be impressed. His "marketing team" consisted of himself, his advisor, and his teachers. Every applicant who is admitted to a selective college markets his or her strengths this way, probably without realizing it. In this step we want you to become a conscious marketer of your strengths.

WHY MARKETING?

We consider self-marketing the great neglected step in the admissions process. Today the rising numbers of applicants veil the individual, who is liable to fall into a classification by merit and achievement and become faceless. What does an overburdened admissions committee do when forced to make choices among candidates whose folders would be virtually indistinguishable if the names were blanked out?

Given several thousand such folders, of which only one third or one half of the candidates can be admitted because of the absolute limit on freshman spaces, a committee is bound to make some decisions that are purely arbitrary. Jack is accepted and Jill is not, despite the fact that each is perfectly capable of doing the academic work and contributing to the vitality of campus life. Marketing yourself therefore becomes essential to overcome this flip-of-a-coin kind of decision making that occurs at most selective colleges. Your objective is to force a committee to choose you because they really are aware of your individuality and what a difference it can make to the next freshman class. Otherwise, the committee is just as liable to choose someone else who is like you. There was no way of mistaking David for some other applicant.

SUGGESTIONS FROM ADMISSIONS DEANS

Be yourself through the process. Don't put on a persona that is not your own.

Susan Murphy, *Dean of Admissions and Financial Aid,*
CORNELL UNIVERSITY

Do not make your application look like it was filled out on top of the mailbox!

William Peck, *Director of Admissions,*
CONNECTICUT COLLEGE

Tell about all your personal credentials. Just being number one in the class is not going to make your application successful.

Herb Davis, *Director of Admissions,*
UNIVERSITY OF NORTH CAROLINA

Students should do their best to let the admissions office know what is important to and about them, and not be shy about their accomplishments. It is hard to capture yourself on pieces of paper but it is important to try because that is all the admissions office has to look at.

Jennifer Rickard, *Associate Dean of Admissions,*
SWARTHMORE COLLEGE

It is important to remember that admissions decisions are not made by gatekeeping computers but by humans who exercise a considerable amount of human judgment. Tell us, therefore, all that you can about yourself.

Richard Nesbitt, *Associate Director of Admissions,*
WILLIAMS COLLEGE

Recommendations can help a student when they shed light on a special quality, experience, or talent, and when they provide strong evidence of a student's enthusiasm for learning or distinguished extracurricular involvement.

John Anderson, *Dean of Admissions,*
KENYON COLLEGE

WHEN TO MARKET YOUR STRENGTHS

Your marketing efforts begin when you have a sure sense of your strengths and know the colleges that are most likely to appreciate them. This usually occurs near the end of the admissions process, when you file your application, and it continues right up to the time when admissions committees begin their final decision sessions — December for Early Decision applicants, January to February for other applicants.

Many applicants do not take advantage of selective colleges' open folder policies: that is, admissions offices are willing to continue to examine the folders of strong candidates right up to the time when final admissions are determined. It is, of course, possible to be rejected early in the process without knowing it. Marketing efforts cannot reverse 99 percent of such decisions. But because you are applying to several colleges of varying competitiveness, you must expect to lose some and win some. We know that marketing your strengths will vastly improve your winning chances.

WHAT DOES MARKETING INVOLVE?

We use this commercial word *marketing* because selective colleges have become in a sense a marketplace dominated by the forces of supply and demand. In the old-fashioned markets that still exist at county fairs and in European cities, the sellers spend much of their time proclaiming the virtues of their wares, and they are not always scrupulous in their claims. In the genteel world of college admissions there is no place for huckstering, but an admissions committee, laden with folders, is wide open to your efforts to make your folder one that has to be flagged and labeled "Admit."

Marketing in college admissions comes down to three things:

- Assessing your strengths
- Assessing the colleges that want students with your strengths
- Communicating these strengths to the colleges

First David, with the help of a counselor, learned to fix his attention on his consuming passion. This overcame the lack of academic self-confidence that had developed from his habit of doing his best only in those subjects that deeply interested him. His second step was to commit himself to a college major, philosophy, and then acquaint himself with colleges known to be looking for philosophy majors. Finally, he had to make it clear to the colleges that he was maturing rapidly and would make an excellent student.

Marketing yourself will take some thought, and it will not bring admission letters from every college. David was turned down by Haverford, University of Pennsylvania, and Penn State, where the competition was tougher. As another example, take Mary Lou, captain of her Boston high school tennis team, winner of her club tournament, and ranked among the top players under eighteen in her region. She believed she could get into the University of North Carolina on the strength of her tennis, despite a mediocre academic record and 1000 combined SAT scores, and she applied for Early Decision. The tennis coach said she was as good as in. But no, Mary Lou was not admitted by Early Decision, and was not even deferred. She was told that she had been rejected.

Marketing herself with the tennis coach was a waste of time. She was not aware that out-of-state applicants must score at least 1200 on their SAT to be admitted. The exception would be some fabulous athlete, musician, writer, etcetera. Mary Lou is a good tennis player, but she misjudged her strength;

had she been state champion, North Carolina might well have admitted her. She might have improved her chances by applying to several selective colleges that have less competitive athletic programs, where her tennis would have outweighed her academic record.

MAKE A MARKETING PLAN

The three marketing steps — assessing your strengths, identifying the colleges that will appreciate your strengths, and communicating your strengths — take time and thoughtfulness. The more colleges you apply to, the more effort you must make. Early Decision candidates should have their marketing plans ready by September. So let's review what is involved.

To help you market your strengths, we have drawn up this Strengths Assessment form, a copy of which appears in the Appendix.

ASSESSING YOUR STRENGTHS

Our form suggests how you might go about reassessing your strengths in the light of all you now know about yourself from earlier introspection begun in Step Two. You have come to a critical moment when doubts must be put aside and weaknesses ignored. Whatever about you is strong must become stronger during your senior year. You are putting your best foot forward for all the world to see.

In using the form, keep your observations to yourself until you have clearly identified your strengths. Then discuss them with your counselor, teachers, and others to confirm your own judgment. No one's judgment is perfect, as we saw in the case of Mary Lou, the tennis player. We are all guided by our wishes, and sometimes they are fanciful. It is wise to be skeptical of praise, because your elders have their wishes, too: they wish for your success, and they want to encourage you.

But after discounting your own tendency to overestimate your strengths and your teachers' possible flattery, you must decide how you are going to help admissions committees bring a blurred picture into focus. You want those committees to see you clearly, while other candidates by contrast are harder to make out.

IDENTIFYING THE COLLEGES

While getting to know the colleges, you will have picked up many hints about their programs, their departments, their facilities, and you may in your pie-charting have spotted a need you think you might fill at one place or another. You know that Minnesota is interested in your hockey ability or Haverford

MY ADMISSIONS STRENGTHS ASSESSMENT

(This form is obviously not exhaustive. Use it creatively to sketch a logical college and postcollege plan, substituting your own ideas where appropriate.)

STRENGTHS

Academic
Grades _____
Class rank _____
Test scores _____
Honors _____
Special projects _____
Extra credits _____
Outside courses _____
Related work experience _____

Nonacademic
Sport _____
Sport _____
Letters _____

ACTIVITIES

School activities
School government _____
Class officer _____
Publications _____
Music _____
Drama _____
Clubs _____
Other _____

Other activities
Community _____
Camp _____
Work _____

OTHER ADVANTAGES

Strengths of Character
Independence _____
Reliability _____
Courage _____
Persistence _____
Patience _____
Tolerance _____

Skills/Talents
1. _____
2. _____
3. _____

COLLEGES LOOKING FOR MY STRENGTHS

College   Strength
_____   _____
_____   _____
_____   _____

IN COLLEGE

Possible majors   _____   _____   _____
Courses to take   _____   _____   _____
Grades expected A _____   B _____   C _____

Honors I seek
Phi Beta Kappa _____ Honors _____ High Honors _____
Highest Honors _____

AFTER COLLEGE

Possible graduate work in _____ _____ _____
Possible job

Family business _____	Education _____
Own venture _____	Government _____
Sales _____	Media _____
Corporate management _____	Arts _____

MARKETING STRATEGY

Communicate strengths to

Admissions committee _____
Faculty members _____
Administration _____
Coaches _____
Alumni _____

By means of

Extra essays _____
Exhibits: tapes, photos, drawings, crafts, newspaper clippings _____

Added recommendations: employer, minister _____
Visits or phone calls to people on campus _____

in your soccer. When you visited the University of Pennsylvania, you noted that its strong anthropology department is looking for more students who want to major in that subject. You should apply to the University of Pennsylvania if you like it; an expressed interest in anthropology would help you be admitted.

Here is a short list of new programs or facilities you should be aware of. If you have strengths that match any of them, you have a basis for marketing these strengths at those colleges.

Dartmouth is looking for women who wish to become scientists.
Princeton's Philosophy Department has a new building.
UCLA's Communications Department would like more students.
Harvard/Radcliffe would be interested in a qualified student who wants
    to major in Polish literature.
Duke has new computer science facilities.
Boston University is expanding its engineering program.
Georgetown welcomes candidates with second-language fluency.
University of Pennsylvania is enthusiastic about good lacrosse players.

Brown wants more students committed to social service careers.

Johns Hopkins, as noted, welcomes good philosophy students.

Stanford needs rowers.

Davidson's Center for Special Studies is a natural for top students wanting combined majors or independent studies.

Notre Dame has a new chemical research laboratory.

Barnard's Program in the Arts should be considered by women interested in the dance, music, the theater, visual arts, or writing.

Claremont McKenna College's five-year management-engineering program welcomes applicants who can do the work.

George Washington University seeks students for its unique spring-semester program in La Rochelle, France, for students specializing in international affairs or international business. All courses are taught in French.

Bates has a new major in biochemistry.

You should query your counselor and your teachers for ideas about college programs suited to your capabilities. It is quite possible that, late in the admissions process, you may discover a college you have not visited. The thing to do is to telephone the department or the coach you think might particularly appreciate your strengths. You will save yourself a lot of trouble by getting information directly from those who know what they are looking for. If you are encouraged to apply, phone the admissions office and tell them about yourself. You will be told either that you ought to apply or that the competition is too stiff. Nothing is lost by this but the cost of phoning.

COMMUNICATING YOUR STRENGTHS BY DOCUMENTATION

Documentation is the key to communicating your strengths to the colleges. It may be paradoxical that you want to be more than a set of photostats in your folder, that you want to bring all that paper in your folder to life, but you have to realize that an admissions committee has to work with pieces of paper, photos, tapes, drawings, or other palpable evidence of who you are and what you can do. When push comes to shove — and it does in committees as members compete among one another for admitting one candidate or another — whoever is in your corner will glance at documentation in your folder. It may be simply a penciled memo that you have brought your grades up during the last marking period, or it may be a tape of a speech you have made for the UN program in your community. It could be a reminder that you sent some plastic sculpture that is over in the art department being admired by the faculty.

If more candidates realized the importance of documentation, there would be less effort spent on ineffective efforts to capture admissions attention. We know of no way to gain admission to a good college by creating a sensation — such as sending an oversized Christmas card to Santa, the admissions director, saying you want to be admitted for Christmas. By "marketing" we do not mean adopting the creative tactics of advertising or publicity. Admissions officers are far from stuffy, but they universally believe flamboyance should be saved for cheering their athletic teams. Showoff applicants usually do not make it past the first cut.

Documentation will be supplemental evidence supporting your claim as a more deserving candidate than others like you. For example, Bernard's résumé of his soccer expertise (see accompanying box) provides all the relevant information a college soccer coach could ask for. With it was attached a packet of newspaper clippings reporting on Bernard's playing; these provide objective appraisal that back up what his coach says.

Now, we ask you, would not this small bit of documentation be more powerful as a persuader than a brief summary standing alone on the application form? You will note that Bernard did not confine his report to soccer, but mentioned his academic strength and other interests. This scholar-athlete was admitted to Dartmouth by Early Decision.

This résumé was attached to Bernard's application, and he also kept the Dartmouth coach informed of his playing during the fall, sending an occasional clipping, with a copy to the admissions office. By decision time this candidate was better known to Dartmouth than most of his competition.

WHY BE BASHFUL?

In telling this success story to other applicants, we frequently hear "I'm just not that pushy. I don't believe in bragging." Neither do we believe in bragging. Marketing your strengths is not bragging; it is communicating. Colleges want to know who you are. They give you an opportunity to reveal yourself on your application through answers to questions and in the personal essay, and most students take advantage of this opportunity, which they do not look on as bragging. But they stop there, despite the fact that colleges beg them to tell them anything about themselves they ought to know in considering these students' candidacies. Remember the words of a well-known executive placement expert: the secret of success is controlled aggression. Adding documents to your file is a form of aggressiveness, to be sure, but selective colleges are filled with aggressive undergraduates.

Another kind of résumé is that of Katerina (see page 233). It helped her get into Williams from a Maryland high school. A B+ student with a combined SAT score of 1200, she also was a varsity swimmer. It was certainly helpful to be the daughter of an alumnus, but Katerina was taking no chances. She made up this résumé because on her Williams application there was only room to list piano, voice, and chorus, plus her church choir. The résumé is impressive without being overstated.

BERNARD'S SOCCER RÉSUMÉ

Midfielder
Lincoln Soccer Association
Lincoln, Connecticut

School Team	Lincoln High School, Lincoln, Connecticut 2-year Varsity Starter — 34 consecutive games Assist — Leader (12) Junior Year (1991) All County 1st Team 1984 All-State — Honorable Mention 1991 Elected Captain for 1992 season Varsity Coach: Steve Walzer
Club Team	LSA Select Team 6 years Teams made it to State Finals 5 times 1990 — Selected to participate in exchange program with West German team 1990–92 — Assistant Coach for 1990 Select Team 1989 — Scholarship Award for Service to Soccer Community (Coach, Referee, Player)
Select Teams	1991 — Ct. 16 1/2 — Under Select Attended Region I Tourney where started all 7 games 1992 — Ct. 16 1/1 — Under Select Region I Tourney — Captain, Starting Center Midfielder
Self-Assessment	Strengths: Intensity, vision Weaknesses: Dribbling
Academics	1290 SAT Combined Score 1st Decile Many Honors Classes
Other Interests	All-State and Captain of Lincoln High School Ski Team Writer for school newspaper
Coach's Comments	"Certainly he has one of the highest work rates of anyone in the county. He was consistently solid, both offensively and defensively all year long." (Steve Walzer, Lincoln High)
Personal Data	Height: 5'7" Weight: 135 lbs.

KATERINA'S MUSIC-RELATED EXPERIENCE

TRAINING

Voice Lessons (alto)	1991–92
Piano Lessons	
Popular/Jazz/Classical	1986–91
Classical	1981–86
Dance	
Jazz — Langton Dance Company	1988–89
General — Thomas Turner Dance Class	1985–87

SCHOOL SINGING GROUPS

Chamber Chorus (High School)	1990–92
Group of 16; perform sacred choral works, mostly a cappella, at school and away	
Festival Chorus	1989–92
Group of 60; perform sacred and secular choral music, at school and away	
Special Chorus (Junior High)	1988–89
Group of 25; perform sacred/contemporary music at school and around state	
1st Prize: Regional Competition	

MUSICAL STAGE PRODUCTIONS

Trial by Jury (High School)	October, 1990
You're a Good Man, Charlie Brown (Jr. High)	May, 1989
Best of Broadway (Langton Dance Company)	April, 1989

MUSIC IN THE COMMUNITY

St. Luke's Church	Summers 1991–92
Musical accompanist for Sunday School	1988–89
Church Choir (Soloist: Christmas/Easter services)	1981–87
Willow Wood Nursing Home	1990–91
Entertain groups (piano); accompany visiting singing groups	1988–90

OBJECTIVE

I plan to pursue the study of music in college, possibly as a major, and hopefully to be active in extracurricular activities that are music-related. I expect that music will be a lifelong avocation, but not a career.

REPORT NEW DEVELOPMENTS

After you send in your applications, keep the colleges informed about new successes: high marks, a research paper that is praised, chairmanship of a committee, an award, an athletic first. Make sure you do not repeat what is already in your folder, and document it — photocopy your report card if it is exceptional, photocopy an award, a news clipping. On page 235 you will see a reading list sent to colleges in February by Deborah, whom Stanford subsequently admitted. She is an English major and plans to get her Ph.D. and teach on a college faculty.

Whatever the colleges do not know about you constitutes a new development, and this can include personal information about your health or your family. One candidate reported that the remarriage of her separated parents had picked up her spirits and encouraged her to improve her grades. SAT I and Subject Test scores will be sent to the colleges, but if the results show a significant improvement, your counselor ought to call this to the attention of the colleges.

GET THAT EXTRA RECOMMENDATION

Your teachers' recommendations will probably be strong, if you have chosen the right teachers. Thousands of applicants get wonderful recommendations from their teachers. When you get an extra recommendation, however, you distance yourself from the pack. Read Beth Ann's supplementary recommendation from her college advisor. You will see that it is not boilerplate, or cliché-ridden, but thoughtful and convincing. A B student in a strong private day school near Philadelphia, Beth Ann was rejected by several Ivies despite her college varsity potential in three sports, but she was wait-listed by Duke, Middlebury, and Carleton, and accepted by Bowdoin. She held out until admitted by Duke for the second term in January. This is not a bad admissions record for an average student. The extra recommendation got her that extra consideration from four selective colleges.

CRITICIZE YOUR EXHIBITS

The tape recorder is a tempting appliance. Why not send in a tape of some music you played or composed, or your valedictorian speech? Because if it is not deemed good, it may sink you! Tapes or works of art sent in by candidates are usually assessed by faculty members, unless an admissions officer happens to be an expert in the subject. Often faculty judgments are harsh and include remarks like "Would not want this student in my courses."

You must therefore never send exhibits of any kind to any college without being assured by outside experts that they have the merit you think they have.

DEBORAH'S READING LIST

REQUIRED

Samuel Beckett, *Waiting for Godot*

Paddy Chayefsky, *Television Plays (Holiday Song, Printer's Measure, The Big Deal, Marty, The Mother, The Bachelor Party)*

Anton Chekhov, *The Cherry Orchard, The Three Sisters*

F. Scott Fitzgerald, *The Great Gatsby*

Frances Fitzgerald, *Fire in the Lake*

Nathaniel Hawthorne, *The Scarlet Letter*

Homer, *Iliad, Odyssey*

Henrik Ibsen, *Ghosts, A Doll's House, An Enemy of the People*

Henry James, *Washington Square*

Stanley Karnow, *Vietnam: A History*

Henry Kissinger, *Years of Upheaval*

Niccolò Machiavelli, *The Prince*

Arthur Miller, *Death of a Salesman, The Crucible*

Eugene O'Neill, *The Iceman Cometh, Long Day's Journey into Night*

Jean-Paul Sartre, *No Exit, The Flies*

Bernard Shaw, *Heartbreak House, Saint Joan*

William Shakespeare, *Coriolanus, Antony and Cleopatra, Hamlet, The Tempest, The Merchant of Venice, Richard II, Henry IV, Part I, King Lear, Sonnets*

Sophocles, *Oedipus Rex, Oedipus at Colonus, Antigone*

August Strindberg, *Miss Julie*

Mark Twain, *The Adventures of Huckleberry Finn*

John Webster, *The Duchess of Malfi*

Oscar Wilde, *The Importance of Being Earnest*

OUTSIDE

Hermann Hesse, *Siddhartha*

Aldous Huxley, *Ape and Essence*

John Irving, *The Cider House Rules*

James Joyce, *Portrait of the Artist as a Young Man*

Jean-Paul Sartre, *Huis Clos (No Exit)* (in French)

Erich Segal, *The Class*

Kurt Vonnegut, Jr., *Breakfast of Champions, The Sirens of Titan, Slaughterhouse-Five, Welcome to the Monkey House, Cat's Cradle*

Alice Walker, *The Color Purple*

Although I enjoyed all of the books listed, *Waiting for Godot, Long Day's Journey into Night, No Exit, King Lear, The Color Purple,* and *Portrait of the Artist as a Young Man* were among my favorites.

BETH ANN'S EXTRA RECOMMENDATION

Bright, motivated, cultured and well-traveled, Beth Ann is an attractive girl — charming and coltish. She is involved in studies, three varsity sports, chorus, yearbook, friends, and succeeding in all endeavors. Additionally she is conversationally fluent in French and German, having lived abroad in 8th grade where she attended a French-speaking Swiss Gymnasium.

Academically, Beth Ann's achievement record and demanding curriculum place her in the top quarter of a competitive class of 80 students, all of whom will attend selective colleges or universities. She is taking an academic overload this year (four courses are required) including English, American History and French V, which are considered "advanced courses" — the equivalent of first year college courses at most schools. Because of her year away, she missed some of our sequential material. On her return, by dint of summer tutoring she skipped Algebra I entirely and went directly into geometry in 9th grade. She also omitted Latin III (having tutored herself during the summer) in order to catch up to her classmates; her "B" in Latin IV is thus a real tribute to her effort, energy and interest. Occasionally Beth Ann feels some academic pressure, but then, who doesn't around here? By and large, she copes well.

Beth Ann's teachers say of her: "The quality of Beth Ann's writing improved during the course. Her final essay was moving and well written. Her other English essays and comments in class reflected her enthusiasm and the accuracy of her reading;" "Beth Ann is a pleasure to have in math class because she is always so involved and focused on what is going on. She should be very proud of her work this year;" "Beth Ann has performed impressively this year in history. Her essays have been well informed, well organized and well written. She puts diverse information together well and differentiates well between the relevant and the trivial."

An excellent athlete, Beth Ann is a starter on our hockey team and a varsity squash and lacrosse player also.

Beth Ann has the brains, the training and the determination to be successful at Duke. She's been a high achiever here and a contributing member of the school community; she's socially adept and appealing, and she comes from a sophisticated and intellectual family. Thus this recommendation gets our very warm support.

Agnes Murphy
College Advisor

You must seek the opinion of someone who does not know you. If you have won a local photography contest, show your work to a professional outside the community. We have seen expensively blown up color photos shot abroad that almost anyone could tell were not quite in focus. But because a local bank allowed them to be displayed in its window for two weeks, the applicant thought the pictures would go over big with her colleges. In fact, photography was not the applicant's strength, and she was persuaded by her advisor to send the colleges articles she had written about England for her local weekly newspaper.

Your short story in the school literary magazine will be sent to the English department for an opinion. At Yale the judgments of creative writing can be very severe. When it comes to sending in things of value, such as an oil painting, it is better to send a photograph of it. Colleges cannot be responsible for your valuables. You should not expect them to take the trouble to return anything sent by you, even if you supply the postage.

TALKING TO ALUMNI

During the winter the alumni schools committees often interview candidates at the request of the admissions offices. If you are contacted by a college alumnus, by all means meet and talk to the person. As we have discussed in Step Seven, the interview is not important in a college's admissions decision. An interview with an alumnus will never have the effect of reversing a positive decision of an admissions officer; as we said, you cannot blow an interview. But an alumnus in your corner is helpful. Usually, alumni reports confirm the judgments of the professionals of the college. A highly enthusiastic report may turn a skeptical reader of your folder into a believer. One major role of the local interviewer is to be aware of high school students in his home area who have received publicity for success in athletics, the arts, or town leadership. He can substantiate for the admissions committee the applicant's achievements.

IF YOU KNOW A TRUSTEE

Not infrequently a parent will say, "George So-and-So has been a trustee of Middlebury for years, and he's a very dear friend." There follows a proposal to get in touch with George right away. George may well be amenable to such an approach and will actually write a glowing letter about a candidate he has known since birth. But, perusing it, the admissions committee finds no additional information that can help them decide the candidate's admission fate. Warmth and friendship are insufficient documentation, no matter who makes the recommendation. The question "Is this candidate a better candidate than dozens of others?" remains unanswered.

When George's letter does not make the difference and the candidate is rejected, a dear friendship may cool. Our advice is the following: never ask anyone of importance in the college — trustee, donor, diligent fund raiser, or administrator — to write a recommendation without doing two essential things: giving the person a copy of your application and arranging for you to talk to that person.

Busy people who may have known you for years do not know the details of your school career. They will, however, usually take the time to look over your application. If they do not feel that they can honestly recommend you, they will say so, and the friendship remains intact in the long run. And if they do recommend you, after an interview, their recommendation will be very persuasive. No admissions committee wants to get a letter from someone in the university asking why a recommended applicant was rejected, while another deemed less attractive was admitted.

WHEN DEFERRED
ON EARLY DECISION

Marketing is particularly necessary for those whose Early Decision applications are deferred for review in the winter. Some deferred applicants have an edge, but many are at risk. A letter of deferral should be taken as a notice to get cracking, for you must now file a number of applications with other colleges, and the college that deferred you must be treated as if you had never applied there. Do not be discouraged. Get your documentation together and send the original college something new while building a stronger academic record for the winter school term.

KEEPING IN TOUCH

You file your application in January and you are notified by the colleges on April 15 that you are admitted or not admitted. More than three months of waiting. It seems an eternity. Meantime, those who have been admitted on Early Decision are keeping it no secret. This can make you envious, and you may ask, what if no college wants me? What will my financial aid package be?

There are two things for you still to do. One is to continue to push yourself academically and nonacademically, to keep on training for college, where even more will be demanded of you. The second is to keep in touch with the colleges. If you are applying to six colleges, you can phone someone at each of them every week — a faculty member, a coach, someone in admissions, the financial aid office, a dean of students, undergraduates you met. Tell them something new about yourself and be bold enough to ask how your chances for admission look. What you will get from such a conversation will be late information and perhaps encouragement. Some colleges issue notices of where you stand; they say you probably will be admitted, or probably you will not be admitted.

This information will probably come to you through coaches and faculty members rather than from admissions officers. Admissions committees theoretically cannot announce to anyone before April 1 that he or she is admitted, because the majority of selective colleges have agreed to adhere to a single announcement date. But they can give you a strong hint, usually through your counselor. If you are going to be admitted, they want you to accept their invitation to enroll. These unofficial hints tend to condition a candidate to a favorable response when the official notice of admission arrives in the mail.

Keeping in touch this way, you are marketing yourself by showing interest. Obviously, you will not be admitted to any college just because you like it. But by Step Eleven you should know the colleges that are within your range — a few may be off target, but not all. And those you have properly targeted will appreciate your enthusiasm for their institution. Would you believe that all those formidable deans and professors you are in awe of have their anxieties too? They love their colleges, for the most part, and they want all you applicants to love them, too.

Funny things happen when you keep in touch. A college that may be last on your list will grow in your affection because of a conversation you have with a professor on the telephone. You may be advised to read an article on the national budget because of your interest in economics, and suddenly you have established a relationship that you want to continue. An undergraduate will say, "If you come here, we want you in our fraternity."

In this kind of marketing by telephone or mail or even by an informal visit to a coach, faculty member, head of an activity you communicated with earlier, if the college is near enough, you continue to present a person to the college; the bureaucratic impersonality of applications and folders is eroded by contact.

APRIL 15, THE MOVEABLE ADMISSIONS DECISION DATE

In the early nineties, the April decision announcement date for selective colleges became unofficially ignored by some of them. Many admission announcements now are leaked to high schools late in March. This is to help the colleges find out who will accept their decisions. By letting counselors know who is going to be accepted, they can get feedback from counselors who query the students. Jumping the decision date has also been used as a psychological ploy to attract appreciative candidates. This helps the colleges determine the size of their wait list and to project the size of the next freshman class.

But if thousands of applicants were to do this, would it not annoy all those people in the colleges? No. Colleges have enough faculty members, coaches, administrators, and other personnel to take the occasional applicant calls. You will annoy someone only by being annoying. To phone a chemistry professor you met and discuss with him an experiment you are starting will please and intrigue the professor. To ask the admissions office if they received the A+ paper you wrote on Machiavelli is no imposition. We said that documentation is essential, but keeping in touch will make the admissions process more human — for you, and for the colleges.

AFTER MARKETING, WHAT?

In the box are further examples of creative marketing. They are there to stimulate you, or to be imitated if you so choose. You and your college advisor are the best marketers of your strengths. Of course, you must keep your college advisor informed about your marketing moves, so that he or she can respond knowledgeably if a query comes from the college about some documentation or phone call of yours.

TAKE A BREAK

There comes a time, usually about mid-March, when you realize you have done your best to put yourself over with several colleges, and the admissions process is just about over. You have completed your marketing efforts, and there will be buyers. There remain the problems of accepting one college which admits you, one out of two or more, of working out the financial details, of considering the waiting-list alternative. All these are discussed in Step Twelve.

So give yourself a break and stop thinking about admissions for a few weeks. Enjoy the onset of spring. Smile. Do not worry. There is an adage to the effect that what we worry about never happens. When something goes wrong, it is usually a surprise. You forget to turn off the parking lights, and the car battery dies. A power outage spoils an hour's work on your word processor. Six inches of snow falls on April Fool's Day.

And then the letters arrive from the colleges, and you open them to read the good news, ACCEPTED.

CREATIVE MARKETING

The only limit to marketing your strengths is your imagination. To stimulate your thinking, here are some marketing stratagems that have worked for others.

Send to admissions:

- a copy of an award or citation received in your senior year
- a newspaper clipping about your achievement
- a particularly striking word of praise written by a teacher about a paper or project
- the school paper carrying results of your election to office or position of honor
- a prize story that has appeared since submitting your application — or a photo, drawing, sculpture, model, etcetera.

Send to the appropriate faculty member:

- a paper or project report of exceptional merit
- a model you have constructed of a building, machine, medical exhibit
- software you have developed
- a report on a business you are running
- music you have composed
- a tape of a speech, musical performance, ceremony honoring you; a relevant videotape
- a painting, drawing, sculpture, or other work of art in disposable form — that is, a copy, or photo of your work, since it will not be returned to you
- a translation prepared by you from a foreign language into English, or vice versa, for a faculty member who reads that language.

Step Eleven Checklist

1. Begin marketing your strengths when you file your applications, and continue right up to the closing of your folder — December 1 if you are a candidate for Early Decision, otherwise late March.

2. Create a marketing plan to make use of all your self-scrutiny, as well as fresh awareness of what distinguishes you from other applicants. Assess your strengths, identify the colleges that need them, then communicate to the colleges the nature of your strengths by means of documentation.

3. Document evidence of your strengths with outstanding essays you have written, creative writing, art, newspaper clippings, recent report cards, commendations, awards, résumés of athletic experience, speeches, tapes.

4. Get an outside opinion of creative work before sending it to admissions offices, which will ask faculty members about its quality.

5. Avoid flamboyancy and gimmickry, but do not be bashful. Admissions committees admire "controlled aggression."

6. If you add recommendations to your folder, give a copy of your application to the person who is writing the college on your behalf. This is especially important if the person is a trustee or an administrator of the college.

7. Alumni admissions volunteers can help you and cannot hurt your chances. Get an interview with an alumnus or alumna if possible.

8. Keep in touch with faculty members and coaches by phone or, if a college is near you, in person. Let them know about your latest achievements.

9. Your college advisor should be informed of your marketing efforts. Send him or her copies of your letters and exhibits sent to the admissions office. An advisor can be more helpful in backing up your candidacy when armed with new information.

STEP TWELVE

Enroll in the Right College for You

ADMISSIONS PROCEDURES
AFTER ADMISSION

You will be reading this before you experience the inevitable elation that occurs upon being notified of admission, so you may wonder why there is a Twelfth Step in our plan to help you enroll in a selective college. It is quite simply because the complex admissions process does not end with admission itself; it ends only after you sign an agreement to enroll in some college. And even then, as you will see, you can nullify this agreement if you are prepared to sacrifice a deposit of up to $500.

You will, of course, experience great euphoria following receipt of any warm letter of congratulations from a selective college that has admitted you to its upcoming freshman class. Astonishment and excitement may last for days as congratulations pour in. This sense of achievement and accomplishment, we almost inevitably observe, is succeeded by nervousness and indecision. Anticipating the options that you will have after receiving admissions notifications will allow for smooth planning without the confusion that often reigns at home as the final decisions in the admissions process draw near.

We have prepared this questionnaire to help you think ahead. A worksheet copy appears in the Appendix.

EARLY DECISION OBLIGATIONS

Usually about a fourth of those applying for Early Decision to the most selective colleges are admitted before Christmas. Among the Ivies this means 400 to 500 students per college. Where competition is not quite so strong, the acceptance rate of Early Decision candidates is about 50 percent. All of you admitted early have already made a contractual commitment to attend these colleges. We warn you once again that you are bound to submit no applications to any other college. The colleges to which you have been admitted have ways of discovering such applications even if you do nothing about an admission from another college.

In other words, if you are tempted to discover what other colleges might have accepted you by filing applications with them, never do this. You can seriously affect your college career. The penalty for breaking this rule is withdrawal of your acceptance. No comparable selective college will admit you, and you will be obliged to enroll somewhere that you probably will feel is beneath your ability.

With your early acceptance comes a financial aid package if you applied for aid. This can be a surprise. It may seem too ungenerous. You should contact the financial aid office and express your feelings. It may be possible to get an improvement in the package, or you may be asked to be patient and wait until spring for a possible increase. At that time the colleges have a clearer picture of the total aid funds to be budgeted for the year. Some applicants promised substantial aid packages may decide to enroll elsewhere, leaving the institution extra money to redistribute.

In practice Early Decision candidates admitted in December face far fewer choices than those admitted in April. This is one more reason why the numbers applying early are rising at the rate of about 10 percent a year — and why the competition for early admission is getting stronger year by year.

EARLY NOTIFICATION

We have explained in Step One the distinction between Early Decision and Early Notification. Those of you who have received Early Notification that you will probably be admitted to one or more selective colleges know that you are free to file applications elsewhere. Chances are you will be admitted to another college or two.

CHOOSING YOUR
PREFERRED COLLEGE

We have assumed from the start that you will be admitted to at least one selective college, but applicants who follow the Twelve-Step Plan are rarely admitted to fewer than two. This is because they apply to some colleges that are an obvious "fit" for them. If, however, you are accepted by only one college, your college career has been determined — unless you have applied to nonselective colleges as "safeties" or because they are less expensive.

Students like Theresa illustrate the problems that arise when you apply to many colleges. Theresa applied to ten schools, and was wait-listed by Barnard, Carleton, Oberlin, Trinity, and Vassar, and accepted by Pomona, Smith, Kenyon, Wesleyan, and Washington University. This put her in quite a quan-

YOUR ADMISSIONS DECISIONS QUESTIONNAIRE

1. I have been admitted to the following colleges:
   _____ _____ _____. (List the dates on which the colleges notified you.)

2. Acceptance deadlines are the following: _____
   _____ _____

3. Financial aid packages compared (from Step Eleven):
   Colleges A $_____ B $_____ C $_____

4. Deposits required: Colleges A $_____
   B $_____ C $_____

5. I have been wait-listed at: Colleges A_____ B_____
   C_____

6. Alumni and/or coach contacts initiated by colleges:
   names _____ dates _____

7. Alumni and/or coach contacts initiated by me:
   names _____ dates _____

8. Campuses revisited: _____ _____ _____

9. I prefer college _____

10. I plan to accept if removed from waiting list at _____

11. I plan to accept deferred admission in January at _____

12. Do financial considerations require me to attend a public college in my state?   Yes   No

13. I wish to renegotiate the financial aid package at _____

14. I am disappointed in not getting into _____. I want to consider: (1) a 13th year of high school and reapplying to _____ _____; (2) enrolling in another college and transferring to _____ in my _____college year.

15. I plan to take Advanced Placement tests in June in these subjects: _____ _____

TRANSITION QUESTIONS

16. I have lined up a summer job and will save $_____ toward my college costs.

17. I am assured of a campus job doing _____ and earning
    $_____

18. I am considering taking the following courses freshman year:
    _____ _____ _____ _____
    _____ _____

19. My roommate will be chosen by the college _____
    by me _____

20. I will be living at _____

21. My academic advisor will be _____

22. Deadlines for paying tuition _____
    room and board _____

dary, as she discovered. "I wish I had made up my mind earlier," she told a counselor. "Who needs all these options?" She was persuaded to drop all the colleges where she was wait-listed. Her applications to two women's colleges suggested that she might not be totally comfortable at a coed school. Theresa was extremely attractive to boys, and she felt that she could end up spending too many nights out at Pomona or the other coed colleges. She enrolled at Smith.

Millicent, accepted by Connecticut College and Colby, also had to decide about Duke's decision to wait-list her. Unable to get any decision out of Duke in the spring, she enrolled at Colby. Then in September Duke announced she could come to Duke in January, which she did; but it cost her family about $500 in deposit money.

Anticipating the choices that lie ahead of you, you should make a note in your notebook of your original observations and feelings when you evaluated colleges after campus visits. Then look at the conclusions you drew after studying your pie charts. There is often a conflict between estimating your chances of admission and loving a particular college. You apply to both, expecting to be turned down by the one you love. Then you are admitted to the one you correctly decided would accept you, and you are also wait-listed, like Millicent, at the college you really prefer. We discuss the wait-list problem below. For the moment we want you to be aware of such surprises. In theory, you have only applied to colleges you would be happy to attend. But when the admissions reach your mailbox, you must weigh one college against another, and sometimes you may agonize for days.

WHEN COLLEGES
PUT ON THE PRESSURE

Until now you have been currying favor with the colleges to let you in. Once they have let you in, they have to woo you. This occurs at all levels of selectivity. One Princeton alumni group in southern New Jersey traditionally invites those who have been admitted to attend a dinner before May 1, the common reply date. Each accepted applicant is flanked at the table by alumni. After the dinner, about four out of five invitees decide to enroll at Princeton. This is more than twice Princeton's national yield.

You can anticipate being importuned by coaches and even faculty members once you have been admitted. This treatment will make you feel important, loved, and wanted. It may also trouble you and render you momentarily indecisive about two wonderful colleges. That is when it may be necessary to revisit a campus or two.

REVISITING CAMPUSES

In April you will see the buses pulling into New Haven. They carry prospective freshmen. Yale's yield is about 54 percent; of those who have been admitted, 46 percent enroll someplace else — mostly at Harvard, Princeton, Stanford, Dartmouth, or Amherst. This is one way to revisit the campus, and it is popular because all your expenses are paid by some alumni group. You get a chance to stay overnight and retake "the 10:30 test" we discussed in Step Seven, to reassess the feel of the college late at night in a dorm.

If you are a scholarship student, arrangements will be made for you to make the trip when there is no bus going from your area to a particular college. Even scholarship students may get all the expenses of the trip paid by contacting the admissions office and saying that they want to revisit the campus. Alumni in your area are most helpful in this matter. You need not feel obliged to enroll just because the college has gone to expense and trouble to persuade you of its merits. Be prepared to be impressed by the presentation. Red carpets are rolled out for prospective freshmen in April — deans and top faculty members or coaches tell you what you can expect during your next four years; student leaders put on a show, and they can be very persuasive. You may be invited to an athletic event in the afternoon, or asked to play tennis or swim in the Olympic pool.

It is not easy to turn down a college after a visit during which you are treated like royalty. However, you need not commit yourself one way or the other. If you possibly can, go to another campus where you have been accepted. Then, with two wonderful experiences and a notebook full of fresh impressions, you approach the moment of truth. You talk the problem over with family, counselor, teachers, your peers — and then it is up to you, and you alone. You do not have to explain or apologize to anyone. Go to your room and think about it.

CONSIDERING
FINANCIAL AID PACKAGES

At the time of your admission you will receive a notice, issued by the financial aid office of each college, of your aid package, consisting of scholarship, loan, and job. From two or more colleges you will receive aid packages that differ in generosity. You may ultimately decide on attending the college that seems to value you most, and this is fine so long as it is your preferred college. But if you would rather attend a college offering you less, you should make this known to the financial aid office (the admissions committee cannot help you get more aid) of the preferred college.

As we have pointed out, colleges that admit you really want your enrollment. If money is an obstacle, selective colleges will listen to a reasonable argument, especially if new circumstances have developed since you applied for aid — family illness, new obligations, business difficulties. Colleges can, if they have the scholarship money, be more generous than the College Scholarship Service advises them to be. They can raise your scholarship, or increase your loan, or arrange for a loan to your parents.

So do not quit on a college because of dissatisfaction over their financial aid package. And here is where you, the student, are likely to be more persuasive than your parents. You really are the needy one; your parents, with few exceptions, have more means than you have. Psychologically, their case is bound to be weaker than yours. What can your father say when the question is asked: "Have you considered a second mortgage?" It is a question, however, that can only be asked of you indirectly, since you have no house to mortgage. Be bold and say that you need X thousand dollars, and you want it in the form of an increased scholarship. At the worst, you will be told that there is no scholarship money available, but that a larger loan can be arranged. There is no end of loan money around, although to leave college heavily in debt is not a pleasing prospect. (Incidentally, statistics show that selective college students seldom fail to meet their obligations to the federal government.)

THE WAITING LIST

Colleges put candidates on waiting lists to protect themselves from a drop in yield. Yield is the actual enrollment as a ratio of those admitted. If 2,000 are admitted and 1,000 enroll, the yield is 50 percent. Colleges keep annual yield records, but they can never be sure that the averages will hold, as unpredictably fewer students may decide to enroll in a college this year than last. If the yield drops to 48 percent, for example, then to make up the 2 percent that were expected, the college goes to the waiting list. But if 50 percent do enroll, then perhaps no one from the waiting list gets in. When the yield is surprisingly high, some of the freshman class must be housed off campus. The following year, the college reduces the total number of applicants it admits.

Colleges are under no obligation to take anyone from the waiting list. If you have been wait-listed, you can congratulate yourself that you are among an elect; you are one who would have been admitted if the class were only a bit larger. But you cannot begin to guess whether or not you will be admitted. You really have no other way to protect yourself than to agree to enroll at another college that has already admitted you.

Meanwhile, in the admissions office where you are wait-listed, the committee is adding up its acceptances and filing them by categories. Let us say there are one hundred on the waiting list and finally it is decided that only fifty of these need to be admitted to fill the freshman class. What fifty will be admitted? No one on a waiting list is ranked, any more than anyone in the freshman class is ranked. If you call up the admissions office and ask where you stand in relation to others on the list, you will be told that there is no way to answer that question.

The reason is that the admissions committee is still balancing the class. Its class profile may show, for example, that the number admitted from traditional private schools is already on target; the college wants to admit no more in this category. If you are of this kind, you will not be admitted from the waiting list — and you will not be told why. Or suppose you are an outstanding woman soccer player and were put on the waiting list in the expectation that another woman soccer player would enroll. When she decides to go to another college, you are sent a letter of admission; you have been taken off the waiting list.

Although it would seem that you are completely powerless to do anything if you are wait-listed, this is not the case. Assume that you prefer the college that has wait-listed you above any others. You are dying to be one who is accepted from the list. Here is what you do:

1. You agree to enroll in the college you like second best, where you have been admitted.
2. You then contact the admissions committee at the college where you are wait-listed and tell them where you will enroll unless you are admitted to their college.
3. You add, "If you take me off your waiting list, I assure you I will enroll at your college."

Is this cricket? Absolutely. It is not dirty pool to accept one college's offer of admission, and then later withdraw from that freshman class in order to accept another offer as the result of being taken off the waiting list. However, it is costly. You have paid a deposit, usually about $500, with your agreement to enroll. This you must forfeit as the price of enrolling in the college you like the best. There is nothing morally wrong with this practice. Colleges accept it as a business proposition. None likes to lose a freshman, but for a fee, so to speak, the practice is tolerable.

From the point of view of the college that has wait-listed you, your assurance to enroll if admitted is a boon. The more acceptances a college can be certain of, the less work and worry for the college. It happens that colleges will still be trying to fill all freshman places as late as the end of August. By that time admissions offices are already working on the next freshman class, so they are anxious to put an end to the process, which should have been over by July 1. You, who promise to come if admitted, become more attractive to the college.

To reinforce your promise, write the college a letter stating your intention, and enclose any new information about yourself that makes you an attractive candidate. Remarket yourself! Send in a copy of your spring varsity letter certificate, or your most recent A+ paper.

Having done this, you have done all you can about the waiting list. You may be on two or more waiting lists, and in all cases your procedure is identical. However, you should not promise several colleges you will enroll if admitted. Be assertive at all of your wait-list colleges, however. Be tough-minded now. If you find yourself in a bind being taken off two waiting lists, smile, accept the college you prefer, and send regrets to the other. You already have reason to cry a little, sacrificing the deposit fee at the college you originally accepted.

And remember, the chances of being taken off any waiting list are very slim. Make up your mind that you will go to the college you have accepted, so if lightning strikes and you are taken off a waiting list, it will be that much more pleasing.

ADMISSION NOTIFICATION BEFORE APRIL 1

The most selective colleges no longer adhere strictly to the historic common notification date, April 15. Like the less selective colleges they try to steal a march on their competitors by unofficially admitting a percentage of the stronger candidates around April 1 or even earlier.

With a two-week head start, these colleges can put psychological pressure on you to accept their offers of admission.

Be prepared for this situation: you have applied to half a dozen selective colleges, four of which adhere to the agreed common notification date; two

WEIGHTY WAITING LISTS

Recent wait-list numbers were almost scary. The increase in applications flooded waiting lists. Exactly half of institutions who use waiting lists in their acceptance process had the same number of students on the list in 1992 as they did in 1991. Sixty percent of responding institutions used the lists, and of these, nearly 40 percent placed more students on the waiting lists in 1992 than they did in 1991. Only 10 percent wait-listed fewer students this year.

Colleges that wait-listed up to 200 applicants include Guilford College, Hampshire, Hanover, Linfield, NYU, Ramapo College, Seattle University, University of Vermont, and Wheaton College (IL).

Columbia, Lafayette, Michigan Tech, Randolph-Macon, and Wesleyan all wait-listed between 200 and 500 students.

To those who remember the not-so-distant past, when the largest number of wait-listed students at any institution was 100, the recent phenomena of 1,000-plus lists seems incomprehensible. Colleges and universities that placed as many as 500 to 1,000 applicants on wait lists include Amherst, Brown, Colgate, North Carolina State, Northwestern, University of Rochester, and Yale.

Oberlin College put 138 more applicants on its wait list this year, bringing the total to 534. Rutgers put a whopping 2,769 applicants on hold, which officials said was roughly the same as last year. And Carnegie-Mellon suspended the hopes of 1,200 applicants, also the same number as last year.

colleges announce in a letter of April 1 that you have been admitted to their freshman classes. These admissions are contingent, the letters say, on your paying a fee prior to the Common Reply Date of May 1, which most colleges honor.

Well now, here's a howdy-do. We have told you that you will be admitted to at least one selective college, and often two, and this latter goal has been achieved. Is it not a bit greedy to wait to be admitted to one or more of the more selective colleges that will not notify you until later? Why not accept a bird in hand?

For these reasons: (1) It is needlessly costly. (2) You may want to review the financial aid package you received. (3) If you are rejected by the other four colleges, you can probably enroll at one of the two that admitted you early, since it is obvious that you are an attractive candidate. (4) The April 1 admissions are a signal that these colleges recognize you as the kind of candidate likely to be accepted by one of their more selective rivals. Therefore, you are not taking a very big risk in waiting two more weeks; you are in a stronger position than you may think. Early admission is an attempt to stampede you into an acceptance at once that you can exercise later.

Your response to these early admissions, then, should be a letter that goes about like this:

Dear Dean _____,

Thank you for your notification of admission. I am deferring my decision to enroll at your college until I hear from several other colleges where I have applied for admission.

[If you are an aid applicant]:
I must also compare financial aid packages from these institutions with yours. It would greatly help me to know as soon as possible what financial aid you plan to offer me.

Please notify me if there is any difficulty in holding a place for me until May 1.

Sincerely,

Now the ball is in the other court. Furthermore, you are not on the hook for a fee as high as $500 to hold your place. This demand is a bluff. Ignore it; you will not lose your place. We regret that some selective colleges have been driven to adopt this tactic, long practiced by colleges that must actively campaign to maintain enrollment at a level necessary to fill freshman places and provide the tuition income needed to keep the institution solvent. Needless to say, the practice infuriates the more selective colleges, which are powerless to fight back without breaking the common notification agreement.

Blind copies of your letter should go to other colleges, which will notify you of your admission or rejection on April 15. Your counselor, armed with a copy of your letter, should be asked to phone these colleges and say, "Can you tell me how this candidate's prospects look now?" Admissions can say, "Not very good," or "Fair," or "Pretty good." "Pretty good" amounts to admission, since the colleges already know in most cases whom they have admitted.

DEFERRED ADMISSION

An option some colleges reserve to themselves is to offer you a deferred admission; instead of enrolling in September, you enroll for the winter term in January. Duke, Middlebury, Mount Holyoke, and Connecticut College are among those that admit a smaller number of students on a deferred basis. These admissions invariably are given to those on waiting lists. Behind the deferred admission is the departure from the campus for overseas or special projects of a small number of students, who do not let the college know this until the summer before they are going to leave. To fill their places, the freshman class is expanded.

Should you accept deferred admission? Most applicants do. There is the drawback of coming on campus after other freshmen have developed their social arrangements. You will not be able to graduate with your class in the spring. These are minor disadvantages. The colleges are aware of them and do their utmost to make you feel welcome on campus.

THE NONSELECTIVE COLLEGE OPTION

Despite all we have said, we know that some candidates will apply to safety colleges, where they will be accepted without question. Many such colleges are excellent, but the student bodies do not perform at the challenge level academically. Having considered yourself a selective candidate from the start, you should not, as you near the finish line, decide to drop out of the race. Stay to the end. There is time enough later to decide on a nonselective college.

Often the nonselective college is a public institution in your home state, where the cost is as much as a third that of the most selective colleges. Opting for such a college may be unavoidable for financial reasons, although we continue to believe that worthy candidates will be able to make it financially through most selective colleges, private or public.

POSTGRADUATE YEAR

There are two reasons to consider a postgraduate year after high school: one is a realization that an extra year of studying before you go to college will allow you to mature, improve your study habits, possibly improve test scores, and in general put you in a stronger position for admission to a selective college. The other is rejection by one or more colleges you hoped to attend, and which you can probably get into after an additional year in high school.

In a postgraduate program you do not repeat a grade. Such programs are demanding and make you stretch. Because you are not in school with your old friends with all their demands and expectations, you tend, in the postgraduate year, to make academic work your chief concern. Of course, you will engage in activities and sports, but these will be more relaxing than competitive. The postgraduate year most typically is taken in a private school.

"We find that our postgraduate year students mature rapidly," one private school headmaster told us. "They are no longer under peer pressure socially. Dating is less on their minds than learning. They improve their SAT and Subject Test scores. When they get to college, they are usually very successful."

A postgraduate year at the local high school may allow you to take a part-time job to build savings for college. In a job you can develop both skills and a deeper sense of responsibility. It is our experience that nothing but good comes of adding a postgraduate year to your secondary education.

TRANSFERRING TO
SELECTIVE COLLEGES

It is extremely difficult to transfer to the most selective colleges, as we have said. They do not have many extra places, and they prefer to have their students on campus for their four years of education, though many take off a term along the way. However, the less selective colleges welcome transfers when the applicant has done well at a junior college or state institution. It is not unreasonable for a strong student to plan to attend an in-state public college or a small private institution for a year or two and then graduate from a selective college. The savings are substantial.

As a transfer applicant you will have to arrange for transcripts to be forwarded by both your high school and your college. Since the transfer applicant pool is small, you are competing in a small pie slice and can quickly learn from the admissions committee what your chances are. Your best strategy is to get one or more faculty members interested in having you enroll. Knowing your major can make you a very attractive candidate at a selective college that has encouraged your transfer application.

ENROLLMENT AT LAST

The rule is: enroll where you will be happy. But how can you know at what college your happiness lies? Have you not always known what pleases you? A wise old headmaster, Francis Boyden of Deerfield Academy, used to say to parents bringing their boys to look over the schools they were considering:

CONSIDER TRANSFERRING

Another difference between the eighties and the nineties is the growing possibility of transferring from a less selective college to a more selective one. At the Educational Consulting Center we've counseled students disappointed in not being admitted to their first choice not to despair and to apply again sophomore year as a transfer.

We can cite Duke, Harvard, Pennsylvania, Stanford, and Georgetown as colleges that have accepted transfers from state universities. We must add that transfer students should not normally expect an aid package.

Economics is driving this trend, as well as an awareness of the maturing and motivation of many transfer candidates. Selective colleges must build up their revenues, and a bright transfer student brings more tuition money. Some state universities have become overcrowded and underfunded, and this has meant a diminished educational experience.

"Let the boy decide which is the right school for him. He'll know." He did not want to take any boy who had any reservations about his school.

This is a good clue for you to follow. Your reservations and uneasy feelings about a college should be respected. They may be quirky and unreasonable to someone else, but you have to live with them. Suppose the students at the college do not appeal to you. You need not feel guilty and tell yourself that they probably are not representative of the whole college. Weighing your reactions to these students and to those of another college where you warmed up to them, you must count one as a negative and the other as a positive. On balance you ought to spend your four years of college among people you like.

You can be happy at a college with which you are in strong disagreement on a basic issue. William F. Buckley's first book, *God and Man at Yale,* was an attack on what he perceived to be the absence of religious emphasis on a campus he loved. You cannot be happy at a place you feel is beneath you. We think of a young man who sincerely believed that he should have been admitted to an Ivy League college. He enrolled in a fine university, but not so highly prestigious as the one he thought he should be attending. The result was a miserable academic performance that finally caused him to drop out. He would have been wiser to stay out of college a year or two until he got over his peeve.

So before May 1 you should come to a conclusion as you go through your notes and try to decide among two or more colleges. You have had all the advice you can get from us, from your parents, teachers, friends, and the clergy. The colleges have decided about you. You are a desirable under-graduate in their eyes. Now comes the moment at your desk when you close your notebook, and listen to what your own heart tells you to do.

Some candidates leap before they look. They are so excited about being admitted to a college, especially a prestigious college, that they accept without a second thought. Who would think of not going to Harvard after being accepted? There are those who should. A Harvard/Radcliffe administrator told us that every year there are a few students who are emotionally not up to the competition they encounter — or imagine they encounter.

"For example, a freshman will tell me he feels inadequate because his roommate has already written a symphony. In his school orchestra he played first violin. We can change his roommate, but it's not so easy to change his negative opinion of himself," the official said.

Another Harvard/Radcliffe administrator calls this *the fallen prince syndrome.* A tennis star back home finds she is cut from Harvard's freshman squad and goes to pieces. Obviously her expectations outran her capacities, but it does happen. Such students would be better musicians and tennis players in a less competitive atmosphere, even though academically they can do the work at Harvard/Radcliffe.

Going to a college to please your parents may be a mistake if the college does not please you. A recent graduate of Amherst, her father's college,

LOOK WHERE YOU'RE GOING

It's hard to avoid hearing, seeing on TV, or reading about the new troubles on college campuses. PC, or political correctness, multiculturalism, the canon content, racism, sexism, anti-Semitism, free speech, and curricula-reform issues are meat for the voracious news media. High schools in general are relatively free of this political activism. In college you are likely to be exposed to — if not personally involved in — public controversy. In the nineties as in the sixties, campuses are battlegrounds for forces of social change and reaction.

"Is this the new enlightenment on campus or the new McCarthyism?" *Newsweek* wondered in a report on student codes of conduct and the First Amendment, suggesting that all the halls of academe are aflame. But in fact some places are more charged with the electricity of confrontation than others. This may be a consideration when choosing which offer of admission to accept. If you enjoy the exhilaration of debates carried on in rallies and radical student newspapers, then the struggles at a University of Michigan or Pennsylvania are places you'll enjoy.

"Disagreement can be fun," says Stanley Fish, Distinguished Professor of English at Duke and an ardent defender of PC. But perhaps not fun for you. As you inquire about life on a particular campus, you can quickly learn whether you will be entering a zone of intellectual conflict.

However, the absence of an outbreak does not guarantee perpetual peace at any college. We cannot guide you to any safe havens where the ivory towers stand tall. Part of your education will be to look where you're going and try to avoid the minefields — or at least be prepared for them.

wishes she had gone to a large university. Such sentiment, of course, does not go over with her father. It would have been wiser to displease him briefly four years ago than to make him feel guilty now for his enthusiasm for his alma mater.

Before enrolling anywhere, picture yourself at the college as a student and imagine how you will feel there. If you have any doubts, you ought to be guided more by them than by the hope that everything will probably work out all right. Trust your feelings, because they usually stay with you a long time.

Decisions to choose Amherst over Princeton, Berkeley over Stanford, Duke over Rice or any other college may be based on seemingly whimsical or even irrational considerations. But obeying the dictates of the heart seems to make good sense when it comes to enrolling at a selective college. Here are some explanations for college choices given to us by recent high school graduates now in selective colleges:

NEGATIVES	POSITIVES
Curriculum too limited	Prestige
Don't want to fulfill a foreign language requirement	Campus spirit
	Candlelight dinners
Orientation too literary	Many community-related programs
Lab facilities outmoded	No core curriculum
No environmental studies	Strong Russian studies
Overemphasis on athletics	Great track coach
Campus too spread out	No sexual harassment
Fraternities dominate social life	Excellent sports opportunities for women
Faculty has liberal bias	
Atmosphere is sexist	Mother went there
Minorities underrepresented	Better bookstore
Lots of drinking	Math tradition
Ivory tower, remote	Beautiful buildings
Noisy, overcrowded	Thesis requirement
Preppy	Year-round tennis
No business courses	Near skiing
Too competitive	Safe campus
Father went there	Independent study program
No art museum	New theater
Too many pre-med majors	Great glee club
Obligatory remedial writing course	Tutorial system
Snobbish	Art history slide collection
Poor balance of men and women enrolled	Strong year-abroad program
	New library
	Alumni spirit
	Friends going there
	Most students have cars
	More dating possibilities

One way to convince yourself that your "reasons" for choosing one college over another are sound is to poll some students during a second campus visit, asking them to give you some reasons they personally like where they are. If you get "bad vibes," you know this place is not for you.

All selective colleges are happy campuses for most of their students, but because each college is unique, you should make sure that a college's uniqueness and your own personal uniqueness harmonize.

Knowing how many young people every year choose wisely, we know you will. Have a wonderful four years in college!

Step Twelve Checklist

1. Become aware of the procedures you must follow after you have received a letter of acceptance.

2. Be prepared to spend time comparing the advantages of attending two or more colleges that admit you. Avoid snap decisions.

3. Expect pressure to enroll at colleges that admit you. College officials and alumni can be very persuasive. Weigh all their arguments carefully.

4. Being wait-listed can cause disappointment when you are never finally accepted. By enrolling at the college you like second best, you take a positive step. You can always change your mind, if you are later admitted from the waiting list. In this case, be prepared to pay a penalty fee to the college you accepted.

5. Selective college applicants rarely settle for a nonselective "safety" school. Stay with the selectives if you belong in one of them.

6. Trust your instincts. You will enroll in the right college for you.

A Twenty-Month Calendar for Your Selective Admissions Process

JUNIOR YEAR

SEPTEMBER

Establish your fall plan for selective college admission steps. This includes:

- a start on considering colleges that interest you by finding out where the information lies in your school or your community library;
- dates of parents' night and meetings with college admissions office visitors to your school; an initial meeting with your college counselor;
- a review of your curriculum to make sure that your courses are making you stretch (see suggested guidelines on pages 64–65);
- making out a reasonable schedule of nonacademic activities;
- getting a copy of the PSAT/NMSQT *Student Bulletin* and consulting the College Entrance Examination Board's *College Handbook* or. . . .

OCTOBER

Note the date of your school's PSAT/NMSQT. Make sure you know your school's College Board/ACT code number, to be used whenever you take tests.

Sign up for the College Board's free Student Search Service (SSS), which matches your background and interests with colleges that are looking for students like you. You will receive information about their programs in spring.

Plan to attend at least one college fair in your area.

NOVEMBER

Begin filling your notebook with preliminary information about colleges that interest you after studying catalogues, viewbooks, software, and other sources such as college newspapers and yearbooks. Talk to recent graduates of your high school about their colleges as well as to alumni (don't forget alumni on your school faculty).

DECEMBER

When you get your PSAT/NMSQT scores, review your test booklet in order to begin preparing for the SAT. (*Note:* if you plan to apply for Early Decision, you must take the SAT I and II in your junior year.)

Get the College Board's *Registration Bulletin,* which includes test dates. Note the deadline date for January, if you plan to take this SAT I.

To register for the SAT I, complete the registration form, including the Student Descriptive Questionnaire (SDQ), and mail it with the fees in time to arrive by the deadline.

JANUARY

Before taking the SAT I, study *Taking the SAT I,* which is available at your school, and take the practice test as explained in Step Four.

Plan to do well on your school exams. They are even more important than the SAT.

FEBRUARY

If you took the SAT I you will receive with your scores your *College Planning Report.* Go over it with your parents and counselor to determine what steps, if any, are needed to improve your college preparation.

Take notes of admissions procedures of colleges that interest you, paying particular attention to Early Decision requirements.

Consult with your counselor and teachers about taking the Advanced Placement tests in May.

Study the *Index of Majors* to help you relate your interests to colleges you plan to visit.

MARCH

Check the SAT test date for this month, since this date varies from year to year to avoid conflict with Easter and term breaks.

Take practice SAT I tests before taking the official SAT I.

Plan to take one or more Subject Tests in June in those subjects in which you are doing well, especially if they are subjects you won't be taking in your senior year. Check with the teachers in each course for their advice. This is especially essential for Early Decision candidates.

Plan your summer. Will you earn money? Or do you need to take enrichment courses? Make your summer constructive by thinking it out in advance. Look into special activities that develop your talents and enhance your profile for college admissions.

APRIL

Begin to schedule campus visits for spring. You will need an appointment for interviews. See Step Seven on visiting colleges.

Discuss college costs with your parents and draw up a tentative needs budget for use when you visit colleges. Check the College Board's *College Cost Book* to study the differences in tuition, room, and board expenses at all accredited colleges.

MAY

Take AP examinations if advised by your teachers to do so.

List courses and possible majors you might study in college.

Start to identify those people you will ask for letters of recommendation. Make sure of teachers, administrators, counselors, coaches, and others you expect to write glowingly about you.

Start thinking about essay topics.

JUNE

Take Subject Tests in subjects you have mastered. If you are considering Early Decision application in the fall, plan to have three Subject Tests completed by the June testing.

Take notes on your campus visits, guided by recommendations in Step Seven. Continue campus visits through the summer if necessary.

Athletes should begin contacting college coaches. Draw up your athletic résumé to send or bring to the coach. Look into special athletic camps. See Step Eleven.

Plan your senior curriculum around the most demanding course schedule you can handle.

Early Decision candidates must prepare for a short few months before applying to college. Of particular importance is the essay. Try to have it ready by early October.

SENIOR YEAR

SEPTEMBER

Consult your notebook to see where you stand in your college preparations. Have you narrowed your college choices?

Plan to retake the SAT I in November (in some states it can be taken in October) if you want to improve your score. Study tests or arrange for tutoring if need be.

Begin practicing essays.

Refer to your notes on the various admissions procedures of the colleges you will apply to.

Early Decision candidates should have applications this month for mailing by the end of October. Don't forget the financial aid forms.

OCTOBER

Meet with admissions representatives of colleges you are considering, and visit more campuses if necessary.

Register for Subject Tests given in December, as well as for the SAT I if you plan to take it.

Talk to teachers and others about recommendations.

Discuss with your counselor the colleges you are going to apply to, and establish deadlines for the mailing of your transcripts.

Early Decision candidates should do their self-marketing this month.

NOVEMBER

Read *Meeting College Costs* and other resource material on scholarships and discuss financial aid further with your parents. Get all necessary financial aid forms from your school. Explore scholarship opportunities.

Finish your essay under teacher and counselor supervision.

Study college applications without actually filling them out yet.

Early Decision candidates should be sure not to miss the application deadline this month. Financial aid forms must also be filed.

Arrange interviews with alumni of selected colleges over the next several months.

DECEMBER

SAT I and Subject Tests are given this month.

Give your counselor, principal, or designated school official the Secondary

School Report section of your college application forms early this month.

Register for the January SAT I or Subject Tests if you plan to take them.

Line up your appropriate teachers and others who will make recommendations. Give them the forms for each college. See Step Nine.

Be sure you give your parents the appropriate financial aid forms (FAFSA/FAF) to begin filling out.

Use vacation to do any extra study needed to do well on your fall term school examinations.

Early Decision applicants who have been admitted must withdraw any other applications.

JANUARY

Financial aid forms must be mailed right after the first of this month.

Take the SAT I and Subject Tests if you are scheduled to.

Applications for admission must be mailed to meet deadlines. Check all details before sealing the envelope.

Make sure recommendations and transcripts are being mailed.

FEBRUARY

Ask your counselor to submit midterm grades to the colleges you have applied to.

Arrange now to take Subject Tests in May.

This is a good month to do self-marketing with faculty members and coaches at colleges.

Note that your last chance to take the SAT I again is in March.

MARCH

This is a good month to nail down sources of financial aid.

Continue to work hard academically and keep colleges informed of your progress and of extracurricular achievements.

APRIL

This month you will receive your letters of admission. Follow the procedures described in Step Twelve.

Visit one or more campuses if necessary to help decide what college to accept.

Make sure that you are getting the best possible financial aid package, and let the financial aid office know of any dissatisfaction you have. Aid packages can be revised.

If you still want to attend a college that has wait-listed you, let the admissions office know your desire, following Step Twelve procedures. Send admissions officers any news, such as high marks or awards.

Don't forget the deposit deadline.

MAY

Notification-of-acceptance deadline is May 1, known as the Common Reply Date. You should also notify colleges you regretfully do not plan to attend, thanking them for their accepting you.

Take AP examinations.

Consider registering for the June Subject Test date if you have excelled in particular subjects during your senior year. This may help you gain extra credits in college.

JUNE

Respond promptly to all requests from your college regarding housing preference and preliminary selection of courses for first semester.

Notify your school to which college it should send your final grades, class rank, and proof of graduation.

Plan to earn money this summer or to get a head start on courses you will be taking.

Drop a note of appreciation to your college counselor, teachers, or others who have helped you in the admissions process.

The Enduring Liberal Arts

Most selective colleges base their curricula on the liberal arts, a tradition of education that began in the medieval universities at Oxford, Cambridge, the Sorbonne in Paris, and Bologna in Italy. Literature, languages, history, mathematics, philosophy, science, and social science are the disciplines underlying the bachelor of arts degree. But many liberal arts colleges also award the bachelor of science degree; academic disciplines include journalism, communications, theater arts, and, of course, computer sciences. These are practical subjects students take as career training. Some see this development as a weakening of the liberal arts, whose defenders say that its courses prepare a student for life, not for any specific profession or occupation. You will hear the boast "this is not a trade school," an echo of the misguided aristocratic scorn of hard work considered beneath the dignity of the upper classes.

But in fact liberal arts colleges continue to educate our future doctors, engineers, corporate managers, bankers, scientists, government officials, teachers, and entrepreneurs. As long ago as the Renaissance Leonardo da Vinci dissected corpses to understand how to make accurate anatomical drawings, but he also learned Latin and associated with humanist scholars for the enrichment of his mind. The link between the practical and purely contemplative disciplines is strong. What good does it do to major in English if you are becoming a lawyer or a doctor? Aside from the aesthetic pleasure of studying great works of literature, you gain an understanding of human nature and how to cope in a competitive world. Georges Pompidou, who succeeded Charles de Gaulle as president of France, was a professor of literature for years before he entered politics.

It may surprise you to learn that one of the strongholds of liberal arts education today is MIT! A former president of Vassar has noted that a liberal arts education "now distinguishes whatever nourishes the mind and spirit from the training which is merely practical . . . . Such an education involves a combination of knowledge, skills and standards."

It would be hard to improve on the case for the liberal arts made by John Sloan Dickey, when president of Dartmouth College.

> Imaginatively taught and pursued, the liberal arts present choices ranging from the largest philosophic issues of wisdom and wrongdoing, through the dilemmas of statecraft, the hypotheses and many wrong ways of science, to the most delicate variants of taste and style in expression and selection in all art forms. Few things are more basically liberating than the conscious exercise of a choice. A man is best known by his choices. I find that as I work my way further and further into the mysteries of education, I place an ever-higher value on the growth in a student, of sensitivity to comparative data, and his growing awareness of the opportunities of choice. Could any field other than the liberal arts yield as broad and as significant an introduction to life's comparisons and choices for men and women who are free not primarily because of birth, but because they learned to use their birthright to choose a way of life?

Unless the liberal arts are misnamed, they should be adaptable to changing circumstances — and they are, as interdisciplinary studies abound: economists study mathematics; physicists study computer science; composers use computers to create new music; historians, art students, anthropologists, and future professors of literature study the principles of psychiatry. The use of personal computers is widespread among students and faculties of liberal arts colleges, where language studies include COBOL and other languages of software.

Still, we cannot ignore the so-called culture wars raging on many campuses, where social issues are debated by faculty and students, where the vogue of multiculturalism has been invoked to question the Eurocentrism of the liberal arts, and where the white male for some has become a kind of white whale to be harpooned. Political correctness has in places given rise to a kind of "thought police" and led to suits that challenge campus regulations as an infringement on sacred First Amendment liberties. Curriculum revision is sought in confrontational ways that wrack campuses and turn ivy walls into billboards for slogans questioning the content of courses and books.

Welcome to the real world! Ivy walls do not an ivory tower make.

LIBERAL ARTS IN AN AGE OF TECHNOLOGY

Frank H. T. Rhodes, president of Cornell, has offered six reasons why the liberal arts are of enduring value today.

Reason 1. Liberal arts provide writing and speaking skills that enable one to perform effectively on a wide range of tasks in any field of endeavor. A New England Telephone Company recruiter is quoted by Dr. Rhodes as saying: "We need managers who can deal with diverse situations, and liberal arts students are perfect for that because they've had a diverse education."

Reason 2. One develops in liberal arts courses an international outlook that is essential for work at a time when 70 percent of American products face foreign competition.

Reason 3. Vocational skills rapidly become obsolescent. Lifelong learning is a national requirement, but it can be built only on "a broad and strong general foundation of undergraduate studies."

Reason 4. "The most useful reason of all for the liberal arts: Life is empty without them." Dr. Rhodes cites this statement from a report by the Rockefeller Commission on the Humanities: "The humanities offer clues but never a complete answer. They reveal how people have tried to make moral, spiritual, and intellectual sense of a world in which irrationality, despair, loneliness, and death are as conspicuous as birth, friendship, hope, and reason . . . they stretch our imagination, and they enrich our experience. They increase our distinctively human potential."

Reason 5. "Science and technology, in a narrow sense, are amoral. But their application involves profoundly moral issues. . . . From the scientist we learn what is possible, but from the humanist we learn what is acceptable, and so define the boundaries beyond which human dignity is imperiled."

Reason 6. The liberal arts have the potential for reuniting the sciences and the humanities. The idea that science is an orderly process is a misconception. "The great leaps in understanding have often been guided not by the systematic methods of scientific inquiry, but by the scientist's vision of beauty and art and sense of the mystical."

Does Dr. Rhodes have any suggestions for the best liberal arts path to take? No, because, he says, "thirty years in higher education has convinced me that trying to determine the 'good majors' in college, at least in the purely vocational sense, is a lot like playing the lottery, and the odds of success are about the same."

As an intelligent selective college student, you will be free, therefore, to choose the liberal arts curriculum today that will prepare you for the tomorrows you cannot possibly foresee. New conditions will best be met by reliance on old, time-tested educational disciplines — the liberal arts, the humanities.

THE VALUE OF A GOOD EDUCATION

Frederick C. Calder, former headmaster of Germantown Friends School in Philadelphia and now executive director of the New York State Association of Independent Schools, reminds high school students that secondary school has a purpose independent of college preparation: preparation for life as an adult.

"Much of the motivation for going to college," he remarks, "has little to do with improving the mind and much more to do with placing one's self, or one's child, where power and prestige unite in a formidable promise of future success.

"If college per se isn't the goal, then what is it? We hope that when our young people graduate from high school that they will be well on the way to becoming cultivated men and women, with sharpened intellects, with developing good tastes, and with a strong sense of civility. We hope that they will have a slightly better sense of humor than when they came; that they will be able to laugh at their own foibles and vulnerabilities with the rest of the world. We hope that the world and how it works will be a great deal clearer and that reality will surprise them much less often than it did before. We hope that they will like themselves a little better, because until they do, they will never be free to love others.

"And finally, we hope that they will understand better that whatever happens to this planet and the creatures that live on it, they can never by themselves alone overcome the eternal obstacles to peace, freedom and happiness."

Applying from Abroad

*I*n revising this edition, we have devoted more attention to the needs of selective college applicants from outside the United States, both citizens and noncitizens. This is because so many more U.S. college applications now come from abroad — about 438,600 in 1993–94, a 4.5 percent increase over the previous year. We anticipate a continuing rise in these applications. Howard Greene's Educational Consulting Center has helped hundreds of applicants from abroad meet the requirements of America's selective colleges by following the application procedures outlined in previous chapters of this book. To the applicant from abroad, American admissions procedures often seem puzzling and needlessly bureaucratic. This is because, unlike most other countries, we have no national education system that establishes a uniform curriculum for secondary schools or standardizes admissions procedures throughout the nation. Our 16,000 high schools are controlled by local communities and their standards are determined by the legislatures of the fifty states. Our approximately 2,200 four-year colleges and universities are governed by boards of trustees or state regents, which establish higher education admissions policies.

In a national system, the state furnishes the money for operating the universities (a college, in many countries outside the United States, usually is the designation for a private secondary school). Our colleges and universities depend on both public and private sources of money and on the tuition and fees charged to each student. The famous private universities like Harvard, Stanford, and MIT have over the years been endowed by private donors, foundations, and corporations with funds invested to provide interest and dividend revenue. Others have small endowments. To complicate the pattern further, some state institutions like the University of Texas have large endowments, and other public universities now raise donations annually from their alumni, their graduates.

This situation is not unrelated to admissions. Colleges lacking large endowments become dependent on enrollments for tuition money and on government grants to supplement funds from private donations, and they compete almost savagely with other colleges for enrollment. Such enrollment is nonselective. Most high school graduates can enroll in some colleges within a few weeks of filing an application. The open enrollment admissions process at these colleges is little more than a registration function. If you, as an applicant from another country, have read this book, you are aware how different selective admissions procedures are from open enrollment at non-selective colleges. Essentially the difference between selective and nonselective college admissions is that in selective admissions, applicants are screened in order to allow selection of those who qualify under each college's own standards. We assume, therefore, that you, by virtue of your strong record, are among the qualified selective college applicants, and that your school has recommended that you apply to a selective college in the United States.

Involved as the process is, it is nonetheless reasonable and fair. We urge you as a top student to file applications with several colleges just as if you were applying from an American high school. Be assured that admissions committees of selective colleges will welcome your applications.

All the conditions for selective college admissions described in this book must be fulfilled by students who apply from abroad. Nonetheless, an applicant from another country does have one advantage: he or she competes only against other applicants who reside outside the United States. You should reread Step Eight — Find Your Place in the Class Pie Charts. Coming from a foreign country, you automatically bring to any college a different perspective, another cultural orientation, another language, and unique experiences that are highly valued. Your slice in any college pie chart will be a small sliver, so that if you qualify as a selective college candidate by virtue of your academic record and your nonacademic interests and achievements, you already have a strong chance for admission to one or more of the colleges we list.

But still you must compete against other interesting applicants, so you must pay particular attention to the presentation of yourself in your application. It is important that you emphasize characteristics that make you distinctive. Merely to be French or Iranian or Argentinian is not sufficient in itself to carry you over the ivy wall; nor are the children of American nationals abroad automatically considered interesting or exotic. You must demonstrate your qualities.

International students have grown tremendously in the last five years — for example, another jump from '91 (1,347) to '92 (1,680).
Dean of Admissions,
University of Pennsylvania

FOREIGN STUDENT ENROLLMENTS
AT SOME SELECTIVE U.S. COLLEGES

The Institute of International Education's figures show that in 1992 the leading field of study among foreign students in the United States was business and management, with more than 79,500 enrolled. Engineering came second, with about 73,500. After that came math and computer sciences, with more than 36,500. Physical and life sciences had about 35,000 and social sciences had more than 30,500.

China had the largest number of students in the United States with 45,130. The number of Europeans grew by 8 percent, and Germany led the European countries with 7,880 enrollments.

Here is a sampling of foreign student enrollment at selective colleges for 1992–93.

College	Number of Students	Percentage of Total Enrollment
University of Texas (Austin)	4,152	8.5%
Boston University	4,084	14.4
University of Southern California	4,038	15.4
University of Wisconsin (Madison)	4,014	9.8
New York University	3,531	10.4
Ohio State University	3,449	6.6
Columbia University	3,338	17.2
University of Pennsylvania	3,248	15.7
University of Illinois (Urbana)	3,089	8.6
Texas A&M University	2,956	7.1
Harvard University	2,660	15.4
Cornell University	2,478	13.6
Stanford University	2,373	15.8
MIT	2,167	22.1
UCLA	1,764	5.0

SOURCE: *Open Doors* (New York: Institute of International Education, 1991–92), as cited in *The Chronicle of Higher Education*, December 1, 1993.

YOUR ACADEMIC RÉSUMÉ

Although your school will be sending colleges your transcript, you should include in your application a detailed academic résumé of your own with the following information: all schools attended from grades 1 through 12, with special descriptive emphasis on your high school, especially its program in eleventh and twelfth grades. Describe your high school, stating whether it is private or public, university preparation or technical. Say in what language instruction is given. Mention graduation requirements — Baccalaureate or Advanced Certificate examinations, for example. You will need to discuss the grading system to make clear your level of performance. Your academic concentration in eleventh and twelfth grades must be spelled out.

When you discuss admissions tests, give the dates on which they were taken. Explain your school's academic calendar: normal school year, graduation, length of courses. Describe the level and degree of difficulty of your courses, since foreign schools vary, and admissions offices simply lack the time to discover their comparable qualities. It is up to you to identify the character of your education as candidly as possible.

THE TOEFL

Your transcript must be in English. If the school does not provide a translation service, you will have to arrange for a translation. Likewise, unless English is your native language, you will have to take one of several English language ability tests, the most common of which is the TOEFL, Test of English as a Foreign Language, administered by the Educational Testing Service, which prepares the College Board tests. Your school will provide you with the most recent *Bulletin of Information* and application form.

The TOEFL, a three-hour multiple-choice test, is administered six times a year abroad or in the United States at five hundred test centers. The fee is $35 for a regular test date, or $42 for a Friday test date. Your test score will be sent to the colleges you indicate, not to you, and you will receive through ISIS, the International Student Identification Service, information from American colleges identified as appropriate for you. You should plan to take the TOEFL at least five weeks earlier than the deadline for submitting your completed application to the colleges.

Some colleges will accept the Michigan Language Test, given at American consulates worldwide as well as at certain test centers. Georgetown University's American Language Institute also offers an English skills test. But the TOEFL is the preferred test to take. It tests listening comprehension, structure and written expression, and reading comprehension and vocabulary. The minimum acceptable score out of 800 is usually between 550 and 600. The test, of course, is given to avoid enrolling students unable to keep up their work in a language foreign to them. Should your score be too low, you can always improve your English and retake the test.

ENGLISH AS A
SECOND LANGUAGE (ESL)

Many American universities and international education programs, such as the Experiment in International Living, offer intensive English-language training courses during both the academic year and the summer. Enrollment is noncompetitive, since the courses are not part of any university degree program. Accredited ESL programs are authorized to issue the Form I-20 that enables students to receive a student visa (Form F-1 Non-Immigrant Student Status) for entry into the United States. Be sure to enroll only in an accredited program. American embassies and consulates keep lists of recognized institutions.

THE VISA

Form I-20 is also obtainable from the college where you plan to enroll. After you have followed the Twelve-Step Plan and are accepted by a selective college, the college you choose will send you this form at your request. With the I-20 in hand, you must take it and your passport to an American embassy or consulate in your country in order to apply for a student visa.

Proof will be required that you are in good health and that you have enough money to cover college expenses and living costs in the United States. Most universities and colleges will ask you to take out health insurance during your stay to cover the cost of major illness.

Your own country's regulations affecting your study abroad must be understood, in order to avoid any delay in your plans. Application for a visa should be made at the same time you apply to American colleges, even though it will not be issued until you have been offered admission to an American institution. Otherwise you risk arriving late for your first term.

Visas are issued for the length of your degree program, usually four years. Students with advanced standing may graduate in three years. You must indicate on your application the exact length of your planned stay in the United States.

FINANCIAL CONSIDERATIONS

Americans complain of the high cost of higher education. Foreign students at first are stunned to learn that selective private colleges cost $15,000 to $25,000 a year for tuition, room, and board. Public institutions are far less expensive: $6,000 to $10,000 a year altogether. In either case, you must also have money for books, personal expenses, and travel and living expenses when school is closed.

Unfortunately, there are few scholarship monies available to foreign students, nor will you be allowed to earn money in America. For this reason, most colleges to which you apply will include a financial information statement to be completed by your family, giving assurance that you have sufficient funds to complete your study. This must be attested to by a bank officer.

YOUR PERSONAL STATEMENT

In addition to following the Twelve-Step Plan faithfully, as a foreign applicant you should add to your application a separate statement explaining just why you wish to attend an American college. This means acquainting yourself with the nature of our higher educational style. Most foreign students begin by assuming that our system is like their own, in which specialization begins early and leads to a professional degree. This is not the case. Your understanding of the American liberal arts curriculum is critical, and you must let the colleges know you are aware that undergraduate education is broad, even in schools of engineering, business administration, and architecture. We tried to bring out this characteristic in the final statement of this book.

In the American system specialization occurs at the graduate level, after you have a bachelor's degree. Whatever you plan to specialize in later, you must first take a number of undergraduate courses in the humanities, social sciences, and the arts. Be at pains to get across to admissions committees your understanding of what an American liberal education means to you personally, how you think it will broaden you and equip you for what you plan to do when you come back to your native country. Speak to the benefits you anticipate from four years in a selective American college. Describe your aspirations for yourself and for your fellow citizens.

Experience in counseling foreign applicants leads us to give the same assurances to qualified students abroad that we give to American high school students: if you follow the Twelve-Step Plan, you as an outstanding student in your country will be able to enroll in a selective American college, and probably you will be admitted to more than one. We wish you luck and welcome you to America.

SOME INTERNATIONAL STUDENT PROFILES

Here are excerpts from essays of seven applicants from abroad.

LORETTA COBURN, Ecole International, Geneva. Turkish mother, American father. Trilingual. Harvard summer school junior year to improve writing. Modest SAT scores. TOEFL 600-plus. Applied Duke, Union, Trinity, and Bates, as well as Northwestern, where she enrolled.

"So, where are you from?"
This simple, straightforward question is probably the one I dread most

when I meet someone for the first time. Oddly enough, I am perplexed by the ambiguity of the question and only able to mutter, almost incoherently, "um . . . well . . . I . . . aah . . ." Where do I begin? Should I tell them where I live, where I go to school, what nationality I am, or something else? How can I answer such a plainspoken question without a tiring recitation of my diverse background. Surprisingly, unlike many, I cannot answer precisely without digression. ". . . well . . . my family lives in Istanbul, Turkey and I go to boarding school in Geneva, Switzerland. I am half Turkish, half American. I have lived in Bahrain, Hong Kong, Turkey, Kuwait, and the U.S. and I have attended nine different schools . . ." (My listener dozes off as I ramble on discursively.) Although my response seems exhaustive, I find it very difficult to express the mere essence of my experiences without profoundly analyzing them.

KLAUS LINDE, German-Swiss School, Hong Kong. Intern at high-tech manufacturing company in Pittsburgh. Very modest SAT scores, TOEFL 590. Essay defined business interests, athletic record. Applied only to one selective university, where he enrolled.

The years I have spent in Hong Kong (6 years) I will always remember as a very important time since it had such a significant impact on my adolescence.

I can still recall the time I have spent in Germany before I moved to Hong Kong. I used to live just outside of Stuttgart in a rather small suburban residential area. My whole world consisted of "Steinpilzweg 41" (street name), where I gathered most of my childhood experience. Up to that point in my life the "horizon" did not stretch far beyond this world.

That was until my family moved to Hong Kong which for me at age 15 was like undertaking a journey into a whole new galaxy full of new surprises. The first adjustments had to be made to the climate; as soon as I stepped out of the airplane I thought I had just collided with a wall. The air was so dense that it felt difficult to breathe. The new challenge was my first day at school which turned out to be easier than I thought. Soon I was accepted by my fellow class mates and it wasn't a problem to follow most of the course work except English class which was naturally much more advanced than what I was used to in Germany.

USTAF DUN, Ecole International, Geneva. Strong curriculum, B+ grades. Modest SAT scores, TOEFL 640. Tufts summer school junior year for English writing and literature. Good marks. Applied Brandeis, Northwestern, Skidmore, and Tufts, where he enrolled.

The student and faculty community of The International School of Geneva is a melting pot of individuals with varying backgrounds, beliefs and cultures. The student body is made up of 97 nationalities, 74 mother tongues, and several religious denominations. I feel that this diversity is the particular aspect of my community that has had the greatest impact on my values and beliefs.

Diversity was not, however, new to me when I came to Geneva. I, myself, am a good example of it. I grew up in four strikingly different environments. I began life in the ancient and mystical city of Istanbul, moved to the corn fields of Peoria, Illinois at the age of three, went on to the hustle and bustle of New York City two years later, and finally settled in the very European and international city of Geneva. Four unique locations, worlds apart, all of which exposed me to a variety of people, ways of life and cultures. Also, being the child of a mixed-marriage (Moslem father, Jewish mother) I was predestined to become a multicultural person, unbiased and free of prejudices. But it was not until I came to Geneva that I began to appreciate the value of my background and experiences as a child.

LOLA AMADAN, American School, London. Lebanese. Good SAT scores, TOEFL over 600. Strong essay and personal interviews led to acceptances at Brown, Connecticut College, Skidmore, Wellesley, Middlebury. Enrolled at Brown.

Like my ancestors I am a nomad, a wanderer who seeks freedom, happiness and peace and harmony between myself and the world around me. The whole world is my home because I have no special bonding to any single nation. Both my parents are Lebanese and I was born in Lebanon in 1975. When I was four months old the civil war started in Lebanon and my family was forced to move from the area of conflict to Saudi Arabia. I have no emotional attachment towards the country where my family was born and lived. I feel awkward when friends around me talk about the great love they have for their native countries and all I can feel is pity for my own country.

Saudi Arabia became my home until I was seven years old. As a spectator looking back upon the actions of my past, I can focus on one day in particular which seems to me was a starting point for my search for myself. That day my father took my brother and me to the desert to see how the Saudi bedouins lived. He took my hand in his and as I looked up I saw the biggest, bluest and brightest sky ever. Looking back down to the sandy earth I saw in the distance a black tent that was loosely pegged into the sand. It was so loosely pegged that it could have flown in to the air any minute and become free to dance in the wind. I felt inside me so much warmth and excitement as I absorbed the sights around me. Now I look back and realize that what appealed to me most was how unfixed these people were. Any minute they could have gathered their meager possessions and moved on. They really were as free as any man or woman could be. From these people's lifestyle I discovered how vital freedom was to my life. After that visit I felt that all there was to life was being free.

ELIAS COPALLOS, Athens College honor graduate. Uneven SAT scores — very low verbal, very high math. High Achievement scores in math, physics. Summer school at Exeter and Harvard with As and Bs. TOEFL 610. Accepted by Tufts, Columbia, Boston University, and Washington University. Entered

Tufts, graduated, and was accepted in several elite American M.B.A. programs.

Although I was born in Salonika, Greece, before I was two months old we moved to Lagos, Nigeria. My early school years at an English nursery school exposed me to the English language and the English educational system, and my first contact with the Greek system was not until I moved to the Greek community elementary school. The Greek community had only an elementary school, so I had to come back to Greece for my secondary schooling. I moved to Salonika for the fifth class of the primary school where, for the first time I got to know something of the real Greek educational system. The next year I finally came to Athens College, which once more involved changing schools and educational systems.

Because I believed that all these changes were, nevertheless, somewhat limited I decided to explore other cultures and educational systems by attending different summer schools, as well (went to England three times, twice to Sherborne, and once to Ascot) once to Austria (OKISTA), and twice to the USA (Phillips Exeter Academy and Harvard summer school). From all this experience I discovered that the most appealing educational system for me was the American one, and I feel I proved this at least, to myself by obtaining excellent grades in both of the summer schools I attended in the United States.

LAWRENCE INGLETON, Eton. Combined SAT scores of 1230. Submitted research papers. Good athlete. Applied Dartmouth, Colgate, Hamilton, Williams, and University of Vermont. Enrolled Dartmouth.

The person who I admire particularly is Colonel David H. Hackworth. Although many might not think of him as prominent, I feel that his story is important to all those who want to understand the tragedy of Vietnam. Hackworth was the youngest full colonel fighting for the U.S. in Vietnam and to this day is America's most decorated living soldier. His military service spanned twenty-five years and he was awarded one hundred and ten medals. However, he put this extraordinary career in jeopardy in order to tell the truth. In April 1971 in Cao Lanh, Vietnam he was interviewed by ABC television and he denounced the doomed war effort. It would be easy for me to write at length about him, but his story is better told in his book "About Face."

The question still remains "Why do I admire him?" To some, he might appear to be a traitor, but I believe he was an exemplary patriot who initially struggled as others did to hide the horror of Vietnam, but in the end felt it was his duty to tell the truth.

I have read extensively on Vietnam and wish that people would try not to ignore it but face its challenge. I share this view with Colonel Hackworth who is determined to see that Vietnam is remembered and the veteran and his family are given the treatment they deserve. He, like me, does not want another tearful chapter to the Vietnam War to be written into America's history and this will happen if the veterans are continually ignored; their generation will be scarred forever.

Colonel Hackworth is one of the few men who tried to warn the American people that defeat in Vietnam was inevitable. I admire him for his determination to see justice done and the Vietnam veteran cared for properly. He is obviously a man of remarkable courage but also of compassion and dedication to the truth, someone with whom one day I would clearly like to be compared.

ANGELENA BOTILIGNI, American School, Tokyo. Modest student, active extracurricular record. TOEFL 650, English Achievement 600, Spanish 750. String essays, interviews. Applied Middlebury, Wheaton, Haverford, and Franklin and Marshall. Enrolled Middlebury and graduated with honors.

What has living in a number of countries taught me and awakened in me? Is the experience of being transferred to a new place about which you know nothing, fearful, educational, enjoyable or disastrous? These are questions that others as well as I have asked. I would respond with a majority of positive attitudes and experiences.

I was born in Italy of an Italian father and Brazilian mother and currently live in Japan. But these are not the only factors that have shaped my life; rather, it has been the wonderful opportunity my parents have offered me — that of travelling and living in different countries — because of my father's international business career. Not only has this allowed me to reside in different cities, but also to meet wonderful people with relatively different ideas, beliefs, and traditions. All in all, it has been a tremendous possibility to form an international background, mind and community of friends. I strongly believe my way of life has been a positive asset for me in developing and shaping my thoughts and emotions; in short, my whole self!

My early school years took place primarily in Italy, Portugal and South Africa. I remember them with great nostalgia as they offered unforgettable experiences. One of them, being that of learning English in South Africa, together with the experience of beginning what was to last for many more years to come, an international relationship with friends. As a matter of fact, I still keep track of them! Secondly, South Africa was an opportunity to learn new skills. Due to the availability of space and facilities, I learned to play tennis, to swim, and I took ballet and horseback riding lessons.

AMERICANS ABROAD

American applicants living abroad can be guided in many respects by our recommendations to foreign applicants. While, of course, you will not need a visa or have to file proof of financial responsibility, you will need to show admissions committees that you are highly qualified. American colleges are acquainted with a certain number of foreign schools, but not with all. They are therefore on the alert for all indications of your strong academic work and of your uniqueness as a person. If you have the opportunity to visit American colleges, by all means do so.

Like your foreign counterparts, you are of interest to selective colleges because your experience in another culture will add a special dimension to your college class. But you must make it clear just what you have gained from your life abroad, how it makes you stand out, what changes in your outlook and life-style have occurred during your foreign schooling. For example, one student educated in an army school in Germany wanted to become an intrepreter. Her program was to spend her college vacations in a German institute that trains interpreters. She was admitted to three selective colleges, attended Georgetown, and after a time at the UN joined a private firm of interpreters in Paris.

THE TIME FACTOR

Living abroad, you are already aware, no doubt, of how long it takes letters to reach their destinations in the United States. You must allow for delay by factoring the slowness of the mails into your plans. Assume that weeks will pass before you get a response to any query or request. Naturally you should always use air mail, except in really urgent cases, when you will have to use express service, whatever it costs.

The application procedure for those applying from abroad begins with a preliminary international application requesting information. If the college decides you are qualified to apply for admission, it will then send a final application form.

RECOMMENDED READING

English Language and Orientation Programs in the United States. A directory of intensive English-language training, academic preparation, and orientation programs for the foreign student who needs English development prior to admission to a selective institution. Published by the Institute for International Education, 809 United Nations Plaza, New York, NY 10017.

Study in U.S. Colleges and Universities: A Selected Bibliography. Institute for International Education, above.

Guide to the Foreign Student Information Clearinghouse: A Service for Students from Overseas Who Plan to Study in the United States. Published by the National Liaison Committee for Foreign Student Admissions, The College Board, 1717 Massachusetts Avenue, Washington, DC 20036.

AFTERWORD

Why College?

*I*n the senior year of high school, all thoughts of good students and their families turn to college admission. "Getting in" becomes the paramount concern, and then, once in the college of choice, the concern becomes grades, or making the varsity, or getting in the right fraternity or sorority, or winning a class election. Suddenly it is graduation time and "getting in" begins again — graduate school or a job. That is the pattern for some, but not all.

Take future doctors: they know where they are going and what they must do to get there, so that the A.B. is just a blip on the chart of their career progress. The same is true for others with professional goals — lawyers, engineers, accountants, corporation executives.

But many of those graduating in the nineties from the best colleges will be brought up short by the realization that their degrees have not opened doors for them, and they will fall back on quasi-lucrative jobs as waiters or waitresses, house painters, tennis pros, or telemarketers. Like Mr. Micawber they believe something will turn up, because in America it always has, right?

Well . . . prophecy is not one of our talents. We can note trends in college admissions and draw conclusions about the future for a few years. Beyond that we are like the many holders of college degrees, wondering just what the outlook is for all the bright, energetic, and talented college graduates in this new post–cold war era. Once among the elect, holders of the bachelor's degree are just part of a crowd. The country is overstocked with high achievers. Are you future A.B. holders part of the solution to the nation's difficulties or part of the problem?

You must answer the question for us and for yourselves, as others in the past have. In the last half-century some of the new inventions have been television, jet aircraft, nuclear fission, plastic, superhighways, shopping centers and malls, frozen foods, supermarkets, personal computers, fiber optics, automatic dishwashers, fax machines, microfilm, paperback books like the one you're reading, answering machines, cellular phones, credit cards, CDs,

VCRs, convenience stores, mountain bikes, and ski lifts, to name just a few of the additions to our life-style.

There have been increased rights for minorities, the end of the cold war and nuclear proliferation (we hope), an expansion of voting rights, and new concern for our fragile environment.

In health care we have seen the cures for many contagious diseases, increased longevity of the population, development of organ transplants, the CAT scan, the pill, prostheses, wonder drugs, intensive care, genetic engineering, and burn centers.

You can counter these positives with drug abuse, gun proliferation, unspeakable crimes, homelessness, overcrowded prisons, global warming, species extinction, gay bashing, racism, pornography, Wall Street chicanery, poor schools, terrorism, hijacking, AIDS, bribery and corruption, crooked elections, political imprisonment, assassinations, smuggling, piracy, satanic cults. Put on your dark glasses. This is the well-known flip side. Does it challenge you or plunge you into despair? Glass half empty or . . . ?

The point is that no one knows what is going to turn up. We Americans are all Micawbers in our expectations for new and remarkable developments. Incurable optimists, we live by Franklin D. Roosevelt's exhortation in the depth of a terrible economic depression that the only thing to fear is fear itself. The answer to our question "Why college?" is: TO DEVELOP THE HABIT OF OPTIMISM AND THE EXPECTATION THAT YOU PERSONALLY HAVE AN IMPORTANT ROLE TO PLAY IN A FUTURE WAITING TO BE BORN. You are the heirs of opportunity and we await with keenest expectation the surprises you have in store for us.

APPENDIX

Your Worksheets

COLLEGE REQUIREMENTS WORKSHEET

Colleges

Name of College   1. _____ 2. _____ 3. _____ 4. _____

Level of selectivity (Demanding, Very
   Demanding, Exceedingly Demanding)   _____ _____ _____ _____

Units of high school courses required (1 unit = 1 year)

  English   _____ _____ _____ _____

  Mathematics   _____ _____ _____ _____

  Science   _____ _____ _____ _____

  Languages   _____ _____ _____ _____

  History or Social Studies   _____ _____ _____ _____

  Electives advised   _____ _____ _____ _____

  Total units required   _____ _____ _____ _____

Is SAT I or ACT required?   _____ _____ _____ _____

How many Subject Tests required?   _____ _____ _____ _____

  Tests recommended   _____ _____ _____ _____

Advanced Placement policy, if any   _____ _____ _____ _____

Is credit given for college courses taken
   while still in high school?   _____ _____ _____ _____

Colleges

5. _____ 6. _____ 7. _____ 8. _____ 9. _____ 10. _____ 11. _____ 12. _____

STUDENT QUESTIONNAIRE

1. What type of college do you see yourself in? Please look over the characteristics listed below and review them with your parents before checking anything.

    GEOGRAPHICAL LOCATION (number choices 1, 2, 3, etc.)

    Northeast_____ Middle Atlantic_____ Midwest_____

    South_____ Far West_____ Does not matter_____

    EXACT LOCATION (please check)

    Urban_____ Suburban_____ Rural_____

    Does not matter_____

    SIZE (please check)

    Small (under 2,500 undergraduates)_____

    Medium (2,500–6,000)_____ Large (6,000–10,000)_____

    Extremely large (10,000–25,000)_____

    Do you prefer a college (undergraduate only)?_____

    A university (undergraduate, graduate, and professional students)?_____

    Does not matter?_____

    Coeducational?_____

    Single Sex?_____ Does not matter?_____

    What characteristics would you prefer in a college?

    What characteristics would you like to avoid?

    How important a consideration is institutional prestige?

    How intensive an academic workload and grading system do you want?

2. Intended major (or possible majors, if you are undecided)?

    Specific academic interests apart from your major?

    Extracurricular interests you intend to pursue in college (please list in order of importance):

3. Will you need financial aid?_____ Do you want a part-time job?_____

4. Father's college and class_____

   Graduate school(s)_____

   Mother's college and class_____

   Graduate school(s)_____

   Does either of your parents teach or work at a college or university?

   Are any relatives significantly involved in any college of possible interest to you? Which ones?

5. At this time are there any colleges in which you are particularly interested? Which ones? Why?

   Have you already ruled out any colleges? Which ones? Why?

6. How would *you* assess yourself as a student?

   What do you consider to be your areas of academic strength and weakness?

   Do you think your transcript and counselor/teacher reports, if any, are a fair evaluation of your academic abilities?

7. How would you characterize yourself?

   What kind of person are you?

   What kind of people do you like to be with?

8. Please list your *most important* extracurricular pursuits (specify years of involvement).

   School activities:

   School sports:

   Outside activities:

   Work and summer activities:

   Hobbies and pastimes:

   Awards (academic and extracurricular):

   Please indicate, after reviewing the items above, the one or two that interest you most.

PARENT'S QUESTIONNAIRE

(Each parent should answer the questions without consulting the other; then they should compare answers. They should write them out but not show them to the children. They may want to use their answers when talking to a school counselor.)

1. What characteristics are you especially interested in finding in a college or university for your son or daughter? You might wish to comment on the college's type, style, atmosphere, academic reputation, and "institutional prestige," as well as its location.

2. Describe to yourself your son's or daughter's relative strengths as a student (organization, motivation, self-discipline, independence, creativity, growth potential, etc.).

3. Colleges often ask for several words that best describe an applicant. They also ask schools to assess individuals in areas such as leadership, confidence, warmth of personality, concern for others, energy, and maturity. How would you describe your son's or daughter's personality and values?

4. What is his or her greatest achievement? In what sense is he or she special in your eyes?

5. Is there anything else you feel (medical background, etc.) would be helpful to your son or daughter regarding the college selection process? Anything in the family history, its educational background, for example?

6. Please list the names of any colleges to which you plan to encourage your son or daughter to apply.

PARENT'S QUESTIONNAIRE

(Each parent should answer the questions without consulting the other; then they should compare answers. They should write them out but not show them to the children. They may want to use their answers when talking to a school counselor.)

1. What characteristics are you especially interested in finding in a college or university for your son or daughter? You might wish to comment on the college's type, style, atmosphere, academic reputation, and "institutional prestige," as well as its location.

2. Describe to yourself your son's or daughter's relative strengths as a student (organization, motivation, self-discipline, independence, creativity, growth potential, etc.).

3. Colleges often ask for several words that best describe an applicant. They also ask schools to assess individuals in areas such as leadership, confidence, warmth of personality, concern for others, energy, and maturity. How would you describe your son's or daughter's personality and values?

4. What is his or her greatest achievement? In what sense is he or she special in your eyes?

5. Is there anything else you feel (medical background, etc.) would be helpful to your son or daughter regarding the college selection process? Anything in the family history, its educational background, for example?

6. Please list the names of any colleges to which you plan to encourage your son or daughter to apply.

COLLEGE VISIT SUMMARY SHEET

Name of College_____ Location_____

Date of Visit_____ Interviewer_____

STUDENT BODY

(Impression of student body in terms of appearance, style, degree of interest and enthusiasm, diversity of their social, religious, ethnic background.)

ACADEMIC FACTORS

(How serious about academics is the school and its students? How good are the facilities for academic pursuits? How varied is the curriculum? How strict or flexible are the requirements?)

CAMPUS FACILITIES AND SOCIAL LIFE

(How complete and modern are the facilities such as dorms, dining room, student center, cultural center, athletic facilities? How active is the social life? How diverse is it? What are the parietal rules for students? Is it predominantly a commuter or dormitory campus?)

OVERALL IMPRESSIONS

(What you liked least and most; what seemed different or special about it. What type of student do you feel would be happiest here? Are you the type?)

RATING

On a scale of 1 to 5 (with 1 being the top grade) rate the college on the basis of your interest in it.

COLLEGE VISIT SUMMARY SHEET

Name of College_____ Location_____

Date of Visit_____ Interviewer_____

STUDENT BODY

(Impression of student body in terms of appearance, style, degree of interest and enthusiasm, diversity of their social, religious, ethnic background.)

ACADEMIC FACTORS

(How serious about academics is the school and its students? How good are the facilities for academic pursuits? How varied is the curriculum? How strict or flexible are the requirements?)

CAMPUS FACILITIES AND SOCIAL LIFE

(How complete and modern are the facilities such as dorms, dining room, student center, cultural center, athletic facilities? How active is the social life? How diverse is it? What are the parietal rules for students? Is it predominantly a commuter or dormitory campus?)

OVERALL IMPRESSIONS

(What you liked least and most; what seemed different or special about it. What type of student do you feel would be happiest here? Are you the type?)

RATING

On a scale of 1 to 5 (with 1 being the top grade) rate the college on the basis of your interest in it.

COLLEGE VISIT SUMMARY SHEET

Name of College_____ Location_____

Date of Visit_____ Interviewer_____

STUDENT BODY

(Impression of student body in terms of appearance, style, degree of interest and enthusiasm, diversity of their social, religious, ethnic background.)

ACADEMIC FACTORS

(How serious about academics is the school and its students? How good are the facilities for academic pursuits? How varied is the curriculum? How strict or flexible are the requirements?)

CAMPUS FACILITIES AND SOCIAL LIFE

(How complete and modern are the facilities such as dorms, dining room, student center, cultural center, athletic facilities? How active is the social life? How diverse is it? What are the parietal rules for students? Is it predominantly a commuter or dormitory campus?)

OVERALL IMPRESSIONS

(What you liked least and most; what seemed different or special about it. What type of student do you feel would be happiest here? Are you the type?)

RATING

On a scale of 1 to 5 (with 1 being the top grade) rate the college on the basis of your interest in it.

COLLEGE VISIT SUMMARY SHEET

Name of College_____ Location_____

Date of Visit_____ Interviewer_____

STUDENT BODY

(Impression of student body in terms of appearance, style, degree of interest and enthusiasm, diversity of their social, religious, ethnic background.)

ACADEMIC FACTORS

(How serious about academics is the school and its students? How good are the facilities for academic pursuits? How varied is the curriculum? How strict or flexible are the requirements?)

CAMPUS FACILITIES AND SOCIAL LIFE

(How complete and modern are the facilities such as dorms, dining room, student center, cultural center, athletic facilities? How active is the social life? How diverse is it? What are the parietal rules for students? Is it predominantly a commuter or dormitory campus?)

OVERALL IMPRESSIONS

(What you liked least and most; what seemed different or special about it. What type of student do you feel would be happiest here? Are you the type?)

RATING

On a scale of 1 to 5 (with 1 being the top grade) rate the college on the basis of your interest in it.

COLLEGE VISIT SUMMARY SHEET

Name of College_____ Location_____

Date of Visit_____ Interviewer_____

STUDENT BODY

(Impression of student body in terms of appearance, style, degree of interest and enthusiasm, diversity of their social, religious, ethnic background.)

ACADEMIC FACTORS

(How serious about academics is the school and its students? How good are the facilities for academic pursuits? How varied is the curriculum? How strict or flexible are the requirements?)

CAMPUS FACILITIES AND SOCIAL LIFE

(How complete and modern are the facilities such as dorms, dining room, student center, cultural center, athletic facilities? How active is the social life? How diverse is it? What are the parietal rules for students? Is it predominantly a commuter or dormitory campus?)

OVERALL IMPRESSIONS

(What you liked least and most; what seemed different or special about it. What type of student do you feel would be happiest here? Are you the type?)

RATING

On a scale of 1 to 5 (with 1 being the top grade) rate the college on the basis of your interest in it.

COLLEGE VISIT SUMMARY SHEET

Name of College_____ Location_____

Date of Visit_____ Interviewer_____

STUDENT BODY

(Impression of student body in terms of appearance, style, degree of interest and enthusiasm, diversity of their social, religious, ethnic background.)

ACADEMIC FACTORS

(How serious about academics is the school and its students? How good are the facilities for academic pursuits? How varied is the curriculum? How strict or flexible are the requirements?)

CAMPUS FACILITIES AND SOCIAL LIFE

(How complete and modern are the facilities such as dorms, dining room, student center, cultural center, athletic facilities? How active is the social life? How diverse is it? What are the parietal rules for students? Is it predominantly a commuter or dormitory campus?)

OVERALL IMPRESSIONS

(What you liked least and most; what seemed different or special about it. What type of student do you feel would be happiest here? Are you the type?)

RATING

On a scale of 1 to 5 (with 1 being the top grade) rate the college on the basis of your interest in it.

COLLEGE VISIT SUMMARY SHEET

Name of College_____ Location_____

Date of Visit_____ Interviewer_____

STUDENT BODY

(Impression of student body in terms of appearance, style, degree of interest and enthusiasm, diversity of their social, religious, ethnic background.)

ACADEMIC FACTORS

(How serious about academics is the school and its students? How good are the facilities for academic pursuits? How varied is the curriculum? How strict or flexible are the requirements?)

CAMPUS FACILITIES AND SOCIAL LIFE

(How complete and modern are the facilities such as dorms, dining room, student center, cultural center, athletic facilities? How active is the social life? How diverse is it? What are the parietal rules for students? Is it predominantly a commuter or dormitory campus?)

OVERALL IMPRESSIONS

(What you liked least and most; what semed different or special about it. What type of student do you feel would be happiest here? Are you the type?)

RATING

On a scale of 1 to 5 (with 1 being the top grade) rate the college on the basis of your interest in it.

COLLEGE VISIT SUMMARY SHEET

Name of College_____ Location_____

Date of Visit_____ Interviewer_____

STUDENT BODY

(Impression of student body in terms of appearance, style, degree of interest and enthusiasm, diversity of their social, religious, ethnic background.)

ACADEMIC FACTORS

(How serious about academics is the school and its students? How good are the facilities for academic pursuits? How varied is the curriculum? How strict or flexible are the requirements?)

CAMPUS FACILITIES AND SOCIAL LIFE

(How complete and modern are the facilities such as dorms, dining room, student center, cultural center, athletic facilities? How active is the social life? How diverse is it? What are the parietal rules for students? Is it predominantly a commuter or dormitory campus?)

OVERALL IMPRESSIONS

(What you liked least and most; what seemed different or special about it. What type of student do you feel would be happiest here? Are you the type?)

RATING

On a scale of 1 to 5 (with 1 being the top grade) rate the college on the basis of your interest in it.

FINANCIAL WORKSHEET

Colleges	1. _____	2. _____	3. _____	4. _____
Tuition	_____	_____	_____	_____
Room and board	_____	_____	_____	_____
Fees	_____	_____	_____	_____
Books and supplies	_____	_____	_____	_____
Travel	_____	_____	_____	_____
Personal expenses	_____	_____	_____	_____
Total one-year budget	_____	_____	_____	_____

KINDS OF AID AVAILABLE

Tuition payment plans Monthly payments	_____	_____	_____	_____
4 years payable in advance	_____	_____	_____	_____
Scholarships	_____	_____	_____	_____
Student loans from the college	_____	_____	_____	_____
Family loans from the college	_____	_____	_____	_____
Government aid plans admin- istered by the college	_____	_____	_____	_____
Campus jobs available	_____	_____	_____	_____
Hours per week	_____	_____	_____	_____
Noncampus jobs available	_____	_____	_____	_____
Summer job leads	_____	_____	_____	_____
Financial counseling	_____	_____	_____	_____

Colleges	5. _____	6. _____	7. _____	8. _____
Tuition	_____	_____	_____	_____
Room and board	_____	_____	_____	_____
Fees	_____	_____	_____	_____
Books and supplies	_____	_____	_____	_____
Travel	_____	_____	_____	_____
Personal expenses	_____	_____	_____	_____
Total one-year budget	_____	_____	_____	_____

KINDS OF AID AVAILABLE

Tuition payment plans Monthly payments	_____	_____	_____	_____
4 years payable in advance	_____	_____	_____	_____
Scholarships	_____	_____	_____	_____
Student loans from the college	_____	_____	_____	_____
Family loans from the college	_____	_____	_____	_____
Government aid plans administered by the college	_____	_____	_____	_____
Campus jobs available	_____	_____	_____	_____
Hours per week	_____	_____	_____	_____
Noncampus jobs available	_____	_____	_____	_____
Summer job leads	_____	_____	_____	_____
Financial counseling	_____	_____	_____	_____

YOUR ADMISSIONS STRENGTHS ASSESSMENT

(This form is obviously not exhaustive. Use it creatively to sketch a logical college and postcollege plan, substituting your own ideas where appropriate.)

STRENGTHS

Academic
Grades _____
Class rank _____
Test scores _____
Honors _____
Special projects _____
Extra credits _____
Outside courses _____
Related work experience _____

Nonacademic
Sport _____
Sport _____
Letters _____

ACTIVITIES

School activities
School government _____
Class officer _____
Publications _____
Music _____
Drama _____
Clubs _____
Other _____

Other activities
Community _____
Camp _____
Work _____

OTHER ADVANTAGES

Strengths of Character
Independence _____
Reliability _____
Courage _____
Persistence _____
Patience _____
Tolerance _____

Skills/Talents
1. _____
2. _____
3. _____

COLLEGES LOOKING FOR MY STRENGTHS

            College   Strength

        _____   _____

        _____   _____

        _____   _____

IN COLLEGE

Possible majors _____ _____ _____
Courses to take _____ _____ _____
Grades expected A _____   B _____   C _____
Honors I seek
    Phi Beta Kappa _____ Honors _____ High Honors _____
    Highest Honors _____

AFTER COLLEGE

Possible graduate work in _____ _____ _____
Possible job

    Family business _____   Education _____
    Own venture _____   Government _____
    Sales _____   Media _____
    Corporate management _____   Arts _____

MARKETING STRATEGY

               Communicate strengths to
               Admissions committee _____
               Faculty members _____
               Administration _____
               Coaches _____
               Alumni _____

                    By means of
Extra essays _____
Exhibits: tapes, photos, drawings, crafts, newspaper clippings _____

Added recommendations: employer, minister _____
Visits or phone calls to people on campus _____

YOUR ADMISSIONS DECISIONS QUESTIONNAIRE

1. I have been admitted to the following colleges: _____
   _____ _____. (List the dates on which the colleges notified
   you.)

2. Acceptance deadlines are the following: _____ _____
   _____

3. Financial aid packages compared (from Step Eleven):
   Colleges A $ _____ B $ _____ C $ _____

4. Deposits required: Colleges A $ _____ B $ _____
   C $ _____

5. I have been wait-listed at: Colleges A _____
   B _____ C _____

6. Alumni and/or coach contacts initiated by colleges:
   names _____ _____ dates _____ _____

7. Alumni and/or coach contacts initiated by me:
   names _____ _____ dates _____ _____

8. Campuses revisited: _____ _____ _____

9. I prefer college _____

10. I plan to accept if removed from wait list at _____

11. I plan to accept deferred admission in January at _____

12. Do financial considerations require me to attend a public college in
    my state? Yes No

13. I wish to renegotiate the financial aid package at _____

14. I am disappointed in not getting into _____. I want to
    consider: (1) a 13th year of high school and reapplying to
    _____ _____; (2) enrolling in another college and trans-
    ferring to _____ in my _____ college year.

15. I plan to take Advanced Placement tests in June in these
    subjects: _____ _____

TRANSITION QUESTIONS

16. I have lined up a summer job and will save $ _____ toward my college costs.

17. I am assured of a campus job doing _____ and earning $ _____

18. I am considering taking the following courses freshman year:
_____ _____ _____ _____ _____
_____

19. My roommate will be chosen by the college _____ by me _____

20. I will be living at _____

21. My academic advisor will be _____

22. Deadlines for paying tuition _____ room and board _____

Bibliography

GENERAL

Barron's Profiles of American Colleges. Woodbury, NY: Barron's Educational Series. An annual directory of colleges and universities.

The Black Student's Guide to Colleges. Edited by Barry Beckman. 3rd ed. Silver Springs, MD: Beckman House Publishers, 1992.

Comparative Guide to American Colleges. By James Cass and Max Birnbaum. 15th ed. New York: Harper & Row, 1993.

The following guides are published annually by the College Entrance Examination Board (College Board Publications, 45 Columbus Avenue, New York, New York 10101).

The College Handbook. A directory of detailed information on 3,200 four- and two-year colleges in the United States.

The College Handbook for Transfer Students. Provides specific information regarding transfer policies at 2,900 colleges and explains the transfer process.

The College Handbook Foreign Student Supplement. Information for the foreign applicant on admission tests and TOEFL requirements, application deadlines, costs, ESL programs, and percentage of foreign students in each college or university.

Index of Majors and Graduate Degrees. "Covers nearly 600 recognized fields of study and the 2,900 colleges and universities that offer them."

Getting into College: A Guide for Students and Parents. By Dr. Frank C. Leana. New York: Hill and Wang, 1990.

The K and W Guide to Colleges for the Learning Disabled. By Marybeth Kravets and Imy F. Wax. 2nd ed. New York: HarperCollins Publishers, 1993.

The Performing Arts Major's College Guide. By Carole J. Everett. New York: Arco, Prentice Hall Publishers, 1992.

Peterson's Annual Guide to Four-Year Colleges. Princeton, NJ: Peterson's Guides.

Peterson's Guide to Colleges with Programs for Learning-Disabled Students. 3rd. ed. Princeton, NJ: Peterson's Guides, 1993.

The Selective Guide to Colleges. Edited by Edward B. Fiske. New York: Times Books. Published annually.

Volunteer: A Guide to Voluntary Service in the U.S. and Abroad. Edited by Max Terry. New York: The Council for International Educational Exchange. Published biannually.

The Winning Edge: The Student-Athlete's Guide to College Sports. By Francis and James Kilpatrick. 3rd ed. Alexandria, VA: Octameron Associates, 1994.

FINANCIAL AID INFORMATION

The A's and B's of Academic Scholarships. Edited by Daphne A. Philos. Alexandria, VA: Octameron Associates. Published annually.

Best College Buys: Money Guide. New York: Time-Warner. Published annually.

College Costs and Financial Aid Handbook. Published annually by the College Board Entrance Examination Board (New York: College Board Publications). Provides cost and financial aid information for 2,900 colleges and a detailed description of the changes in federal methodology for determining qualification for grants and loans.

Don't Miss Out: The Ambitious Student's Guide to Financial Aid. Edited by Robert Leider and Anna Leider. Alexandria, VA: Octameron Associates. Published annually.

Financing a College Education: The Essential Guide for the 90s. By Richard Lewis. Holbrook, MA: Bob Adams Publishers, 1993.

Need a Lift? Indianapolis: The American Legion. Published annually.

Paying Less for College. Princeton, NJ: Peterson's Guides. Published annually.

Test Preparation

Introducing the New SAT: The College Board's Official Guide. New York: College Board Publications. Offers a description of the changes in the math and verbal sections of the SAT introduced in March 1994, as well as practice questions and strategies on how to take the test.

TestSkills: A Preparation for the New PSAT/NMSQT. Provides sample questions and strategies for taking the new PSAT introduced in October 1993.

Index

314 / INDEX